GOOD
FIGHT

The

GOOD FIGHT

The Life and Work of
CAROLINE WALKER
Bestselling Food Campaigner
and Co-author of
THE FOOD SCANDAL

~

GEOFFREY CANNON

EBURY PRESS

PUBLISHED BY EBURY PRESS
a division of Random Century Ltd
20 Vauxhall Bridge Road
London SW1V 2SA

Copyright © The Caroline Walker Trust 1989

Designed by Nigel Partridge

C.I.P catalogue record for this book is available from the British Library

ISBN 0–7126–3769–9 – Paperback only
ISBN 0–7126–3808–3 – Hardback only

Typeset by ℞ Tek Art Ltd, Croydon
Printed in Great Britain by Mackays of Chatham.

To Jean

And though with great difficulty I am got hither, yet now I do not repent me of all the trouble I have been at to arrive where I am. My sword, I give to those who shall succeed me in my pilgrimage, and my courage and skill, to those that can get it.

John Bunyan: *Pilgrim's Progress*

CONTENTS

———•■•———

Acknowledgements

In her last summer Caroline said to me 'When I die, you will thank everybody, won't you?' And so from Caroline and from me, and from our families: thanks, to the thousands of people who, at different times in Caroline's life, gave her love and help and gifts, and who held her hand, even when her hand was held in fire. Love can turn the pain of flame into light.

So many people enriched Caroline's life, and in mentioning a dozen, all are thanked.

Thanks, to Dr Keith Ball, who encouraged Caroline to pursue her just cause; to Professor Philip James, whose own work gave Caroline her grand theme; and to Sir Francis Avery Jones, who assured Caroline her place in the history of public health.

Thanks, to Professor Aubrey Sheiham, who stood up for Caroline when she was alone; to 'Charles', a mole who cared more for public health than his job; and to Vanessa Harrison, who gave Caroline her first regular national platform.

Thanks, to three women who gave Caroline hope: Sister Keiren Towlson, whose vigilance saved Caroline's life; Sister Marie Louise, whose serenity inspired Caroline; and Dr Anne Naysmith, whose strength and skill let her be at home in her last days.

Thanks, to Jean James, who opened her heart and her house to Caroline, giving us a new home; and to Caroline's dear friends Sandra Hunt and Lesley Morrison, whom she chose to be with in her time of dying, and who shared her death.

I myself am thankful to many people, and mention my sons Ben and Matt, and my daughter Lou, for all their gifts. Above all my own thanks are to Caroline, whose gifts, enthusiasm, faith, goodwill, smiles and laughter, showed me the way.

Geoffrey Cannon

INTRODUCTION

My wife Caroline began to look forward to her death, at the beginning of August in 1988.

In successive years she had become a godmother again, to our neighbour's little girl Anna, and an aunt for the first time, to her sister Olivia's baby. Then my son Matt's daughter Florence was born on 13 June 1988, a few minutes after Caroline's 38th birthday. 'Imagine! I'm a step-grandmother!' she wrote to her family, rather tickled.

On Caroline's birthday we travelled to Aberdeen, for a special occasion. In public life, as a scientist, campaigner, writer and broadcaster, she led the fight for good food in Britain. *The Food Scandal*, our book mostly written by her, became an emblem of the campaigns for better British public health. That was in 1984. In 1985 and 1986 Caroline was chief advisor to the BBC TV Food and Health campaign, and in six months wrote six booklets on good food and good health that altogether were requested by half a million people. 'Her knowledge, her intellectual honesty, her brilliance as a communicator, her fearlessness, made her outstanding,' wrote the great nutritional scientist Dr Hugh Sinclair.

In the summer of 1988, Caroline's last adventure was private. As a young research scientist she had worked at the Dunn Clinical Nutrition Centre in Cambridge; her boss, Phil James, then became a successor to Lord Boyd Orr as Director of the Rowett Research Institute in Aberdeen, and with his wife Jean, a dear friend. Like Caroline, the Rowett is dedicated to public health by means of good nutrition; and in June we joined in its fortieth birthday celebration. Sadly, though, Caroline herself was dying.

A few sunny days later we walked the clifftops of Buchan among seabirds and wild flowers; then Caroline flew to the island of Jura to continue her holiday. Her journey would end three months later, with her burial under a Scottish hill.

I wrote to friends to let them know how things were. The Conservative MP Jonathan Aitken wrote in reply: 'How strange are the pathways of fate and destiny. When I last saw her she was on cracking form, scaring the living daylights out of certain food moguls and lifting all the rest of us to new heights of healthy nutrition. It seems so cruelly ironic that she who brought good health to millions has now lost it for herself. She will be much in my thoughts and prayers as she battles through her last campaign.'

Hugh Sinclair went on: 'We cannot replace Caroline's contribution to nutrition – and this at the most important time when we want such a person in the campaign for the proper provision of the right foods to keep people healthy rather than to keep certain industrialists rich. But so many of us always will treasure the privilege of having known her and admire her immensely brave struggle against adversity.'

Withal the irony, Caroline's style in her public and private lives was all of a piece: tenacious, endearing, funny, frank, and altogether memorable. Much of what she said and did was valuable – 'inspiring', 'illuminating', 'encouraging', are words often used of her. Geoffrey Glazer, her consultant surgeon, put it simply. 'I don't need to say how fond I was of her and how brave she was. I will never forget her.' Therefore, this book.

Which is not another 'Twenty Top Tips On Living And Dying With Cancer'. Caroline was exasperated rather than fascinated by her illness. We did learn a lot, though; enough to make another book. For example, when a doctor says you have cancer he (it's usually a he) will no doubt go on to say what will become of you. Our advice, is take note, say thank you, shop around, and take your own decisions. After all, if a builder says you have dry rot, you do not immediately take his word for it, sign his estimate without looking at the small print, shut your eyes and resign yourself to the pickaxes. (No disrespect intended, to doctors or builders.)

There again, just as there are societies to encourage home births, there should be societies for home deaths. Being looked after at home is more trouble, of course, just as home cooking takes more time. But dying in hospital as most people now do, stuck full of tubes in white rooms, surrounded by suffering and strangers, with those you love kept at the end of a telephone, is a sad and bad ending. Caroline thought being sent to hospital to die is like being put in a skip. (Again, no disrespect to builders or doctors.)

At home in August, Caroline finished planting our garden, with seeds and bulbs identified with little flags, so I would know what to expect the next spring and summer. She gave two interviews: one at the beginning of the month, for the *Guardian* on her sense of death, as we ate lunch; the other from her bed, at the end of the month, for 'The Food Programme' on the meaning of her work.

Our home filled with family and friends and flowers. Pain was the only uncertainty. The surgeons had warned me that obstruction caused by the cancer would eventually be horribly painful. Not so; Dr Anne Naysmith, consultant at our local community hospital, a woman about Caroline's age, disagreed; and with a careful cocktail of drugs, Caroline rested at home, and took responsibility for her death, simply by stopping eating, two weeks before she died. Around midnight as her last day began, she foresaw her death. How was it – what did the thought feel like? 'Oh, *lovely*,' she said; and we laughed. And it was lovely to be with her when she died.

So, here after all is more advice. Starvation is a gentle way to let go. Find a general practitioner who will be your friend. And share.

'I want to share with you why I shall always be grateful to Caroline,' wrote a friend. 'She could always make me laugh, with her wonderful sense of the absurd and her sharp wit. But it was the last few months of her life that were a real inspiration to me. She showed me that the time of dying can be an enriching and growing experience.

Just over a year before Caroline died, a very close and old friend of mine also died of cancer. It was one of the most traumatic times I have ever been through, and I had nightmares for months afterwards.

When Caroline began to approach the last stages of her life, I must admit I didn't know whether I would be able to cope with seeing another friend die. Her summons to come and say goodbye made me face up to it. In the last month just sitting with her reading, or doing my embroidery, I felt an incredible sense of peace. I was aware that Caroline was still giving to me and helping me right up to the end of her life. She took away some of the horrors of my previous experience and healed some of the scars.

So it was not only her living but also her dying that makes her a very special person to me.'

Professor John Garrow is one of the British Government's most senior advisors on food and health policy. He is now head of the department of Human Nutrition at St Bartholomew's Hospital, London. In his inaugural lecture, he said that in the mid-1980s in Britain, a great shift in national mood took place. This sea-change was from the belief, shared by the public and the scientific community, that the British diet was OK, to the belief that the British diet is not OK. When and why the change? He projected a slide, of the cover of *The Food Scandal*, mostly Caroline's work.

She 'had a striking impact on our view of health because of her rigorous mind and her great courage as a whistle-blower,' wrote Caroline's old friend and colleague John Rivers, in his obituary for the *Independent*.

'Like every good scientist, Caroline was passionate about her work, but where she differed from her colleagues was in the way that passion was expressed. Caroline eschewed the stereotype of scientific behaviour that claims to itself Newton's modest disclaimer that he "was but a child walking along the seashore here and there picking up a smoother pebble or a prettier pebble".

Throughout her career, Caroline looked unerringly for the uglier pebbles, picking them up only to hurl them back at their source. She was made so angry at what she saw as the cynical exploitation of people that she determined to do something about it. Since her field was nutrition, the inevitable target of her attacks was the food manufacturing industry and government nexus, and its complacency about food and health.'

Working in public health, Caroline gave her science a meaning, gave it heart and soul. Scientists like to say they deal in facts, but there is more to truth than facts. The opposite of truth is not just inaccuracy, but also lies. Caroline told the truth, and was right to do so, as we know, now that food scandals have been followed by bug scandals, and we realise that nobody is safe from illness caused by bad food.

John Rivers continued, 'Although her public attack on our diet brought scorn and dismissal from the manufacturers, it also created change. While the food manufacturers prevaricated and waved solicitors' letters, they were also preparing to retool and readvertise. The industry dismissed her as queen of the cranks, but progressively adopted the kinds of dietary guidelines she so fiercely advocated.'

If that were true, this book would be no more than a memorial. What

Caroline did achieve, as Dr Garrow perceived, is a change in the nation's mind. Change in the nation's food is yet to come, and so this book is meant as a call to action.

Phil James wrote, in his *Guardian* obituary:

'She was just beginning to develop the framework of a sustained and coherent approach to food policy when she became so grievously ill. Within days of major surgery, she was discovering for herself the inadequacies of hospital food and the nutritional ignorance of surgeons and vowed to write a book on hospitals.

Slowly, however, she realised that she could not do everything: she was tired of incessant lobbying and coping with senior academics and industrialists who were often ignorant rather than unscrupulous. She began to write about the food problems facing Britain over the next ten to fifteen years. How, for example, could the public's food supply be improved when compositional food standards are to be replaced by a free market where all products are liable to be labelled with a wealth of information – but in forms unintelligible to the ordinary consumer?

Where shall we find a successor to this young, engaging, warm and immensely effective campaigner?'

The answer, is that we are all citizens as well as consumers; we are all Caroline's successors. She is an inspiration to us all.

Each chapter in this book touches on a theme of Caroline's life and work: her love of nature; her humour; her care for children; her work as a scientist, and as a campaigner; her heroes, source of her courage. And her advice; the sub-title of *The Food Scandal*, is 'What's wrong with the British diet – and how to put it right'.

Each chapter is in two parts. The best bits come second; Caroline's writing. I have not selected passages from *The Food Scandal* or from her contribution to *Additives: Your Complete Survival Guide*, and to *Eating For A Healthy Heart*: these books are in the shops or in libraries. This book ends with accounts of Caroline's life and work, and an introduction to the Trust set up in her name.

The idea is to take Caroline's work forward. In the first chapter on nature, she sees the need to develop markets for organically grown food; and more generally, the place of good agriculture within the countryside. Next, the chapter on humour, giving what she said about chemical additives as an example, calls for an end to dodgy cosmetic chemicals in food meant for babies and young children; and more generally, for a new partnership between government, science and industry in which the consumer really is sovereign.

Caroline campaigned for good school meals for ten years. More generally, she believed that compositional standards guaranteeing the quality of staple foods should be maintained. These campaigns failed, as the chapter on children shows. They could succeed.

On a grander theme, the quality of our food and therefore our health as a nation, can be protected only by a national food and agriculture policy designed with health as its first priority. A self-confident country may aspire to high standards. Building on previous work, Caroline and many others converted the medical and scientific community to this view, together with many legislators and much of the food industry. As the chapter on science tells, this campaign has only just begun.

In the chapter on campaigning, Caroline looks forward to an end to the secret state of Britain, and to the creation of new tough brave consumer groups. Her heroes speak out as she did, for a land free for animals to range in, and for the celebration of whole, fresh, delicious food. The chapter on Caroline's courage sets out a life's work for a couple more of her successors: getting hospitals, and doctors, interested in good food. This chapter also addresses a question on everybody's mind: Why did Caroline of all people die as she did?

'Don't set her in aspic,' said our friend and guide Margaret Wynn, who has been fighting for good food for fifty years and more. 'We move on. Caroline would have moved on.' The next to last chapter is Caroline's advice on food and health, as good and fresh as when she wrote it. Now, though, she would be saying quite a lot about the bugs in our food . . . .

Thanks to Caroline, so many people share her vision, and so often say, 'What will we do without her?' The answer, is that she is with us. This book is not meant as a memorial, but as a reminder.

CHAPTER ONE
NATURE

———————————◆———————————

'But what about traditional British fruits? What has happened to the Blenheim, one of Britain's highest prized apples in the nineteenth century?'

'I am sitting by a bowlful of wild orchids, vetch, pink campion, thrift, buttercups, bladder campion and other unidentified herbage gathered from the clifftops north of Aberdeen, which Geoffrey and I visited last week.' This is from a letter to relatives Caroline wrote from Aberdeen on 23 June 1988:

> 'The Bullers of Buchan is a birds' housing estate – stuffed with kittiwakes, pelicans, fulmars, guillemots and gulls galore, some sitting within hand's reach with their fluffy grey chicks – a most precarious start in life for the little chaps: the adults seem to spend much of their time pushing the youngsters back on their perch. The clifftop is awash with pink and yellow flowers, up to the edge of the fields (plenty of ammunition here for the herbicide-haters . . .). It is some time since I saw wild flowers in such profusion. I had to go to buy a book to find out what they all were.
>
> On Friday we visited the Scottish National Trust Agricultural Museum at Pidmedden where, apart from being able to eat a lot of nice fresh scones, you can sample the life of a Scottish agricultural worker and see all the old implements of farm and kitchen laid out before you, complete with woodworm and faded instructions for use of the seed-drills and corn-sorters.
>
> Geoffrey is today at the House of Commons eating organic strawberries and cream for the launch of the Soil Association's 'Living Earth' campaign. They are being hosted by Charles Irving, MP for Cheltenham, who is in charge of H of C catering and venomous about all chemicals in his dinners!
>
> Tomorrow if I am all right I'm off to Jura. Last week I had an attack of gut-block, which has now sorted itself out, and I am fully rehydrated, remineralised, and relatively energetic (i.e. normal for me, for my condition). It is my impression that my intestine

is probably beginning to seize up again, and I will then die. Goodness knows how long it will take to kill me off – it might be weeks of starvation – say 3–6 – and given that my kidneys, liver, lungs have all kept in good shape, it looks as if I am in for death by starvation. Frankly, I'd rather have an overdose in the event, as it's not a nice way to go, particularly if I can still absorb fluid and would keep going longer as long as I drank. Without fluids, and if I could stop them giving me a drip, I wouldn't last much more than three days.

However, until it happens, I will go on living as normally as I can, which requires acceptance and restraint both from myself and from everyone with whom I am in regular contact. While I have been so unwell this year, I have had an enormous amount of love, care and support from people, both family and friends, and I very much doubt that I would be here without them.'

We in the West are trained to block thoughts of death, to think of it as a horror that must be hidden – as obscene, in the original meaning of the word. Death at home in the family, normal throughout history and all over the world, is evaded now in Western countries. We sterilise death. Caroline referred to the places where people like us are sent to die, the white rooms full of tubes, as technological skips. 'I hope you don't have to put me in a skip,' she said.

So reading what somebody has to say about their own imminent death is rather fascinating; the more so when, like Caroline, they are young. In an interview she gave to the *Guardian* published a couple of weeks before she died, Caroline said, 'Dying is an alien state. You have to make the effort to communicate otherwise you are totally cut off. And you have to help others come to terms.'

In the event, Caroline was able to choose when, where and how she would die, and with whom. That is another story. When she was prepared for death, and was able to bring people to share her own acceptance, in her conversation and letters she referred continually to the fundamental inspiration of her life and work: nature. A month after her sojourn in Aberdeen, and her holiday in Jura, she was back in London, in hospital. She wrote to another relative, on 24 July:

'Here I am back in my second home – with my own eighth-floor room and bathroom in the splendid new wing. I've come to be topped up with calcium and other goodies to help my stupid little gut. I go home for the day to do the gardening, and come back to sleep – a good temporary measure which is a relief to Geoffrey at night time. Needless to say the garden is a wash-out this summer, but we have improved it from last year's buttercup patch. I've put in lots of honeysuckle, clematis, roses and shrubs, and even have a few runner beans, and about twenty herbs, which the next door pussycats appear to enjoy (particularly basil, which I don't quite understand). Nothing they like better than to dig the plants up. The modern pussy is a bit delinquent – can't bury its waste and has a destructive urge.

The little isle of Jura was really splendid. I stayed with friends in their croft, and had ten days' sunshine. The island is smothered with wild flowers – orchids by the thousand – and is well-stocked with birds, deer and wild goats, and only 200 inhabitants. I always used to think that artists who painted Scottish islands were inclined to a vivid imagination, so hazy and colourful were their pictures, but sitting and watching the skyline change by the hour is quite extraordinary. I stupidly forgot my paint box but spent much of my time with bird- and flower-books. Needless to say I've forgotten most of them already. I flew back to London – 4½ hours door-to-door on stand-by which was very easy.

I hope you are enjoying your new home and surroundings. I'd love to visit you, but my condition is unpredictable – death's door one minute, mowing the lawn the next. I may ring you sometime and see if you can manage a visitor or two for the weekend.'

And so on. The letter Caroline received in reply also expressed joy in nature. But more than that; Caroline's matter-of-fact approach to death inspired love of life in others, as here:

'Such a wonderful letter mixing the bare facts of having to leave this life with descriptions of the flora of your own garden and Jura. I was lucky to live for six months in the Kyle of Lochalsh just before the war and though I was supposed to be working at the hotel there I must have had a lot of time off duty.

One of the most memorable journeys was the rail line between Perth and Kyle. It took all day and was most beautiful, taking routes between lochs and mountains. I used to walk the line to Plockton and the flowers on it were as you said. I suppose the damp makes the orchis grow so high.

We did achieve a patch of the scented butterfly orchis in the moor below the farmhouse in St Columb. I hope the present owner will not try and reclaim that twenty acres. Probably not as he will not want to grow more corn nowadays.

It would be wonderful if you could hover around at times and give us all descriptions of the next world! My mother fancied green fields full of flowers and streams running through. She probably had her wish as she lived a good life. I fear that my next life will probably serve me right.'

Friends who visited Caroline in the summer and early autumn of 1988, in her last months and days, often said they were enlightened: for knowledge of death enhances love of life. If Caroline is anyone to go by, people who live with knowledge of their death do not go in for pronouncements in which the secret of the universe is revealed. I seem to remember Caroline herself enjoying the story of the pilgrim who toiled up and down the Himalayas in search of a holy man. Mission achieved, he sat on the mountain-top at the feet of the sage who, after a while, said, 'You didn't happen to bring any fish and chips with you, did you?'

What is true, though, is that given the chance, people who are close to death are more themselves. And without saying much about it, Caroline encouraged the realisation that the force of her work as a scientist and campaigner for better public health came from her love of the natural world. Oddly enough, most nutritionists do not know or care much about food, and have no feel of where food comes from. Caroline did. She grew up in the countryside, and as a child enjoyed working with her father in his vegetable garden, and eating the meals her mother made from fresh home produce. Her first degree was in Biology, and an early academic influence on her was Jack Edelman, then Professor of Botany at Queen Elizabeth College, where she gained her BSc. (Dr Edelman was later Head of Research for Ranks Hovis McDougall, and Caroline extracted two confessions from him: first that he ate wholegrain bread, and saw Chorleywood mass-produced sliced white bread as fit only for the punters; second, that he was somewhat ashamed of his part in the invention of that abominable technofood, the Pot Noodle. She also influenced Ranks in their decision in 1986 to take bleach out of their white bread. ('No more Vim!' she said. 'Well done, Jack!')

Much of her professional confidence came from her understanding of the place of food in the natural world, and from an avid reading of the evidence, amounting to a general agreement among the most knowledgeable independent scientists by the early 1980s, that whole, fresh food is vital for good health, and protection against many Western diseases.

Not that scientists talk like that: and much of her work at that time was spent translating the jargon of scientists into good, earthy English language not about nutrition but about food – 'you know,' she might say, 'the stuff people eat.' This story by the food writer Yan Kit-So says it well:

'I first became aware of Caroline at a meeting of the Guild of Food Writers when she stood up, a slender figure with an attractive but determined face, and argued with crusading passion against a representative from the Sugar Bureau. Her sharp intellect and forceful yet logical arguments impressed me no end, yet I wondered if she was one of those nutritionists who has forgotten that food is also for eating and enjoyment.

A couple of days later I was on the platform at Notting Hill Gate. Suddenly a gentle and warm smile greeted me, and I recognised Caroline. Throughout our albeit far too short journey together, she asked me about Chinese vegetarian dishes, their component ingredients, their tastes and flavours and their availability in London. To my surprise and great relief, she did not mention a word about nutrition, something about which I know very little.

So taken was I by her friendliness that I suggested that we should go to a Chinese restaurant together. She said 'yes please' but then I had to get off before we could make a date. I never saw her again, but I will always remember her gentle smile and our conversation.'

Caroline was infuriated by the destruction of the fields of East Anglia, now prairie; contemptuous of academics who praised crisps as ideal snacks for children, instead of an apple; and fascinated by the fact that the wars between the English and the Dutch in the seventeenth century were fought over the North Sea herring grounds, essentially for the same reason. The health of a nation depends on the integrity of its food supply. Continental Europeans eat better food than the British because the French, the Italians and the Germans come from an unbroken tradition

of peasant farmers. They value the earth and its fruits. They love true
variety in food. And there is more to health in a nation – or a person –
than absence of illness. Good food is part of the joy of life. Good food,
farmed, grown and made well, creates beautiful landscape, respects wild
life, and encourages pride in work. Good cooking is integral to family
life. The culinary arts are part of every civilisation.

The guns Caroline trained on the manufacturers of mug-a-soup and
their ilk, were not pea-shooters; they are the heavy artillery of a moral
intelligence who knows the meaning and value of good food. That's a
reason to write about her work: she was right, and she is right, and
what she said should be borne in mind by everybody concerned to
restore the integrity of Britain's food.

In *The Food Scandal* Caroline lamented the loss of variety in our fresh
food, with knowledge learned from her father, who at the time of his
retirement was adviser on apples and pears to the Ministry of
Agriculture. 'What about traditional British fruits?' she wrote. 'Cox's
Orange Pippin, Golden Delicious and Granny Smith have overrun the
apple market in recent years. What has happened to the Blenheim, one
of Britain's highest prized apples in the nineteenth century? Or James
Grieve, or the Pitmaston Pine Apple, or Ashmead's Kernel or the dozen
of apple varieties listed in old horticultural journals? New varieties of
apple have been introduced in this century, but many more have
vanished, dismissed as poor croppers, or because they store badly. Most
supermarkets and greengrocers only sell one or two varieties. They do
not seem to be interested in stocking new varieties as they come into
season. Maybe it is too much trouble.'

Things are looking up now; there is more real variety in the shops.
And as I write, in a room overlooking the garden in which Caroline's
flowers now bloom abundantly, the sun is beginning to shine on
traditional, or 'organic' farming. Derek Cooper of BBC Radio 4's 'The
Food Programme' interviewed Caroline at home on the last day of
August, three weeks before she died. She had plenty to say, and her final
words were about organic food:

> 'Water can be added unscrupulously to raw food. The way you
> do that, if you're a farmer, is you sprinkle fertiliser on your crops;
> and the rain comes free out of the sky. What fertiliser does, of
> course, is to encourage plants to grow much faster, and to increase
> their water uptake. So what you end up with is a diluted product.

Ask anybody what they think of the average British tomato. 'Disgusting,' they say. 'No flavour.' Why has it got no flavour? It's got no flavour for several reasons, one of which is it's grown with far too much water. It's grown far too fast. So the nutrients and the flavour in it are diluted.

I believe a big project should be undertaken to measure the difference between food that is produced organically. I think if you did that you'd be very surprised. Because organic food has a reputation for being expensive. But if you knew it was expensive because it's got more in it, then – why not buy it?'

What follows is a profile Caroline wrote in celebration of Christopher Baker, or 'Mr Toothy' as she fondly called him, who supplied Arjuna, the wholefood shop in Mill Road at the end of her street in Cambridge, with his own organically grown vegetables and fruit. The feature, which was rejected by the *Telegraph* Magazine and published later in the Soil Association's magazine, is characteristically earthy.

CHRISTOPHER BAKER OF CAMBRIDGE: AN ORGANIC ODYSSEY

Early Saturday morning, Mr Christopher Baker sets off from his home in Harston, six miles south of Cambridge, with his elderly maroon Volvo estate stuffed to the roof with boxes, bags and buckets full of leeks, potatoes, carrots, parsnips, beetroot, brassicas, spinach, lettuces, parsley, apples, peppers, cucumbers and cut flowers. In his car he also takes a table, a cash box and a biscuit tin for the change, weighing scales, handwritten price tags and plastic bags.

His destination is Mill Road in East Cambridge where for the last few years he has run a market stall on the pavement outside Arjuna, a wholefood cooperative. Regular customers have become very fond of Mr Baker, who can be seen from far up the street as he hurries to prepare his stall. He wears a woolly hat and large blue jacket, and his buckets of marigolds and chrysanthemums decorate his weekly harvest festival.

He grows all the fruit and vegetables himself, with 'no artificial fertilisers or pesticides', advertised on a handwritten piece of cardboard propped on his stall. He sells both direct to the public, and also to Arjuna. His prices are on the whole cheaper than those of the central Cambridge Guildhall market, and he earns less than £1 an hour on his work.

'I spend six and a half days a week growing vegetables, and on the remaining half day I sell them – quickly as I often have a queue. I had the Soil Association inspector for Cambridge and Norfolk round to see me. He knew of nobody else who is both producer and retailer of organic vegetables in this area.

My satisfaction comes mainly from satisfying my customers. I don't need the money, as I have a pension. I like to think I'm doing a useful service.'

Enthusiastic and satisfied shoppers for Mr Baker's organic produce have followed his Saturday stall for over seven years, as have the planning authorities. He started on a derelict bomb site, then moved to the old Bath House (first back, then front), then underneath the railway bridge on Mill Road, and finally came to rest on the pavement outside Arjuna. The early sites he shared with half a dozen bric-à-brac stalls, which one by one gave up the struggle. 'This is much the best site I've had, and it is very good of Arjuna to let me be here.'

Mr Baker's agricultural career began when after he had spent three years in the Civil Service, the war came and as a conscientious objector he worked for four years with a pacifist farming community which had leanings towards organic methods. His job was to mind the five horses.

After the war he spent three years as a field worker in agricultural research. 'In 1980, when I was 62, I realised that the thing I had enjoyed most during my life was growing vegetables for the family, so I decided to retire early to grow them for other people.'

In 1946 Mr Baker had bought a twenty year old overgrown and unproductive apple orchard of three acres for £600, onto which he moved his new home, an anti-aircraft battery recreation hut previously sited in Grantchester meadows. He added extra bits over the years to accommodate his expanding family, a wife and eight children. And he also bought more land, and cows. 'At one point, I had eight acres, eight cattle and eight children,' he says with satisfaction.

To improve the fertility of the orchard and its land, he used a little fertiliser, and a lot of dung. 'I dug out two whole cattleyards by hand.' In addition he grazed his own cattle and goats and hand milked twice a day for thirty years. By the early 1950s the orchard was so fertile that he recouped the £600 in two years: 'I advertised in *Mother Earth*, the Soil Association's magazine, and sent boxes of apples all over the country by train.'

When he went into full time vegetable production in 1980, he started with plots of highly fertile land from which he had grubbed up the apple trees. Now he has no cows, but relies on his neighbour's pig manure, and is entirely organic.

Mr Baker showed me round his three pig-scented acres of organic produce (he recently sold five acres) on a cold November afternoon. He was wearing shorts. We inspected the rows of fat juicy leeks ('one of the easiest things I grow'), spinach, cabbages, sprouting broccoli, sprouts, red lettuce and carrots, suffering from a bad attack of carrot fly: 'My first really bad attack, but the flavour is still good.' The parsley was protected against frost under a row of old car windscreens.

Weeds were thin on the ground. 'Weeds are of course one of my worse problems. I mustn't let them seed. As the farmer's proverb says, "One year's seeding is seven years' weeding".' There are no fast acting selective chemical weed killers on Mr Baker's land, only mechanical removal. 'I have a wheel hoe – a piece of intermediate technology – which I push up and down between the rows. It's invaluable. I couldn't possibly manage without it.'

Then he has two rotavators, two mowers, and a hand drill, all of which are obtained from, and serviced by, his son who runs a mower service business in nearby Haslingfield. 'Without my son, my profits would be very much less. It's a tremendous advantage.'

Mr Baker does almost everything himself – digging, rolling, harrowing, planting, weeding, picking, selling. Once or twice a year he might hire a contractor. 'I'm temperamentally a loner, like Francis Chichester, my hero.'

He has little free time, often works from dawn till dusk, and little more than covers his costs. 'I do it mainly for my own, and my customers', satisfaction. Being entirely self-sufficient, I know my customers. If I grew fewer varieties, the business would be easier, and more profitable. But if I grew fewer, my customers would not be so happy. Nor would I. But I have given up some things, such as strawberries and peas, which were hopelessly unprofitable.

I don't know whether increasing the scale would increase the profitability. But then I would need more specialised machinery, which is expensive. Personally, I have no need or desire to expand. Rather, I want to do less work for less money – but the disadvantage of this would be less satisfaction for myself and my customers. At first my idea was to do twenty hours a week for £10 profit, but I have got into the way of doing much more.'

The quantity, and quality, of Mr Baker's produce is impressive by any standard. It looks good, and, most important, it tastes good. He produces, roughly in order of quantity: leeks, potatoes, brassicas, spinach, beetroot, carrots, parsnips, lettuce, spring onions, chicory, radishes, flowers, sweet corn, runner beans, broad beans, early onions, rhubarb, apples, courgettes, and in his glasshouse, peppers, cucumbers and tomatoes. He tried herbs, but found they did not sell.

His family grew up on the products of his labour: milk, cheese, fresh fruit and vegetables. Mr Baker is fitter and more agile than many men half his age. 'I started jogging in 1937 when it was more or less unheard of. I did two and a half miles three times a week for about twenty years and finally gave it up a year ago. I never enjoyed it, but I found it made me feel better.

I'm not a vegetarian, but three of my children are. I drink a lot of water – three pints a day. Water is certainly the cheapest medicament, and probably the most effective. We filter it to get rid of the chlorine. I scarcely drink any alcohol.'

'Every day I insist on having some raw brassicas. I once read that the Romans only had one herbal remedy for all diseases, and that was cabbage. I think there's some special virtue in cabbage. Cabbage water is supposed to contain a happiness drug.

One of my ideas is that because protein is the basis of life, its quality is most important. It's much more important to produce one's protein organically than one's lettuces, because it is the chemical basis of life. I was always very keen on milk for my children, and I produced it myself.'

The attitude of the public towards organic farming has changed enormously. It used to be considered eccentric. Now people are much more interested. Mr Baker has certainly done more than his fair share to ensure that the people of Cambridge have had a taste of organic produce. Through his charitable, one-man operation, based on his delight in pleasing others, I and many of my friends have enjoyed many a plateful of his fine produce.

CHAPTER TWO

HUMOUR

---◆---

'Put yourself in the shoes of Sam Sludge, managing director of Sludge International PLC, purveyor of Bulldog Brand Boil-in-the-Bag Soyburger . . . .'

Without humour campaigners, and campaigns, are lost. Des Wilson agrees. 'First, it keeps you from going round the bend. Second, it can be the most effective way to make a point. Third, signs of a sense of humour can be surprisingly reassuring to others. It suggests to them that you have a sense of perspective,' he writes, in his *A–Z of Campaigning*.

If you want evidence of a change in national mood, look at the funny pages in newspapers and magazines. Caroline accumulated a file stuffed with cartoons. Three in particular enlightened her lectures. In the days that Mars bars sponsored the London marathon, one of Fantoni's pocket cartoons for *The Times* showed two exhausted marathon runners; one says to the other, 'I don't know about a doctor but I could certainly use a dentist.' Austin in the *Spectator* sketched a café with 'The English Grill' on the awning and, in the window, a notice saying 'Good British Food. Cardiac unit in attendance.' And in the summer of 1983, as an illustration of the Government's attitude to food and public health, Heath in the *Sunday Times* drew two civil servants smiling down at the crowds hurrying along Whitehall: one says to the other, 'Let them eat cakes, sliced bread, sugar, fats, plus additives.' Humour is the weathervane of change.

How about a weekly column on food and health? Caroline asked *The Daily Telegraph* in the spring of 1986. 'Most newspaper features about food and health are written by agricultural, medical or health service correspondents who are generally only familiar with part of the story. Consumer correspondents all too often swallow the story given to them by trade associations and other industry representatives.' What's wanted in such a column is 'plenty of humour. No patronising stuff about eating roughage because it makes your bowel movements better. No weirdo stuff about ginseng twigs curing bald patches. The emphasis to be on what we all eat today, and health issues that affect us all.'

She wrote eighteen features for *The Daily Telegraph* and then for the *Independent* in 1986. The most memorable are the most amusing.

In June she congratulated the Meat and Livestock Commission for encouraging lean cuts, in a feature entitled 'Making no bones about meat'. It began: 'The *Meat Trades Journal* is a jolly good read. Almost weekly it has a go at vegetarians, loony nutritionists and anybody else who has had a stab at the meat on their plate.

It makes no bones (well, almost none) about the quality of meat products, and puts up a spirited defence of all things meaty. "Cancer prevention – new hope in meat" ran a headline in 1985, followed closely by "Pork Pie Month" featuring the Son of Pork Pie Man 1984, and the pattern for a knit-your-own-pork-pie-man-doll.' A bemused *Journal* leader responded, 'It is not often that the *Meat Trades Journal* gets a pat on the back in the national press. *Daily Telegraph* writer Caroline Walker is obviously a keen reader of the *Journal* and takes delight in our activities on behalf of the trade . . . .'

'And you thought milk came from cows?', published in September, commented on the new world advertised by enthusiastic food technologist Professor Alan Holmes, head of the industry- and government-funded food research station at Leatherhead.

'Lunch is a microwaved plastic pack of Fungisnack, nuggets of mycellar protein harvested from a cosy stainless-steel fermenter where it grows on a nutritional broth . . . .

At intervals throughout the day you help yourself to snacks produced by extrusion technology, which can turn sticky dough into a myriad of shapes, sizes and textures. The flavours for these and other foods are silently churned out by billions of genetically engineered bacteria, whose metabolic products are harvested, blended and encapsulated in microscopic carriers for maximum effect.

Dinner begins with imitation crabs' claws, moulded from a mass of farmed tropical plankton . . . . The meal is accompanied by the best that biotechnology can produce: synthetic wine from the laboratories of Omnitec-sous-Loire.'

Answer came there none from Professor Holmes. But Geoff Harrington, Director of Planning and Development at the Meat and Livestock Commission, became a friend; as did Dr Bryan Nichols, Legislation and Health Policy Manager at Unilever subsidiary Van den

Berghs, the giant margarine manufacturer. In August Caroline teased Van den Berghs with a feature entitled 'Buttering up the Royals':

'I made an interesting discovery at the margarine counter of a large supermarket, examining the extensive range of low-fat spreads, plastic churns, other dairy look-alikes, and solidified plant and fish fats that nowadays pass for butter substitutes.

You will be aware that different margarines are made of different types of fat. The most highly 'saturated' or hardened fats can cause blockages in blood vessels, leading to heart attacks, whereas polyunsaturated fats help to keep the arteries smooth and clean.

My discovery was that of the thirty or so varieties on sale, the only ones embellished with the exclusive Royal Warrant were Blue Band, Krona, Stork and Echo, the last three of which are among the most highly saturated margarines on the market. Does the Palace dine exclusively on saturated fats? And is the public thereby encouraged to buy them at the expense of more healthy varieties?

Horrified at the thought of blood cholesterol in the Royal Household solidifying in its tracks, I telephoned the manufacturers . . . . 'I am concerned about the royal arteries,' I said. 'Have you no Royal Warrant to stick on some more polyunsaturated product instead, Flora for example?' This caused a certain amount of emulsification in the Unilever tracks down at Burgess Hill, but the spokesman was finally able to tell me that the Royal Warrant applied to all Van den Berghs margarines.

Then why, I asked, do you not plaster it all over a more healthy variety? . . . Why not indeed, pondered the gentleman, and went off to unclot the packing and labelling departments.'

I pause from writing now, to look in to the local mini-market . . . and I find no Royal Warrant on any Van den Berghs margarine. Another triumph!

In September 1986 Caroline was invited to debate 'Food additives: for the benefit of the manufacturer or the consumer?' at the annual meeting of the British Association for the Advancement of Science. The slides she projected at the Bristol meeting were full of fun, and all made serious points. Showing a picture of a 'schoolburger' concocted from a technocopia of processed starches and sweetened hard fats, tarted up and made evidently palatable with cosmetic additives, typical of the stuff heavily advertised for kids, she said, 'Here is a new weapon. It's called the junk food bomb. It destroys people but keeps profits intact.' Now that food manufacturers are bound by Eurolaw to declare E numbers on labels, she said, 'Consumers are beginning to learn that what they're eating isn't food, but chemistry sets.'

Pointing to a series of pictures of the packs of products she had purchased in local shops, she said: 'Asparagus soup. That asparagus soup on the left, you may be astonished to hear, did contain "Brilliant Blue FCF". But Bachelors have very wisely decided to take it out, after I kept on putting up this slide at lectures.' [Chuckles of appreciation from the audience.] 'It is now reduced only to green colouring, you'll be pleased to hear.'

She didn't mention that two months earlier, at a lunch laid on by Sir Derrick Holden-Brown, boss of Allied-Lyons and then President of the Food and Drink Federation, she had a long and friendly discussion with Dr Iain Anderson, then the Chairman of Bachelors, another Unilever subsidiary. 'I felt we had something to share albeit we were ostensibly from opposite sides of the fence,' Dr Anderson wrote after Caroline died. 'In any case there was much common ground.' After the FDF lunch, we had a strong feeling that Dr Anderson went back to Sheffield and put it to his scientists that less chemistry and more food might be better for business as well as for Bachelors' reputation.

At the British Association, as her time for debate ran out, Caroline turned off the slide projector, switched on the lights, dipped into her shopping bag, and to the consternation of the chairman and delight of her audience, produced some goodies proving that additives are needed by the manufacturer, not the consumer. 'Cheese and onion flavour snacks. No cheese, no onion . . . . "Tropic Ora". Costs 75p. It smells absolutely disgusting. No tropical fruit in it . . . . Here are some fish fingers. "10 Value Fish Fingers." There's an awful lot of water in them. If you want a drink of water I suggest you get it out of the tap.' [Gales of laughter from the audience.]

After the debate the men on the manufacturers' side, from the Society of Chemical Industry and from Unilever, were no doubt relieved that despite protestations from the floor, the Chairman ruled that there should be no vote. But Caroline had the last word. In the Radio 4 'Food Programme' made to commemorate her, broadcast in October 1988, extracts from her British Association frolic were used; and in April 1989 that programme won the Glenfiddich award for best radio programme of the year. It is the 'smiles and laughter' that remain bright in the mind.

Producer Vanessa Harrison says, 'When Caroline appeared on "The Food Programme" two things would happen. All the phones would start ringing, and she would have cheered us all up. She was direct and challenging and funny, with a sincerity and passion that lifted the spirits. After that last programme, as the phones rang and the letters poured in, I found one letter which I thought neatly captured her spirit. "She delivered her message," wrote a Gloucestershire listener, "like a good meal. Wholesome, nourishing, and attractive. Long may the flavour linger".'

The flavour of 'Tropic Ora' certainly lingered. At the next conference on chemical food additives, held at the Dorchester Hotel in London at the end of October 1986, Caroline poured a dose into a medicine glass and invited anybody from the audience to partake. Nobody stirred among the industry representatives present. Finally Paul Levy of the *Observer* took up the challenge. He wrote:

> 'Caroline Walker embarrassed me into sipping a blue liquid that was the nastiest thing I have ever tasted. It had the longest "finish" I have ever experienced: half an hour afterwards, I was chewing unhealthily salted peanuts and quaffing an over-seasoned Bloody Mary in a vain effort to take the taste away.
>
> It strikes me, more seriously, that products like these have a corrupting effect on children's palates. If drunk before or during a meal, no child would be able to taste his food, unless it was very highly seasoned or laced with MSG. In short, only junk food would satisfy the hunger of a child who had drunk this indescribably filthy liquid.'

It was humour that made Caroline's message, that food matters, memorable; enabled others to see what she saw; and contributed to the change in national mood about food and health in Britain that is, above all others, her achievement. The message that we will all do well to value food, is not only good for personal and public health, but also for the future of the food industry as a whole. For, after all, if we don't value food, we won't want to pay much for it.

Meanwhile, cheapened food is what most people get. Added capital value, and new product development, is the name of the technofood name, as she explained in *Additives: Your Complete Survival Guide*:

'Put yourself in the shoes of Sam Sludge, managing director of Sludge International PLC, creator and sole purveyor of the Bulldog Brand Boil-in-the-Bag Soyburger, Iron Lady Wonder Whip, and Honey Crunch Rainbow Jelly Toppings. Last year's profits up, surplus cash to spend. Sludge Puddings reports good trade in the previous year. So do Sludge Snacklets and Sludge Sweeties. So rather than write out a hefty cheque to the Inland Revenue you pay a visit to your top secret Sludge Laboratories where Professor Crackling is putting the finishing touches to his latest creation, a new instant chocolate flavour pudding . . . .

"A complex multiphasic hydrocolloidal system of water, lipids, protein, carbohydrate and air," mutters Professor Crackling, tingling with excitement and doing a little skip as he deftly tips the brown powder into cold milk, does some energetic whisking with the Sludge Whisk-o-Pud (yours for just twenty Sludge Pudding packet tops) and artfully swirls the resulting light and creamy fluff . . . "Perfect!" he proclaims. "Organoleptic bliss! Now I can create twenty other puddings exactly the same, but they will all be different!"

For there is no tiresome chocolate in the mixture to prevent the basic recipe being turned into peach, pear, strawberry or his newest tropical tutti-frutti fizzy flavour: all the flavour is artificial. A quick shake of reliable artificial yumminess and the mixture can be endlessly transformed. All it needs is a good supply of processed sugars, starch, saturated fat, a few by-products of the dairy trade (nice and cheap courtesy of the EEC's ludicrous farming subsidies) and the all-important additives to make the whole thing work.

Emulsifiers to keep the fat and water properly mixed and make air stand up (that's where the whisking comes in), gelling agents to encourage solidification, antioxidants to encourage immortality and stop the fat going rancid when the packet sits on the shop shelf for weeks on end, flavour enhancers to enhance the flavour of the artificial flavours, and a dash of colour for visual appeal. Sam Sludge could not ask for more. All it needs is some clever packaging and advertising, and it'll be ready to send on a promotional tour.'

So looking at a label now, you get an idea of what the 'modified starch' and 'emulsifier', and other items in the small print, signify.

Caroline planned a book that needs writing: an account not just of additives, but of all the ingredients and processes that go to make modern food, and of what all the claims and descriptions on food labels really mean. Did you know, for example, that 'hydrolysed protein' on a label may signify a process whereby lorry-loads of meat and/or vegetable refuse are 'degraded' into constituent amino acids in pits of hydrochloric acid, mimicking vast stomachs, so big that a man could be dissolved in them? Well, now you know. The book waits to be written. Its title is *Better Read Than Dead*.

Some things are too serious not to joke about. John Rivers, Caroline's friend from student days, shared this 'ghetto humour' with her; he called it 'the joke that is separated by a fine line from the explosion of grief or anger' and, in her, 'the way in which, resolutely, jokes and all, she joined the side of the underdog. Because the underdog was there, and needed support. That was no joke, but she wrapped it in humour.'

In December 1985 Caroline was a co-founder of FACT, short for the Food Additives Campaign Team. To the consternation of the CIA, which in Britain stands for the Chemical Industries Association, FACT was launched in the Houses of Parliament, with support from what became thirty consumer representative organisations, and MPs from all parties. 'Food additives under fire,' was *The Times* headline. 'Tougher controls urged on use of food additives,' said *The Daily Telegraph*. 'Give this secrecy the bird,' proclaimed Sir Woodrow Wyatt in his *News of the World* column. 'If you buy a frozen turkey this Christmas, look out,' said Sir Woodrow. 'Most contain additives . . . . No one knows how much harm is done to our health by these tricks. They're designed to make us buy things we wouldn't if we knew what was in them.'

'Add a pinch of chemical to the Christmas fare,' was the *New Scientist* headline, inspired, like Sir Woodrow, by Caroline's Christmas hamper, on show at the FACT launch in Commons Committee Room 6, and then taken by her and the other co-founders of FACT down Whitehall and to Downing Street, for the delectation of the Prime Minister and her then Minister of Agriculture, Michael Jopling. What follows is the story Caroline wrote for the *Guardian*, published on 13 December, the day after FACT was launched. Like the contents of the Christmas hamper, Caroline's story packed a punch. And with all its smiles and laughter, the reader may feel other moods, thinking of those who in 1985 and in 1990 dream of a happy Christmas but are deceived by a tarted-up, chemicalised version of the real thing.

◆

CHRISTMAS DAY IN THE DOGHOUSE FOR MR JOPLING

I have a hamper of Christmas goodies for Mr Jopling; a tasty morsel or two for him to chew over on 25 December. Its contents will be no surprise. But surprises there are, in plenty, in the small print on the wrapping. For these 30 or so foods contain 64 colours, 22 emulsifiers, 13 antioxidants, 11 preservatives, 11 flavour enhancers, 8 gelling agents, 3 acidity regulators, 2 glazing agents, 1 anti-caking agent, 18 other processing aids and 16 mentions of flavours! In this season of goodwill, what *can* be in the minds of food manufacturers so to pollute our Christmas dinner and tea?

The Ministry of Agriculture, Fisheries and Food is fond of innovation and improvement; and fonder still of Added Value, which is the fate of many a deep-frozen turkey. With some skilful engineering, our feathered friend can be transformed into a ready-basted sponge, pre-injected with water, oil, emulsifiers and flavourings. 'The perfect turkey every time,' runs the blurb on the plastic wrapping.

Into one end of our watery beast goes Whitworths 'original recipe' country stuffing mix, complete with a dose of everybody's favourite flavour enhancer (monosodium glutamate, MSG) to make the taste buds tingle. Into the other goes more flavour enhancer, this time enhancing the flavour of the artificial flavour contained in Paxo's 'speciality' beef sausage stuffing mix. These Bisto instant gravy granules are so well formulated that the 'Best Before' date is December 1986 – a bargain – two Christmas lunches for the price of one! On to Knorr's instant bread sauce mix – certainly the oddest I've come across – containing beef fat, MSG and glucose syrup, with emulsifiers and other processing aids to turn the gritty powder into an instant sludge.

Sausages (OK, we all know about them), bacon, cranberry sauce – in her nineties, my granny always relished the trimmings. Well, there's no shortage of them in this lot – no fewer than 169!

Next is Mrs Peek's 'original' Christmas pudding: colour enhanced with caramel, flavour with artificial flavourings, sweetness with glucose syrup.

But the crowning glory of this meal is the sauce, and for the price of 29p, a kettle of boiling water, and some energetic whisking to whet your appetite, you too can join Mr Jopling as he slurps up the Bird's Whisk and Serve Brandy Flavour Sauce Mix. And if you find the brandy flavour a bit thin, well, there's always instant Brandy Flavour (20p for 1 fluid ounce), with the colour of pale pee (created with five coal tar dyes) and the smell of model aircraft glue. Or, if you prefer it, why not some lightly sweetened, ready stabilised aerosol cream? But you have to eat it all at once, before it collapses into a greasy puddle on your pudding. Finish off the meal with coal-tar-dyed and artificially flavoured mince pies, and you're all set for another batch of delectable goodies at afternoon tea.

Let us suppose you make your own cake. Flour contains bleaches and improvers; dried fruit preservatives and glazing agents; *glacé* cherries, mixed peel and marzipan are embellished with coal tar dyes, and ready-to-roll icing (concocted with hardened fish fat) contains emulsifiers. If you join the rest of the population and buy one, chances are you'll get all that lot and maybe more besides. And if you glorify your purchase with Supercook's pretty Marzipan Fruits you'll be lapping up five more coal tar dyes, which is as nothing compared to what you could be licking off the icing if you used the whole range of food colours available.

Assorted biscuits, sweets, savoury snacks – the eating goes on and on, the list of additives stretches towards dinner. It all represents Added Capital Value. The more products a manufacturer can make from the same amount of raw materials, the better for the economy. Food processing creates jobs, machines, advertising, packaging, design, transport. Additives are good for business. They create diversity, long shelf life, colour, flavour, texture, fizz, tingle, crunch, sludge, globbo. They allow manufacturers to replace the expensive bits of the recipe with water, air, cheap fats, starches, sugars, artificial colours and flavours. They lower the nutritional value of food. Even at Christmas.

If you shopped laboriously, you could avoid many of these 170 additives. But for those in a hurry and, worse, for those who are poor, there's little choice. So it's a Christmas box around the ear for Mr Jopling. And to spur him into action here is his New Year's Resolution: as Minister of Food, I promise that the Great British Christmas dinner in 1986 will be fit to eat.

Christmas dinner

Turkey Turkey, water, vegetable oil, salt, emulsifiers, flavourings.
(Swift Butterball)
Paxo rich sausage meat stuffing mix Breadcrumbs, beef sausage (beef, rusk, beef fat, spices), onions, beef fat, sage, wheat flour, salt, chives, parsley, modified starch, flavour enhancer (MSG), hydrolysed vegetable protein, sodium polyphosphates, flavouring.
(RHM Foods)
Whitworths Country Stuffing Mix Breadcrumbs, beef suet, hydrolysed vegetable protein, salt, flavour enhancer (sodium glutamate), parsley, oregano, thyme, sage, nutmeg, black pepper, flavouring.
(Whitworths Holdings)
Paxo Sage & Onion Stuffing Mix Breadcrumbs, dried onions, salt, beef suet,

dried sage, dried chives, dried parsley, wheat flour.
(RHM Foods)

Paxo Golden Breadcrumbs (for ham) Breadcrumbs, colours (E102, E110, E122, E142).
(RHM Foods)

Knorr Bread Sauce Mix Breadcrumbs, wheat flour, onion powder, salt, beef fat (with antioxidant E320), flavour enhancer (MSG), starch, dried glucose syrup, dried skimmed milk, caseinates, mace, acidity regulator (E340a), emulsifiers (E471, E472b), thyme.
(CPC UK, Knorr Division)

Mrs Peek's Original Christmas Pudding Vine fruits (in variable proportion), flour, sugar, invert sugar, syrup, animal fat, rusk, crumb, citrus peel, caramel E150, glycerine, glucose syrup, salt, spices (in variable proportion), citric acid (E330), preservative (E280), flavourings, antioxidant E320.
(Nabisco Group Grocery Division)

Birds Whisk and Serve Rum Flavour Sauce Sugar, starch, dried skimmed milk, hydrogenated vegetable oil, emulsifiers (E477, E322), lactose, caseinate, whey powder, flavourings, antioxidant (E320), colour (E160a).
(General Foods)

Birds Whisk and Serve Brandy Flavour Sauce Sugar, starch, dried skimmed milk, hydrogenated vegetable oil, emulsifiers (E477, E322), flavourings, lactose, caseinate, whey powder, caramel, antioxidant (E320), colour (E160a).
(General Foods)

Budgen Deep Mince Pies Wheatflour, sugar, animal and vegetable fat, apple, water, currants, sultanas, apricot and apple jam (containing gelling agents, liquid pectin, citric acid and acidity regulator E331), flavour and colours (E102, E110). Dried glucose syrup, mixed peel, suet, salt, spice, acetic acid, colours (E102, E110).
(Budgen, a Booker McConnell Company)

Moorhouse's Mincemeat Sugar, apples, vine fruits, glucose syrup, orange peel, rusk, suet, gelling agents (liquid pectin, acetic acid), citric acid, spices, colour (E150), flavourings.
(Premier Brands)

Pan Yan Cranberry & Apple Sauce Sugar solution, water, cranberries, apples, gelling agent (E440b), colours (E122, 155, 133), preservative (E220).
(Rowntree Mackintosh Sun-Pat)

Bisto Rich Gravy Granules Starch, animal oil, hydrogenated vegetable oil, salt, beef fat, hydrolysed vegetable protein, concentrated meat stock, colour (caramel), maltodextrin, wheatflour, emulsifiers (E472e, E482), anticaking agent (sodium aluminium silicate), dextrose, flavour enhancers

(monosodium glutamate, sodium 5-guanylate, sodium 5-inosinate), flavouring, antioxidant (E320, E321).
(RHM Foods)

Whitworths Dried Fruit Mixture Sultanas, currants, seedless raisins, candied citrus peel, glazing agent (905), preservative (E202, E220).
(Whitworths)

Whitworths Glacé Cherries Cherries, sugar, glucose syrup, preservatives (E202, E220), colour (E127).
(Whitworths)

Sainsbury's Cut Mixed Peel Orange peel, glucose syrup, lemon peel, sugar, citron peel, salt, preservative (E220), colours (E102, E124, E142).
(J. Sainsbury)

Whitworths Ready-to-Roll Icing Sugar, glucose syrup, hydrogenated marine and vegetable oils, emulsifier (E471).
(Whitworths)

Supercook Marzipan Fruits Almonds, sugar, invert sugar, glucose, edible colour E110, E127, E102, E131, E122.
(Supercook)

Tesco Red Food Colour Water, isopropyl alcohol, ponceau 4R (E124), carmoisine (E122), tartrazine (E102), acetic acid.
(Tesco)

Tesco Green Food Colour Isopropyl alcohol, tartrazine (E102), green S (E142), acetic acid.
(Tesco)

Whitworths Almond Marzipan Sugar, almonds, glucose syrup, colours (E102, E110, E122).
(Whitworths)

Park Cakes Iced Rich Fruit Cake Sultanas, brown sugar, marzipan (E110, E102, E122), wheatflour, whole egg, margarine, orange and lemon citrus peel, glucose syrup, rice flour, apricot jam, soya flour, whey powder, egg albumen, salt, colours (E150, E142, Chocolate Brown HT).
(Northern Foods)

Yule Log Sugar, milk chocolate (20%), flour, animal and vegetable fat, invert sugar syrup, egg, dextrose, fat reduced cocoa, skimmed milk powder, modified starch, emulsifiers (E435, E471), salt, starch, flavouring, preservative (E202).
(Allied-Lyons)

Savoury Snacks Flour, wholemeal, vegetable and animal fat, cheese, yeast extract, salt, flavourings, sugar, yeast, whey powder, wheat starch, flavour enhancer (monosodium glutamate), pepper, emulsifier (E481), colour (160a), antioxidant (E330).
(Nabisco)

Golden Wonder Choice Savoury Biscuits Wheat flour, vegetable fat, sesame seeds, salt, sugar, cheese powder, skimmed milk powder, glucose syrup, raising agents (sodium bicarbonate, ammonium bicarbonate), poppy seeds, flavourings, acidity regulator (524), caseine, malt, whey powder, yeast, emulsifier (E471), flavour enhancer (621), milk powder, spices.
(Dalgety)

Tea Time Assorted Biscuits Flour, sugar, edible fat (vegetable oil, animal fat and hydrogenated vegetable oil, antioxidant E320), oatmeal, rolled oats, dried whey, wholemeal, glucose syrup, currants, dried skimmed milk, invert sugar solution, raspberry jam (contains gelling agent: liquid pectin, citric acid E330), salt, fat-reduced cocoa powder (0.34%), raising agents (sodium bicarbonate, ammonium bicarbonate, tartaric acid, acid calcium phosphate), cornflour, wheatstarch, cocoa mass, butter fat, colours (E150, E120, E160a), emulsifiers (E322, E472e), carob flour, flavouring, invert sugar syrup, dried egg yolk.
(Nabisco)

Rowntree Mackintosh Selection of confectionery in special Christmas wrapping:

SMARTIES Milk chocolate, sugar, wheat flour, edible starch, colours (E171, E122, E102, E127, 133), flavourings, glazing agent (carnuaba wax), antioxidant (E320).

JELLY TOTS Sugar, glucose syrup, edible starch, citric acid, sodium bicarbonate, acetic acid, colours (E102, E122, E127, E142, 133, E124, E132), antioxidant (E320).

FRUIT PASTILLES Sugar, glucose syrup, gum arabic, gelatine, lemon juice, blackcurrant pulp, raspberry pulp, orange juice, citric acid, apple juice, flavourings, sodium bicarbonate, acetic acid, vegetable fat, colours (E102, E122, E110, E153, E142, E132), antioxidant (E320).

KIT KAT Milk chocolate, wheat flour, sugar, vegetable fat, cocoa mass, butter, raising agent (sodium bicarbonate), salt, yeast, calcium sulphate, emulsifier (lecithin), flavouring.

LION BAR Milk chocolate, glucose syrup, sugar, vegetable fat, cooked rice with added wheatgerm, wheat flour, sweetened condensed skimmed milk, butterfat, salt, flavourings, emulsifier (lecithin), yeast, raising agent (sodium bicarbonate), calcium sulphate (milk chocolate contains milk solids 20% minimum and vegetable fat).

AERO No ingredients listed.
Aerated milk chocolate contains cocoa solids 22% minimum, milk solids 20% minimum and vegetable fat.

ROLO No ingredients listed.
Milk chocolate contains milk solids 20% minimum and vegetable fat.

Bacon (streaky) Pork, water, salt, dextrose, sodium polyphosphate (E450c), flavour enhancer (monosodium glutamate), preservatives (E252, E250), antioxidant (E301), honey.

(Honeydew bacon, Pork Farms)

This bacon has the Charter Bacon Seal of Approval.

Sausages – Walls Pork Chipolatas Pork (minimum 67%, minimum lean 42%, maximum fat 25%), water, rusk, starch, salt, soya protein concentrate, spices, sodium polyphosphate, dextrose, herbs, flavour enhancer (621), antioxidant (E304), E307, sugar, flavouring, preservative (E223), colour (128).

(Walls)

Cream – Sainsbury's Real Dairy Cream UHT (aerosol) Cream, sugar, emulsifier (E471), stabiliser (E407), propellant (nitrous oxide).

(J. Sainsbury)

Additives used in the foods for the Christmas dinner

Colours		*Times used*
E102	tartrazine	11
E110	sunset yellow	7
E120	cochineal	1
E122	carmoisine	9
E123	amaranth	1
E124	ponceau 4R	3
E127	erythrosine	4
128	red 2G	1
E131	patent blue V	1
E132	indigo carmine	3
133	brilliant blue FCF	3
E142	green S	6
E150	caramel	6
E153	carbon black	1
155	brown HT	2
E160a	carotene	4
E171	titanium dioxide	1
	Total	64

Flavourings		
	Declarations of added flavourings	16
	Total	16

Flavour Enhancers		
621	monosodium glutamate	8

621	sodium glutamate	1
627	sodium guanylate	1
631	sodium inosinate	1
	Total	11

Antioxidant

E301	sodium ascorbate	1
E304	palmitoyl ascorbic acid	1
E307	synthetic vitamin E	1
E320	butylated hydroxyanisole	9
E321	butylated hydroxytoluene	1
	Total	13

Preservatives

E202	potassium sorbate	3
E220	sulphur dioxide	4
E223	thiabendazole	1
E250	sodium nitrate	1
E252	potassium nitrate	1
E280	propionic acid	1
	Total	11

Glazing agents

903	carnuaba wax	1
905	mineral hydrocarbon	1
	Total	2

Anticaking agent

| 554 | sodium aluminium silicate | 1 |
| | Total | 1 |

Gelling agents

E260	acetic acid	3
E440	pectin	5
	Total	8

Emulsifiers

E322	lecithin	5
435	polyoxyethylene sorbitan monostearate	1
E450a	sodium polyphosphate	4

E471	glycerides of fatty acids	4
E472b	lactic acid esters of fatty acids	2
E472e	esters of fatty acids	2
E477	esters of fatty acids	2
E481	sodium stearoyl -2-lactylate	1
E482	calcium stearoyl -2-lactylate turkey emulsifier	1
	Total	22

Acidity regulators

E331	sodium citrate	1
E340a	potassium dihydrogenorthophosphate	1
524	sodium hydroxide	1
	Total	3

Other processing aids

E330	citric acid (flavouring, raising agent)	6
E334	tartaric acid (antioxidant)	1
500	sodium bicarbonate (raising agent)	6
503	ammonium bicarbonate (raising agent)	2
516	calcium sulphate (firming agent)	2
540	acid calcium phosphate (raising agent)	1
	Total	18

| | Total additives plus flavours | 162 |

CHAPTER THREE

CHILDREN

———◆◆———

*'Without the discretion to provide a free meal for a poor child, what is a school
to do? Throw the child out in the street? Chuck away the left-over food?'*

One sure sign of the integrity and good sense of any government,
is its record on public health. In the nineteenth century,
revulsion against contamination of food and water, inevitable when
private industry is unregulated, led to enlightened laws designed to
protect the public against rapacity, fraud and disease. Besides which,
good public health is in the national interest: people who enjoy clean
air, safe water, a pleasant environment and food that is healthy as well
as safe and clean, are more productive.

A failing of the Conservative administrations of the 1980s is that Mrs
Thatcher and her advisors and ministers seem not to understand public
health. In the late 1980s an increasing number of traditional
conservatives and liberals turned away from the Thatcher government
because its enthusiasm for unregulated business evidently ignored the
public interest. The general outrage against dismemberment of the
National Health Service and privatisation of the national water supply,
and the food health and safety scandals of the mid and late 1980s,
exposed the Thatcher government as evidently uncaring or ignorant of
public health. If Thatcherism cannot accommodate public health in its
ideology, it is in that respect a throwback to the primitive politics of
laissez-faire, generally discredited over a century ago.

Caroline's commitment as a nutritionist was always to public health.
She was therefore bound to contradict the rhetoric of Thatcherism, just
as the Victorian reformers, who demanded closed sewers as the means
to conquer cholera and other water-borne diseases then epidemic,
collided with the government of their day.

Above all Caroline's commitment was to child health; and in her ten
years of public life, she showed again and again that government policy
was breeding not a rising but a falling generation; that the food and
therefore the health of the nation's children was – is – unprotected and
therefore deteriorating.

Her thesis for her higher MSc degree at the London School of Hygiene and Tropical Medicine, completed in 1977, has a pun with a sting, in its title: 'Single-parent families and social insecurity'. In this and a subsequent academic paper written with Dr Michael Church, 'Poverty by Administration', she showed that the official definition of minimum subsistence used then and now, derived from the old Poor Laws, is liable to condemn the poorest people on the dole, notably children of one-parent families, to basic malnutrition of a type generally supposed to have disappeared in Britain after the 1930s.

Professor John Waterlow, her supervisor, saw this work as 'a very useful contribution to our understanding of the relationship between poverty and food – which I knew absolutely nothing about at the time. She got a distinction for her thesis. I remember reading it and thinking "this is jolly interesting. I really ought to know more about this".' And at the time he wrote to her saying, 'I am very much impressed by your performance this last year . . . . I don't know whether in the long run you are interested in an academic career. If you are, I would like to get you back into the department.'

She had other ideas. In her early work on poverty she walked in the steps of the great social reformers Charles Booth and Seebohm Rowntree. Writing in 1989, her colleague Joyce Doughty says of her thesis 'Caroline's historical analysis was followed by her report of her survey of some fifty single-parent families . . . . A high proportion of these families spent about 40 per cent of total income on food while the national average was 22 per cent. Her detailed report of these families gives an idea of their social conditions.

'In 1977 it was estimated that there were 700,000 single-parent families and half were depending on social benefits. Three-quarters of all children on supplementary benefit were aged ten or less. Some 650,000 children were estimated to be growing up in poverty. In 1989 the number of one-parent families has passed a million, and Caroline's concern about the needs of children and the inadequacy of help remains relevant.'

In 1979 Caroline was working not in the Third World, as she would have liked, but in South Wales, at the Medical Research Council Epidemiology Unit in Cardiff. Following her thesis, she had become nutrition advisor to the Child Poverty Action Group. Academic nutritionists do not usually bite the official hand that feeds them with research grants. However, one of Mrs Thatcher's first personal initiatives on coming to power in 1979 was to introduce a new Education Act abolishing nutritional standards for school meals, and allowing local education authorities to decide whether or not to provide meals, and to charge any price they liked. In a well-publicised conference organised by the Advisory Centre for Education, Caroline challenged this new *laissez-faire* policy. 'Left to their own devices and given money to spend at will, many children will buy sugary and/or fatty snacks for lunch,' she wrote. 'Many children already have sweets and fizzy pop for breakfast – will they be having sweets for lunch in the future? The whole of the fast food industry must be rejoicing at the prospect.' And she predicted, following the then orthodox view, that a school meal free-for-all put children at risk not only of obesity but also stunting.

Her phrasing was trenchant, and she hit her first national newspaper headlines. 'Short fat kids of tomorrow' was the *Daily Express* story. An accompanying leader started, 'Caroline Walker of the Medical Research Council claims that children will grow shorter and fatter when local councils are free to scrap school meals . . . . Instantly our minds conjure up a picture of tubby dwarfs. But is it really true? Miss Walker declaims, 'Some children will be born short, others will achieve shortness, and it looks as though some will have shortness thrust upon them.' All of which sounds just a trifle melodramatic.' The conclusion, written in January 1980, was 'it will be right to keep an eye on what happens after April. But the days of the State, or local authorities, as an all-purpose nanny are over.'

Caroline's academic training in nutrition coincided with the beginnings of a revolution in thinking about children's food and health. In the 1970s, official policy was the same as that of the 1920s: go for growth. Big, heavy, 'bonny bouncing' babies were defined as healthy, because the most serious public health problems of British children half a century ago were those now seen in the Third World: emaciation and stunting. 'I have a photograph of the first school meals,' Caroline wrote in 1986.

'The rows of puffy-faced children stare solemnly up from their wooden benches. In front of them is a bowl of soup and a hunk of coarse bread, which they are, no doubt, itching to get their teeth into. The sequence of photographs in this East London school in 1900, 1925 and 1950 is remarkable and revealing.

In 1900 the boys sit, gormless and boss-eyed, rachitic and with the despair that comes from chronic underfeeding and infection. In 1925, they are more cheerful; many of the boys are strong and fit, but still there are many sunken eyed weaklings. In 1950 the school had gone co-ed; perhaps that had something to do with the cheeriness of the boys, but there is no mistaking the improvement in physical condition.

The same school is still doing business in 1986, and a photograph today would also show boys and girls of Asian, Caribbean and Mediterranean extraction. And in an area like the East End of London in the 1980s, we see a curious mixture of health problems. Some children are still too thin, and shorter than their chums. But some are too fat, and are useless at games.'

What Caroline saw in the 1980s were the ill-effects of a child health policy that had gone too much for growth, by means of fatty, sugary foods, heavy in calories but short of nourishment. Her conversion to this point of view can be dated back to 1979, and a correspondence with Margaret Wynn of the Maternity Alliance, who with her husband Arthur had written a revolutionary book, *Prevention of Handicap and the Health of Women*, which ten years later is still ahead of its time. Margaret Wynn summarised the evidence showing that a fatty, sugary diet in early life is liable to cause cancers and heart attacks in later life; what children need, she said, is the nourishment, including vitamins and minerals, of whole fresh food.

Caroline was impressed, and wrote back: 'Many nutritionists are prepared to sit on the academic fence until "proof" of the links between diet and disease have become established. I am not, partly because we will probably never get proof, and partly because I think the food industry has gone too far. There are now hardly any tinned foods on the supermarket shelf which do not contain sugar, and neither of the two bread companies producing over 60 per cent of the bread in the UK makes 100 per cent wholemeal bread on a national basis. I think these are the issues that pressure groups should now take up.'

Margaret Wynn replied: 'Of course you are right about "proof" which is a Euclidean or Cartesian concept in pure mathematics. Science has always advanced from hypothesis to hypothesis, abandoning or amending hypotheses as they are found to be inconsistent with the facts. But administrative decisions are virtually always based on hypotheses and rarely on anything which has been "proved"!'

So what should children eat? The old school of child health professionals, trained with textbooks written at a time when deficiency diseases were common among the poor in Britain, recommends that children be 'built up' with fatty, sugary foods. The new school, led notably by doctors concerned to prevent heart disease later in life, as well as tooth decay, obesity, and a multitude of other diseases, recommends the same food for children as for adults: plenty of whole, fresh food, and a minimum of processed fatty, sugary, salty food. Working with the Coronary Prevention Group, as she did from 1980, Caroline was resolutely of the new school. In all her writing she encouraged mothers to introduce their babies (after weaning from breast or formula milk) to the food that's best for all the family, and therefore to avoid fat and sugar. 'When you introduce "doorstep" cows' milk to your baby's diet, make sure it is semi-skimmed,' she wrote, in the first, hardback edition of The Food Scandal, published in June 1984.

The next month, in July, the Government published the report of its COMA panel on 'Diet and Cardiovascular Disease', recommending that everybody will do well to cut down consumption of fats, especially hard, saturated fats. Everybody, that is, but children under five. Why the exception? Caroline found out that a group of old-school child health professionals, led by Dorothy Francis of the Hospital for Sick Children in Great Ormond Street, had persuaded the Department of Health to insert the recommendation that young children drink full-fat milk. In the second, paperback edition of The Food Scandal Caroline wrote, 'There was no scientific debate, no evidence was produced to show that milk fat is essential for children . . . . When questioned about this [by Caroline] a member of the COMA Child Nutrition sub-committee [Dorothy Francis] replied, "I've signed the Official Secrets Act: I cannot comment". After all, healthy children throughout history and all over the world have grown up without cows' milk, and in any case 'the valuable nutrients of milk are in the watery part, the skim: this is where all the important vitamins, minerals and protein are to be found.' Caroline encouraged Parliamentary Questions on the issue, and invited Dorothy Francis to debate the issue. There was no satisfactory response.

Breast milk is of course best for babies, as Caroline indicated in an intriguing story she told about new-style wet-nursing, in a letter to BBC TV's 'Food and Drink Programme' in November 1985. According to a Farley's Milk rep, 'Princess Diana breast-fed her two boys for only six weeks, whereupon they were put on to bottle milk. But not the sort of bottle milk that ordinary citizens have to put up with. Her babes were fed on expressed breast milk purchased from Harrods' special breast-milk bank, which, at a price, supplies the chosen few. This milk is collected and prepared by Queen Charlotte's Hospital. Over-producing mothers take their surplus milk there, where it is used in the premature baby milk. It also goes to the Hammersmith premature baby unit.' But do these mums know, Caroline wondered, that some of their milk is going to the *crème de la crème* via Harrods?

What, though, of the schoolchildren on their anything-goes diets, that Caroline had warned against in 1979? All (well, some) was revealed in 1986. Someone in the Department of Education and Science leaked a draft of an official government report on 'The Diets of British Schoolchildren'. This, it turned out, was Government's response to the urgent request of its advisors who, in 1980, had like Caroline been worried about the abolition of standards for school meals. Not that 'response' was the right word: the report had been blocked. With me, Caroline organised a scoop for *The Daily Telegraph*, immediately followed up by the *Guardian* and other papers; and a 'World In Action' special for Granada Television: 'The Threatened Generation'. This media blitz forced the Department of Health to publish a rapidly edited version of the report.

Caroline knew what the Granada programme-makers needed. She suggested whom they should interview, checked the script, and brought the programme and its message to life by starring in the show, in front of a mound of food, the month's diet of a typical British schoolchild. This she had devised in a few days, working flat out at home poring over the obscured nutritional details in the draft report, and then translating this data into food by shopping in the local supermarkets.

Fat? The camera panned over the display. Caroline socked it to the viewers. 'A lot of fat comes from full-fat milk, thirteen pints of full fat milk . . . but what might be a surprise to some people – cakes, biscuits and sweets, chocolates too, these are very high in saturated processed fats. And then that huge mountain of four and a half pounds of chips; and there's another mountain of crisps in front. All these things contain a great deal of fat.'

Sugar? 'First of all there's a pound and a quarter of ordinary sugar that comes out of packets, but that's by no means all of it. There's an amazing amount of sugar in these cakes and biscuits and of course in the sweets, that's an obvious place. But what about these soft drinks?

There's nine pints of soft drinks there and each of those cans might contain anything from five to seven or eight teaspoons per can . . . . So what we have is not only a fatty kind of diet, but also a very sugary kind of diet.'

Whole foods with fibre? 'I practically had to get out a microscope to find them. What these children are eating is remarkably small amounts of fresh fruit and vegetables. And a remarkably small amount of wholemeal and brown bread, less than a third of a slice a day. They're eating far too much white bread.'

Caroline's confidence came from the academic company she kept. After Cardiff, she worked from 1980 to 1982 in Cambridge, at the MRC Dunn Clinical Nutrition Centre, for Dr (later Professor) Philip James and Dr John Cummings, world authorities on obesity and on fibre. From 1980 to 1984 she was joint Secretary of the Coronary Prevention Group with Professor Michael Crawford of the Institute of Zoology, London, an authority on essential fats. And from 1983 to 1986 she worked in the community for City and Hackney Health Authority, responsible for the heart and stroke prevention programme, where a colleague was Maggie Sanderson, chair of the British Dietetic Association community dietitians' group. Encouraged by Caroline to appear on 'World in Action' and speak their mind, they all agreed, and all were appalled.

As – in a quiet way – was Dr John Garrow, another authority on obesity, and chairman of the Government advisory committee that had commissioned 'The Diets of British Schoolchildren' in the first place. Why the delay in publication? 'What has been happening during that time I don't know,' he said. Caroline had a jolly good, informed idea what had happened. 'I think it's quite obvious why the report has been delayed. Because the results are an embarrassment. Because . . . what it shows is that children are eating highly processed unhealthy food. It shows that we are storing up an enormous problem for ourselves as a nation.'

Ray Whitney, Edwina Currie's predecessor as junior Minister at the Department of Health, was questioned. 'One in three are probably having too much – or were then – having too much unsaturated [sic] fat or too much sugar in their food,' he said unhappily. 'Well, that is absolute rubbish,' replied Caroline, 'and the Government is clearly incapable of doing arithmetic. Because you only have to look at the report – the figures are there, in black and white – and what these figures show is that three-quarters of the children in this survey are eating more fat than the Department of Health recommends. If the Government can't see that, they can't read.'

Mr Whitney, who returned to the back benches shortly afterwards, claimed that the Government had in any case started a heart disease prevention programme. From her position in City and Hackney Caroline was well placed to contradict him. 'Any campaign to improve the nation's eating habits has been done despite the Government, not because of the Government or with the Government's backing. There's hardly a health authority in the country that hasn't tried to organise some kind of healthy eating policy . . . . But they've had to pinch money off other budgets to do it. I don't see any campaign by the Government and I don't see any reason why the kind of food children are eating today in 1986 is likely to be any better than what children ate in 1983.'

And she had the last word. Bearing in mind Mrs Thatcher's personal involvement first as Milk Snatcher then as Meal Snatcher, Caroline said of Government:

'They're trying to show us that children are not keeling over from starvation. Well, we all know that. We only need to look around us; in fact, many children are overweight. But . . . these children are eating fatty sugary food which is low in essential nutrients, in proper nourishment; and that kind of food can only be bad for their long-term health.'

Two months later Mrs Thatcher's Government announced plans to prohibit local authorities from offering free school meals to poor children. Sir Douglas Black, a former Chief Scientist at the Department of Health, and later President of the Royal College of Physicians and then the British Medical Association, wrote, 'This constitutes too great a risk for the nation's children. The Government should abandon the proposal.'

Caroline wrote in *The Daily Telegraph*: 'Without the discretion to provide a free meal to a poor child, what is a school to do? Throw the child out in the street? Chuck away the left-over food? Any responsible government would never dream of privatising public health. But that is what this Government seems set to do. Good school meals are vital to raising the new generation. How many people would refuse a meal to a poor child? Would you?'

Since 1986 nothing has changed for the better, and a national campaign for school meals of guaranteed high quality is needed now just as much as it was in 1986, 1979, or indeed in the 1930s.

Caroline always had a lot of time for kids. Dr Peter Mansfield remembers staying the night with us in preparation for the Dorchester food additives conference in October 1986. In the morning, waiting on the doorstep for a cab, three of our neighbours' children came up.

'For a moment her own concerns were forgotten: the youngsters had her complete attention, and the mutual affection was obvious. They chatted with her about the day in prospect, off school to look after mum. She amiably threw out one or two ideas, sensible but right up their street. They clattered off with carefree, cheerful waves.

This was clearly not an isolated event, and displayed Caroline's chief stock-in-trade: her ability to listen to ordinary people and set her sound practical wisdom at their disposal, without patronising them in the least. There must be many industrialists reformed by her influence who never felt the blow.'

Dr Lesley Morrison remembers Caroline in the summer of 1988.

'On holiday with us on Jura, three months before she died, sharing her pleasure in good food with our 2½ year-old, with astonishing patience tutoring him in the art of bread-making. The origin of all ingredients carefully explained, the need for time and care in the process emphasised, the delight in the finished product shared. Sharing also with him her attitude to her illness, explanations given in clear, simple, truthful language which provided him not only with information but also with trust in and respect and fondness for the person giving it. A person could "have a sore tummy" and yet be a friend and fun and firm and fair.

Pity was not allowed. There was "proper" breadmaking to be done. "Banging" the bread had to be carried out for the required time. Good food was something to be valued, on no account wasted, and enjoyed – along with the company of your fellow breadmaker. Caroline wrote a poem for Neeps our son about our time together on Jura. There is a verse about their work together:

> We made a small bread hedgehog
> With currants for her eyes
> We pinched the spines across her back
> And left it warm to rise.

He still quotes things Caroline said to him. She planted seeds of ideas in his head which are continuing to grow. He trusted her, respected her, and knew she was honest. Children are perceptive.'

For me the most touching recollection of Caroline came from Margaret Wynn, forty years older than she, who had put her on a new path a decade previously. Margaret and Arthur were guests at our wedding in September 1987. A year later Margaret wrote, 'I have a memory of Caroline that will never fade. She stood against the pillars of the crypt in her wedding dress with a baby in a coloured mob-cap blissfully asleep in her arms. She was saying goodbye to wedding guests and her face had a calm, serene happiness. This was a side of her rarely seen by admirers like myself of her writings, her platform firmness and wit. Everyone will miss her public value and her promise in the world of nutrition but for the loss of the woman I can think only of the poet's "Could you not, Persephone, leave us one beautiful girl when there are so many thousand lovely women among the dead?" Her courage and humour and concern for anguished friends is already a legend among the young friends who surrounded her. To the old to whom death is but a long acceptance it seems against all course of nature.'

What follows is one of the several features Caroline wrote in 1986 about school meals and the suppressed 'Diets of British Schoolchildren' report. This one, which she called 'Mrs Thatcher's Children: A Falling Generation', was published as 'The Fats of Life' in *Nursing Times*.

◆

MRS THATCHER'S CHILDREN: A FALLING GENERATION

What do British schoolchildren eat? Biscuits, cakes, crisps, chips, soft drinks, sweets, sugar, white bread and the odd bit of 'real' food is the answer, revealed in a Government report entitled 'The Diets of British Schoolchildren', leaked to *The Daily Telegraph* on 3 April 1986, and officially released by the Department of Health one week later.

The survey details might never have reached the public, for its results have been drifting around Whitehall for over a year, awaiting ministerial approval to publish. Mrs Thatcher may personally have intervened to suppress publication of a report whose contents can only horrify those who care about the health of the nation's children.

Mrs Thatcher's personal interest in the food eaten by schoolchildren dates back to 1971, when as Education Minister she saved some

£9 million a year by withdrawing free school milk for seven to eleven year olds, and was promptly labelled 'Mrs Thatcher Milk Snatcher'. If kids drank pop instead of milk would their health suffer? Recollecting events of the time recently, science writer Bernard Dixon remembers Mrs Thatcher dismissing all worries. 'Nobody but she, it seemed, really understood what this was all about. All of her medical and scientific critics were wrong. And the rest was media mischief.'

In 1980, as Prime Minister, Mrs Thatcher was responsible for abandoning nutritional standards for school meals in favour of a free-for-all. The Government's theory was that children nowadays are well fed and need no special protection. With a personal background as a food scientist, Mrs Thatcher no doubt was especially confident that there would be no problems, and furthermore that the privatisation of school catering was good for business. Food choice was, after all, an individual responsibility, a matter for parental concern and guidance. It was not a matter which should be dictated by Government. That was the official line. However, the Department of Health's nutrition advisory committee, the Committee on Medical Aspects of Food Policy (COMA), was not so sure, and asked for a special survey to be carried out, to monitor the effects of Mrs Thatcher's policy. This survey was 'The Diets of British Schoolchildren'.

Between January and December 1983, a representative sample of ten to eleven and fourteen to fifteen year old children from state schools in England, Wales and Scotland kept a detailed weighed record of everything they ate and drank for seven days. The survey covered 3285 children, and was weighted to provide good coverage of social classes IV and V, one-parent families, the unemployed, and those receiving Supplementary Benefit and Family Income Supplement. Headed by Mrs Molly Disselduff, a senior nutritionist (recently retired) in the Department of Health's Nutrition Division, the survey was the biggest of its kind since the war, and cost £650,000.

Preliminary results of the survey were shown to COMA in December 1984. In April 1985, a fuller document was given to the committee, and was discussed further at their meeting in June 1985, when one of its members remarked than the fat content of school meals seemed to be higher than that of meals eaten at home, and that there was room for improvement. Three of the COMA members asked for the report to be published. But in December 1985 it was still sitting in the Minister's in-tray, awaiting permission for publication.

So what was going on, on the political front? MPs, like COMA members, wanted to know when the report would be published, and a series of parliamentary questions was asked. Here are the Government's replies. First of all the Prime Minister herself said, in February 1984, 'later this year.' Then John Patten, junior Health Minister, said in December 1984, 'spring 1985.' In March 1985, MPs heard it would be released 'in the very near future.' In January 1986 the Prime Minister declared that the government 'is currently considering whether to publish an interim report'. The final question came from Simon Coombs (Conservative MP for Swindon) on 17 February 1986, and was only answered two months later (an unusually long time), on 10 April by Ray Whitney, Mr Patten's successor at the Department of Health. He finally announced publication of the report, saying that the results were 'encouraging and show that our children enjoy adequate nutrition'.

After stalling for so long, what made the government publish? The report was leaked. *The Daily Telegraph* described in detail how the nation's children are growing up on a diet of pop, chips and biscuits, and how leading nutritionists, including the government's own scientific advisors, are extremely concerned about the results of the survey.

In a special Granada Television 'World in Action' report, broadcast on 14 April, Professor Michael Crawford of the Institute of Zoology, Regents Park, said, 'If you put the wrong oil in your motor car at the beginning . . . you're going to wreck it for the rest of its life . . . . And this is precisely what we are doing with our children.'

Dr John Cummings, of the Dunn Clinical Nutrition Centre, Cambridge, a member of the COMA committee, said, 'This is the sort of diet which has been condemned both in this country and in many countries . . . as the one likely to lead in later life to a whole variety of ill health.'

Professor Philip James, Director of The Rowett Research Institute, Aberdeen, said, 'I think that if . . . children continue to eat the same sort of food, we can pretty confidently predict that we will continue to have the highest heart disease rate in the world. Indeed, one might predict that the heart attack rate will go up.'

And Dr John Garrow, also of the main COMA committee and chairman of its nutritional surveillance panel that asked for the report in the first place, said: 'Whatever criterion of obesity you use with children, the proportion of obese children is increasing . . . . The younger you become obese, and the longer you have been obese, the more likely you are to develop diabetes, high blood pressure and other problems.'

Look carefully at the table overleaf. This information, straight out of the report but turned into pounds and ounces for the benefit of old-fashioned brains, shows the foods eaten over one month for the average child. We do not know the range of amounts eaten, because the report doesn't tell us. But if your reaction is, oh well, that's only average, it only applies to children with ignorant parents, then consider that for every child who eats better than these results show, there is one who eats worse. These figures are a disgrace, and demonstrate just how badly British teenagers are being fed.

One month's supply of food for the average British teenager.
(In the DHSS report, quantities were given in grams. Here they have been scaled up to one month's supply, in pounds and ounces.)

Food	14–15 year olds		10–11 year olds	
	boys	girls	boys	girls
Milk (full fat)	15 pt	10 pt	14½ pt	11 pt
Milk (skimmed/semi skimmed)	3 oz	3 oz	4½ oz	4½ oz
Yoghurt	9 oz	11 oz	14 oz	14 oz
Cream	1 oz	2 oz	1 oz	1 oz
Cheese	10 oz	6½ oz	6½ oz	5½ oz
Beefburger	11 oz	6½oz	6½ oz	5½ oz
Poultry	1 lb 3 oz	1 lb	14 oz	13 oz
Meat, pies	7 lb 8 oz	5 lb 7 oz	5 lb 9 oz	5 lb
Fish	1 lb 1½ oz	14 oz	1 lb 3 oz	1 lb
Eggs	10½ eggs	7 eggs	8½ eggs	7 eggs
Butter	11 oz	9 oz	9 oz	7½ oz
Margarine	6½ oz	5½ oz	6½ oz	5½ oz
Vegetable oils/other fats	1 oz	1 oz	1 oz	1 oz
Sugar	2 lb 1 oz	1 lb 1 oz	1 lb 6 oz	1 lb
Jams etc	4½ oz	3 oz	4½ oz	4½ oz
Baked beans	2 lb 4 oz	1 lb 6 oz	1 lb 9 oz	1 lb 2½ oz
Peas, lentils	1 lb 1½ oz	15 oz	14 oz	12 oz
Other vegetables	3 lb	1 lb 4½ oz	2 lb 12 oz	2 lb 11 oz
Chips	7 lb 8 oz	5 lb 7 oz	4 lb 5 oz	4 lb ½ oz
Other potatoes	5 lb 12 oz	4 lb 14 oz	5 lb	4 lb 2 oz
Crisps etc	12 oz	15 oz	1 lb ½ oz	1 lb 1½ oz
Fruit	4 lb 3 oz	4 lb 13 oz	4 lb 14 oz	5 lb 10 oz

Food	14–15 year olds		10–11 year olds	
	boys	girls	boys	girls
Nuts	1 oz	1 oz	1 oz	1 oz
White bread	6 lb 8 oz	4 lb 11 oz	4 lb 8½ oz	3 lb 14½ oz
Wholemeal bread	8 oz	8 oz	8 oz	5½ oz
Brown bread	5½ oz	4 oz	3 oz	3 oz
Other breads	10 oz	6½ oz	6½ oz	4½ oz
Biscuits, cakes	7 lb 14 oz	6 lb 5 oz	8 lb 7 oz	7 lb 13 oz
Breakfast cereals	2 lb 7 oz	1 lb 4 oz	2 lb 6½ oz	1 lb 9 oz
Pasta, grains	15 oz	13 oz	10 oz	9 oz
Confectionery	1 lb 15 oz	1 lb 9 oz	1 lb 13½ oz	1 lb 14½ oz
Milk shake/ice cream	12 oz	6½ oz	15½ oz	15½ oz
Soft drinks	7¼ pt	6¾ pt	9 pt	8¾ pt
Alcohol/shandy	1 pt	½ pt	¼ pt	¼ pt

Children now eat more cakes and biscuits than fruit or vegetables (excluding potatoes), more chips and crisps than plain potatoes, more sweets than wholemeal and brown bread, more sugar than fish. Taking into account all the sugar in soft drinks, cakes and biscuits, soft drinks, ice cream, flavoured yoghurts, and all the other processed foods these children eat, their total consumption of sugars must come to at least one fifth of their energy (calorie) intake. This is a nutritional disaster, because processed sugars supply no nourishment, only calories. Saturated fats, too, from cakes, biscuits, chocolates, fatty meats and margarines, and from high-fat dairy foods, are present in large quantities in this food. The total amount of whole fresh foods, lean meats, fresh fish, fruit, vegetables, brown and wholemeal bread needs to be increased a good deal to bring this teenage diet in line with medical recommendations of the Royal College of Physicians, the Department of Health, and the World Health Organisation.

Younger boys are eating half a packet of cakes and biscuits a day, and the rest of the children do their bit to keep Britain's biscuit industry busy. Our teenagers are growing up on a diet of chips, cakes, biscuits, sweets, sugar, soft drinks, white bread, fatty meat and fatty milk. The report does not tell us much about the types of meat eaten, but we know that most meat produced in Britain is too fatty, and that families with young children, particularly poorer children, buy more of the cheap cuts, and meat products which are often little more than a refuse tip for piles of unwanted fat in the meat trade.

So how much harmful saturated fat is disappearing down the teenage gullet? The report doesn't tell us. How much of the essential polyunsaturated fats? Or sugar? Fibre? Zinc? Folic acid (folate)? The report doesn't tell us about any of them. The nutritional analysis is done strictly according to criteria which are twenty or thirty years out of date. It has nothing to say about the likelihood of this generation growing up to develop premature heart attacks, diabetes, overweight, piles, diverticular disease, colon cancer, breast cancer, and the other illnesses which are now agreed by more than fifty independent expert medical committees around the world to be caused in large part by this sort of food. The report makes much of the fact that children are 'taller and heavier' than the official growth standards, but says nothing about the likely consequences of lifelong overweight. It only gives analyses for those few nutrients which are recognised by the Department of Health, and for which there are Recommended Daily Amounts (RDAs): iron, calcium and riboflavin were low in some children, particularly girls. But it tells us nothing about trace elements and minerals like zinc and magnesium, which are important, particularly when children are growing.

It hardly needs to be said that teenage children are at one of the most vulnerable stages of their life, when their food should be of the best possible quality. But the Minister appears not to have understood this point. Mr Ray Whitney's press release on the report said, 'The preliminary results are encouraging and show that our children enjoy adequate nutrition. They reveal no significant difference in nutrition as between various groups of children or children in different social classes.' (The survey could also be interpreted as showing that the teenage diet is of uniform awfulness right across the board.) However, he did concede that 'some children and their parents need more information and education about healthy eating'. How many children need this service? On the subject of numbers, the civil servants who advise Mr Whitney could perhaps benefit from changing places with the schoolchildren they were studying: '1 in 3 children ate more fat than the experts would like,' continued the press release. But the report showed that 4 out of 5 children ate too much fat, judged by the Department of Health's own recommendations. The 1984 COMA report 'Diet and Cardiovascular Disease' said that national fat intake should be reduced to 35 per cent of energy (calories), a level exceeded by about 80 per cent of all the children studied.

What about school meals, so dear to Mrs Thatcher's heart? Very fatty, and not likely to do a lot for the hearts of the kids who eat them. The least fatty midday meals tended to be those eaten at home. The worst nutrition was obtained by children, particularly 14–15 year old girls, who paid a visit to the local takeaway or cafe. They never made up the shortfall in essential nutrients in their other meals, and their overall nutritional intake was the worst in the survey.

What lesson does the Department of Health draw from this sorry state of affairs? That a speedy return to mandatory nutritional standards for school meals is needed, and that all children should be encouraged to eat them, rather than trundle round to the chippie? No. The report concedes that 'there may be some scope for improvements by reducing fat content to bring school meals closer to the recommendations of the COMA report', but the minister's statement merely says that 'children need more education about healthy eating'.

Is education likely to solve the problem? Is it realistic to suppose that a ten year old child will choose food because it is good for her/him, in the face of glamorous and exciting advertisements about less healthy alternatives? The food industry spends around half a billion pounds on advertising a year, much of it directed at children. As a general rule, the more heavily a food is advertised, the worse it is likely to be for your health.

The only sensible conclusion is that education authorities should be compelled to provide food of an optimum nutritional standard to children in their care. They are, after all, *in loco parentis* (in place of the parent). Many schools and education authorities are already doing this, and have discovered that children, like adults, appreciate healthy food when it is imaginatively prepared. Education authorities should be helped in their difficult task, by – at the very least – provision of nutritional guidelines from the Department of Education and the Department of Health.

Is it an erosion of choice and liberty to provide healthy rather than unhealthy food? Some people think it is. If children want fizzy drinks and chips for lunch every day, should they be allowed to have them? When I was at school (and at home for that matter), we had to eat what was put in front of us. Many adults have memories of ghastly institutional meals, which should be an encouragement to us to show that it can now be done better. Those schools which have succeeded in changing from sausage and chips to fish pie and spinach, and have kept their customers, have done it with the help of their children. Many have used school meals to teach about nutrition, but their job could have been made a lot easier with proper support and funding.

If the next generation is to rise, rather than fall, it is essential that children are supplied with food which will enhance their health.

CHAPTER FOUR

SCIENCE

———◆———

'A very strange attitude has developed in science, whereby many scientists feel that they shouldn't have an opinion; they shouldn't have a point of view. . . .'

'Before, during and immediately after the Second World War, scientists had a very clear idea of what their responsibility and what their duty was. They felt they were part of public health. They felt a real responsibility in making their contribution.'

This is Caroline talking to Derek Cooper for the BBC Radio 4 'Food Programme' broadcast after she died. But since then, she said, 'A very strange attitude has developed in science, whereby many scientists feel they shouldn't have an opinion; they shouldn't have a point of view. That as soon as they start to make a decision about one issue or another, whether saturated fat causes heart disease, whether too much sugar – processed sugars – causes tooth decay, as soon as they come to a conclusion, yes or no, the rest of the scientific establishment sees them as cranks, sees them as unscientific, emotional.

So if you're a scientist, and you come off the fence, then you're condemned as a bit loopy. And this makes it difficult for your future career. I've heard scientists say it, myself: "I can't possibly come out and make a positive statement, because people will think I'm crackers, and I won't get another job." And I think that's very sad.

For after all, the whole point of scientific investigation is to arrive at a conclusion. That's the whole point. Why do it otherwise?'

With two degrees, one in biology, one in human nutrition, Caroline was fully qualified to work as a research scientist, which she did for the Medical Research Council between 1978 and 1982. She signed professional letters with the same words she used to introduce herself at conferences: 'Caroline Walker, nutritionist'; and she remained a fully paid-up member of the establishment body, the Nutrition Society.

Therein lay her value to everybody she addressed outside the academic world. She had the credentials. She couldn't be ignored by academic nutritionists. Although some labelled her an 'activist' – as if there is some virtue or meaning in being a passivist – nobody suggested that she was a quack. She spoke from the heart, but also from the head: she knew her stuff. And most leading nutritional scientists not only liked her, but also respected her. John Waterlow, her professor at the London School of Hygiene and Tropical Medicine, and a man of immense influence, wrote a testimonial for her in 1978. 'In the [MSc] examination she obtained, as I recollect, the highest marks ever achieved,' he wrote. 'Her essays are lively and well-informed; one was so good that I have kept it as a reference source for my own work.'

Other scientists rather admired her, for having the guts to state publicly what they said privately. 'Keep going,' some said, during tea breaks at conferences. Some sent letters of support with the handwritten afterthought 'Confidential!', and Caroline would charm them into going public, on radio or television. Documents arrived in the post, sometimes sent anonymously: relevant evidence from learned journals; records of secret meetings in which government and/or industry representatives perverted the evidence that cheapened processed food is unhealthy and unsafe; drafts of official reports on national food and nutrition policy showing how science is betrayed and corrupted by those in power.

And those scientists who have convictions and courage know the temptation to be silent. Caroline was guided by the old saying that 'all that is necessary for evil to prosper in the world is that good people do nothing'. Dr Kenneth Heaton, a leading scientist steadfast in his view, based on science, that Western food is now far too sugary, has endured abuse from industry. He describes Caroline as 'a dauntless warrior in the cause of truth and integrity'. Sir Francis Avery Jones, Dr Heaton's predecessor as Chairman of the Royal Society of Medicine Forum on Food and Health, asked Caroline to join the Forum's Steering Committee. He wrote, 'I chose her because of her superb writing and ideas. One of the Committee (from the food industry) resigned – so I knew I had chosen well!'

Like Sir Francis, Dr Denis Burkitt is a champion of wholegrain bread, and can tell many stories about pressure put on scientists by the hanky-panky artists from the white bread trade. At the beginning of 1985 Caroline and I wrote two Review Fronts for the *Observer* showing, based on Caroline's historical and nutritional research, that the quality of the food people typically eat in Britain now is much the same as the diet of the working classes in the 1930s analysed and condemned by John Boyd Orr. 'I must congratulate you on the research you do so carefully,' wrote Dr Burkitt. 'I want to express my gratitude to you, for your courage and your convictions.' It was Caroline of course, who put her reputation as a scientist at risk.

'I don't have a burning desire for publicity myself,' she told Derek Cooper. 'I've turned down far more television and radio appearances than I've accepted.

The line I always took, was that I was paid with government money – through the Medical Research Council and other organisations – and so are most scientists in this country. I think if they are paid by the public, they have a duty to tell the public what they're doing. If somebody rings you up, and it is your area, then I think you have a duty to say something. You don't have to come to a conclusion.

Another thing, is that scientists are afraid not to know the answer. The great art is to be able to say to somebody when they ring: "Yes, I can do this." Or: "No, I can't." In the beginning, an awful lot of the interviews I did were for producers and editors desperate to get somebody to talk; and they'd say: "Sorry it's you again. I've tried ten others, and they won't do it!"'

This was all after Caroline had become well-known, and her views sought as a champion of public health. In 1977, armed with two degrees, and with experience as an editor for Elsevier Scientific Publishing in Amsterdam, her main concern as a scientist was to get a job. She applied for work in Kuwait, Bahrain, Morocco, Tunis, Greece, Oman, Italy, Jamaica, Libya, The Gambia, Israel, Malawi, the Philippines, and Switzerland; and anywhere overseas, for the Medical Research Council, the Food and Agriculture Organisation, or Oxfam. Nothing doing. Why, with her outstanding academic record? I asked Professor Waterlow.

He didn't know. 'Perhaps her health record stood in her way,' he said; for throughout 1976 she suffered a severe illness from which she never entirely recovered.

In July 1978 she settled for a job as a nutritionist with the Medical Research Unit Epidemiology Unit in Cardiff, working to Dr Peter Elwood, best known for his view that an aspirin a day keeps the heart attack away. She supervised field work involving meticulous 'weighed intake' measurement of the food people eat. In one trial added bran was given to 125 men who had suffered a heart attack, to see if a high-fibre diet might protect against heart disease. In another study she measured what 210 women in Caerphilly were eating during one week, to see if their diet had anything to do with the quality of their blood (specifically, their high-density lipoproteins). Caroline became very skilled at dietary surveys and their interpretation, but she did not believe that the work in Cardiff had much value except as a means to employ scientists, as her sardonic account of a third study in a job application written in November 1979 indicates. 'Body frame size. Data on wrist and knee diameter (and left and right-handedness) are being collected in 800 men and 800 women. The extent to which frame size "explains" variability of weight for height will be examined.'

This application answered an advertisement in *Nature* for a nutritionist at the Dunn Clinical Nutrition Centre, Cambridge 'to participate in a two-year programme funded by the EEC Biology Medical Research Division concerned with food intake data in EEC countries', working to Dr W.P.T. James. She got the job, and worked at the Dunn for two years, from May 1980 to May 1982.

There was more field work to do at the Dunn. The 'March Study' (after the Cambridge town in which it was centred) designed to see if a high-salt diet is a cause of high blood pressure, involved the meticulous measurement of urine, ferried to the laboratory in the back of Caroline's trusty Mini-Morris van. She wrote a guide to 'The Collection of 24-Hour Urines' for field-workers, including practical tips, like '(e). The subject will need to be reminded about the collection. Therefore give each person a safety-pin (as used for babies' nappies). Men should pin their underpants together.'

This work had its funny side. In an associated study, Caroline and Dr James experimented on themselves, supplementing sodium chloride (salt) with lithium in their diets. This study, requiring care because lithium can kill, taken in excess, was not only for the sake of humanity but also in aid of a PhD for Caroline's friend and colleague Claudia Sanchez-Castillo or 'Miss Mexico', to whom Caroline wrote a long poem. Here is an extract:

> Phil has swallowed sodium chloride,
> No changes felt he in his inside
> No extra water did he drink
> Although he might be on the brink
> Of changing from a normal being
> Into one who can't stop peeing . . . .
> Miss Mexico, you must not hide
> The dangers that you put before us.

> Many they are, extremely treacherous,
> When lithium and sodium treats
> You offer us with meals to eat
> All wrapped in tasty orange pills.
> Many invisible horrid ills
> Might we develop all the while
> That you pursue this nasty trial.
> Clad in lab-coat there you stand,
> Machine exploding, pee in hand
> As gleefully you calculate
> The lithium excretion rate . . . .
> Not that we ever wish to be
> A hindrance to your pee-H-D . . . .

Early in 1981 Dr James asked Caroline to go on a trip to France, to advise whether or not the Dunn should collaborate with researchers in Lyons, in a study on diet and colon cancer. The French proposed to use the 'dietary recall' method by which people remember what they eat, rather than the tedious but precise 'weighed intake' method. According to Caroline's report, the French scientists explained that 'Cambridge does not understand French cuisine, which is so incredibly complex that weighing is impossible. Englishmen who dine on HP Sauce may find it easier.' In any case, Caroline was told, 'Dr Geser can remember what he ate thirty years ago with no difficulty whatsoever. Either he ate cauliflowers or he didn't.' She gave the proposed collaboration a thumbs down.

Her first EEC project at the Dunn was also on colon cancer. For many years, scientists all over Europe, and indeed the world, had been accumulating data on diet and cancers. Such studies had multiplied after Dr Hugh Trowell and Dr Denis Burkitt had concluded, after decades of observation and analysis of research then available, that high-fibre diets, preferably rich in whole cereals, probably protect against cancers of the digestive system, and that high-protein, high-fat diets as typically eaten in Western countries are an important cause of common cancers. Data was pouring out of the laboratories into the learned journals, throughout the 1970s.

But so what? All this work had little meaning or purpose until it was collected together and analysed. Only then could anybody judge whether or not Western food is a cause of cancers, which can therefore be prevented, at least in part, by new food and agriculture policies designed to alter the balance of national and international food supplies, with public health in mind. Individual studies are inconsequential. The question is, do many studies taken all together, contradict each other? Or do they add up, like jigsaw pieces of the same big picture? Caroline set to work, collecting the European data on diet and colon cancer together.

In 1971 Dr E.F. (Fritz) Schumacher, author of *Small is Beautiful*, gave a Presidential Address to the Soil Association. His subject was organic farming and growing, but what he said is a watchword for everybody who cares about the relevance of science to our world. He said, in part:

> 'We now should be concerned with "research on research". We should accumulate, assess, systematise and communicate to the public the evidence that already exists and that is being currently produced . . . We should know everything about developments in the USA, Canada, Australia; and what of Sweden, Holland, Germany and France?
>
> The future belongs to the young. We must find out how to get to them and how to present research findings in such a way that the young will take to them. Things exist only in the minds of people, not on paper. We must make our message into a story.'

I don't know if Caroline ever read these words. Dr Schumacher finished with a call for partnership. 'Right ideas, in order to become effective, must be brought down and incarnated in this world, and the commercial interests must be made into servants of correct ideas. In spite of many experiences that seem to point to the contrary, the world is ruled by ideas and not by vested interests.'

Caroline's second EEC project at the Dunn was epic: a critical review of the state of the scientific art not just on diet and cancer, but of diet and the major Western diseases in Europe, starting with heart disease. She scoured the literature, did computer searches, and began a vast correspondence with scientists in Austria, Belgium, Czechoslovakia, Denmark, Finland, France, East and West Germany, Greece, Greenland, Holland, Hungary, Iceland, Ireland, Italy, Luxembourg, Norway, Poland, Portugal, Romania, Spain, Switzerland, Turkey, the USSR and Yugoslavia. When scientists had moved, she pursued them from place to place, country to country. Only Albania and Bulgaria seem to have escaped her scrutiny.

Piece by piece, the big picture took shape. Caroline was not the first person to see that Western food is a major cause of Western diseases; but her immense survey gave her complete confidence in her judgment. In October 1980 she went in place of Dr James as a speaker at a conference on diet and patterns of disease in Europe. The conference, organised for the European Parliament, was a grand occasion at the Palais de l'Europe in Strasbourg.

Caroline was not daunted. John Rivers said of her, 'She came from that English social class that was born, if not to rule, then at least to argue imperiously.' She enjoyed the European stage, but was not beguiled. At the Strasbourg conference the talk was about diet and health in theory, not in practice. Afterwards, she wrote a long letter to Bertrand Schneider of the *Comité National de Prévention Médicale* in Neuilly, France, the Strasbourg conference organiser. The letter is the testament of a scientist committed to public health, and is as cogent now as then; also as relevant, alas, because nothing has changed. What Caroline said is that talk of 'healthy food' or 'healthy diet' is meaningless until these terms are defined; that talk of changing diet for the better is purposeless unless targets are identified; that nutrition research and education are used as substitutes for action; and that public health is too important to be left to doctors. In her own words:

'The second half of the Strasbourg meeting seemed to concentrate on ideas for making undefined changes in diet in undefined groups of people and using educational methods to achieve them. I am still uncertain about how we came to this conclusion regarding strategy for change. Which disease(s) were we talking about? What changes in diet?

Do I assume we had tacitly accepted most of the main conclusions arrived at by the twenty-two international and national committees who have looked at the whole subject of, for example, diet and heart disease, decided that heart disease is preventable, and that dietary measures, among others, are needed? If so, then I presume that our general aim might be along the following lines:

(a) Increase consumption of complex carbohydrates, for example cereal products, particularly bread, pasta, rice, etc. (b) Decrease consumption of fat, which implies less meat and meat products of a fatty nature (for example, beef, lamb, pork) and increase less fatty meats (chicken etc) and fish. (c) Decrease refined carbohydrates. (d) Increase fresh fruit and vegetables. (e) ? Less salt. (f) ? Less alcohol.

It seems to me that the great strength of the nutritionist's position today is the fact that the same general diet can be recommended for the prevention of so many disorders: heart disease, gastrointestinal disorders, obesity, and so on. This general conclusion developed over the last five to ten years should mean that we are less fragmented in our approach, and should also mean that we start thinking about national strategies for primary prevention. But perhaps there was no such acceptance of these twenty-two committees' deliberations? I do not know, because we did not define the changes we thought necessary. We talked vaguely about screening, and vaguely about education . . . .

At the meeting, I accused the general assembly of picking on screening and education because they see them as essentially "non-political" actions. I am sticking to my criticism! The setting up of screening and education programmes implies a large input from the medical, nutritional and associated professions . . . and such programmes are often run within medical establishments. It could be argued rather unkindly that they recommend such programmes merely to ensure their continued employment! . . . It is time that those who ask for large amounts of public money to be spent on such things (and that is a political decision) should evaluate what they are doing. Politicians will soon demand that this be done and we should anticipate this reasonable request.

Those who demand money for such programmes seem to find them infinitely more acceptable than other forms of government action. Indeed, when I mentioned taxes, subsidies, and laws at the meeting, visible shudders went around the room and there was a hurried response to slam the door in the face of impending revolution.

I find this attitude to change quite extraordinary. One does not have to be a political scholar to realise that almost every stage of food production, from plant breeding to advertising, is in some way influenced by government – by taxes, subsidies, loans, laws, and so on. One does have to be rather more scholarly in approach, however, before deciding which change(s) will be the most effective in changing diet.'

Caroline continued to stand up in conferences, and to write, lecture and broadcast, making these points, for the rest of her life. With those who thought like her, she was beginning to set a new agenda. Public health needs public money spent for the public good: and in standing up and saying so, Caroline insisted that scientists are – or should be – servants of humanity.

Towards the end of the 1980s, the medical establishment, the leading consumer representative bodies, and many legislators, agreed that major Western diseases, starting with heart disease, can be largely prevented by whole, fresh food which on a national basis can be supplied only by a new food and agriculture policy with public health as its goal. Intellectually, scientifically, morally, Caroline's argument is won. Ten years previously, a good handful of people in Britain agreed with her. She was outstanding in having no thought for herself; she had the stubborn integrity of somebody who, to use Sir Francis Avery Jones's words of her, was 'ahead of her time'. Some say that she would have done better to be more protective of herself.

A story from my own experience confirms that while the argument is won, the battle is not. On 28 July 1989 the British Government issued a White Paper following the Great Bug Scandals: 'Food Safety: Protecting the Consumer'. This included a section on 'Government advice on nutrition' which began, 'The Government is keenly aware of the need for sound dietary advice and information to the public. A good diet is essential to the proper growth of children and the maintenance of health in adulthood.' It went on, 'The Government welcomes what food manufacturers and retailers are doing to promote healthy eating.' At the press conference I asked the Rt Hon Kenneth Clarke, Secretary of State for Health in Mrs Thatcher's Cabinet, if he could define a 'good diet' or 'healthy eating'. He glowered and would not answer.

A month after the Strasbourg conference, on 17 November 1980, Dr James sent Caroline a letter. 'I wonder if you would be willing to help a group of us in a somewhat difficult task?' he began, disarmingly. 'We have been asked by the National Advisory Committee on Nutrition Education (NACNE) to present to them a set of principles on which future health education in Britain can be based. Our concern, of course, is to deal with dietary questions . . . .

The plan is to have a meeting from 9.00am on Friday 9 January 1981 to Sunday lunchtime, the 11th . . . . I appreciate we are making very heavy demands on your time, but this is a very important problem and

I think that if we can get it right it could in the long term be of considerable importance . . . .'

And so Caroline became Secretary to the working party commissioned by the National Advisory Committee on Nutrition Education, itself set up by government. The story of the NACNE report and its betrayal is well known, and best told in the paperback edition of *The Food Scandal*. In 1980 Caroline may have suspected what was to come: NACNE's predecessor set up by government in the 1930s was the Advisory Committee on Nutrition: no 'Education', notice.

NACNE changed Caroline's life; mine too, since the suppression of the NACNE report by government and industry was the occasion of my meeting Caroline in 1983 and our professional and personal partnership. As a scientist, Caroline came off the fence. While her colleagues waited, she acted. She had enough of the academic world and moved into the community in 1982, from the Dunn to City and Hackney Health Authority, responsible for its heart disease and stroke prevention programme.

Caroline retained her identity and integrity as a scientist by applying her knowledge. While the NACNE report remained marooned, she used its drafts as a basis for new food policies for Health Districts, in London, and nationally. She wrote accounts of the scientific basis for the NACNE recommendations. And at the end of 1983, after the NACNE report was eventually published as a 'Discussion Paper', she wrote one of a series of papers for the *Lancet* designed to show how the plans of the NACNE report can be put into action.

By this time her knowledge of food policy was formidable. She had a special interest in eating habits, or 'dietary patterns' as academics say, and how these change over the years. 'Dare to suggest to many British citizens that it would be healthier to eat less fat and sugar,' she wrote in *The Food Scandal*, 'and you might get a good ticking off for trying to ruin British food and culture. Take your peculiar ideas to the funny food shop round the corner that sells beans and prunes in sacks . . . .

Yet the food we eat today has little to do with the food we ate 150 years ago, or even in the 1950s. Pasta, noodles, yoghurt, hamburgers, muesli, Camembert cheese, roasted peanuts, aubergines, peppers, satsumas, garlic sausage – none of these things are British, and all of them have been introduced recently.

In the last twenty or thirty years, Greek, Chinese, American and Italian restaurants and take-aways have been springing up all over the place . . . . Did you think that Colonel Sanders served in the Royal Fusiliers, or that McDonald of the hamburgers hails from the Highlands, or that the Pizza Express was the London to Carlisle mail train?'

The language in the *Lancet* was more measured, but its message, made plain by Caroline's meticulous analysis of dietary surveys and the breadth and depth of her knowledge of food and nutrition, is the same.

THE NEW BRITISH DIET

The long-term dietary goals set out in the report of the NACNE working party (1) propose substantial reductions in the national consumption of fat (25% for total and 40% for saturated fat), sugar (50%), and salt (25%) and a rise in consumption of dietary fibre (50%). A reduction in alcohol consumption is also recommended. Changes of this scale have been criticised as being draconian, (2) unenjoyable, (3) un-British, (4) and difficult to achieve. (5) Yet there is nothing new about these goals. The British diet, in common with nearly all national diets, is constantly changing. (6) Until about 200 years ago, sucrose was eaten in very small amounts and only by the affluent. (7) For the mass of the population, total fat consumption was below 30% of total energy until well into this century. (8) Those who doubt the practicality of change may overlook the substantial changes in the British diet (9) since 1945 and even in the past decade, towards a higher level of processing and the introduction of many new foods not British in origin (eg, hamburgers, yoghurt, pasta).

I have set out here one simple scheme demonstrating that it is possible to construct a British diet with the foods now eaten in the UK which goes a substantial way towards meeting the long-term NACNE goals. This guide is inevitably schematic, but it points to changes which consumers could make by exercising an informed choice. It also points to the scale of response that will be required from industry; a change to a new British diet will not come about only because of consumer demand.

Method

The Household Food Consumption and Expenditure Survey (NFS) records weekly food purchasing data from a random sample of approximately 7500 private households throughout Great Britain. It is conducted annually and throughout the year. It omits alcoholic and soft drinks, sweets and chocolates, and meals eaten outside the home, and therefore underestimates total food consumption. However, since it provides detailed information about the individual foods people buy, shows the contribution of different foods or groups of foods to average nutrient intakes (NFS, table 34), and takes account of household wastage, it is the most suitable source of national data for calculations of this type. The data used here are taken from NFS, 1981. (10) Other national data (Consumption Level Estimates) give the total quantities of all foods and alcohol moving into consumption from agriculture and the food industry. They give no information about wastage along the distribution chain, how meat is turned into joints, the diversion of meat and fish into pet foods &c. Their use is therefore severely limited.

To work out how the NACNE recommendations can be achieved I examined the contribution of different foods or groups of foods to the national intake of fat, saturated fat, sucrose, and fibre (Table 34, NFS 1981) and proposed changes on this basis. The precision with which changes can be proposed is constrained by the way in which NFS nutrient analyses are presented. For example, large numbers of different foods are grouped together in "other meat and meat products", and "other cereals and cereal products", so nutritional changes resulting from changes in the quantities of these foods cannot easily be specified.

The new diet

Table 1 shows the differences in weights of foods between the 1981 NFS diet and the new diet. Table II compares the contribution of different groups of foods to national nutrient intakes (NFS, Table 34; additional calculations have been made using McCance and Widdowson's *The Composition of Foods* (11).

Dairy Foods

Dairy foods provide 30·8% of total and 41·3% of saturated fat in the national diet. Liquid milk (3·8% fat by weight) alone provides 12·6% of total and 16·9% of saturated fat. Butter is the only other single food providing as much saturated fat (16·0% of total saturated fat). The widespread provision of skimmed (<1% fat by weight) or semi-skimmed (<2% fat by weight) pasteurised milk could have perhaps the greatest immediate effect on total and saturated fat consumption. The new diet (table I) has the same quantity of milk (0·55 pints/person/day), but specifies that it is semi-skimmed, thus preserving milk's valuable contribution towards nutrients other than fat. (Vitamins A and D are fat-soluble, but occur in small quantities in milk; other sources are available.) Butter has been reduced by a third. Other milk and milk products, cream, and cheese have not been altered, their contribution to national fat and sucrose intakes being small. However, there is scope for the food industry to make less fatty cheeses and less sugary yoghurts. Cream accounts for only 1·3% of total fat in the national diet, and no changes have been made.

Table 1. Changes in weights of foods consumed from 1981 NFS diet to new diet (g head/day unless otherwise stated)

Food	% change	Weight 1981	New diet
Liquid milk (litres)	0*	0·31	0·31
Dried milk (litres)†	0	0·003	0·003
Other milk, cream (litres)†	0	0·03	0·03
Cheese	0	15·6	15·6
Butter	−33	15·0	10·0
Beef, veal	−33‡	28·1	18·7
Mutton, lamb	−33‡	17·0	11·3
Pork	−33‡	15·3	10·2
Bacon, ham (raw)	0	16·7	16·7
Liver	+110	2·8	5·9
Poultry (raw)	+50	28·1	42·1
Sausages	−50	13·6	6·8
Other meat and meat products	−50	36·3	18·1
Total meats		157·9	129·8
Fat fish	+100	2·5	5·0
All other fish	+100	17·3	34·6
Total fish		19·8	39·6
Eggs (number)	0	0·5	0·5
Margarine§	−33	16·7	11·1
Other fats§	−33	13·0	8·8
Total fats (excluding butter)		29·7	19·9
Sugar and preserves	−50	53·0	26·6
Fresh potatoes	+50	157·3	236·4
Other fresh vegetables	+50	93·3	139·8
Other vegetables and vegetable products	0	67·2	67·2
Dried beans	300	1·7	6·8
Total vegetables		319·5	450·2
Fresh fruit	100	74·3	148·6
Other fruit and fruit products	0	32·0	32·0
Total fruit		106·3	180·6

Food	% change	1981	Weight New diet
Bread	+50	126·4	189·7¶
Flour	0	24·1	24·1
Cakes, pastries	−33	11·3	7·6
Biscuits	−33	20·7	13·9
Other cereals and cereal products	100	43·1	86·2
Total cereals		225·6	321·5
Beverages	0	11·9	11·9
All other foods	0	38·3	38·3

*Change to semi-skimmed. †Milk litre equivalents. ‡Less fatty cuts. §Low saturates.
¶Half wholemeal, quarter white, quarter brown.

Meat and Meat Products

Meat and meat products provide 27% of total and 25·3% of saturated fat in the UK diet. Sausages, and "other meat and meat products" (pies, convenience meats, pastes, spreads, &c) together provide 9·7% of total and 8·9% of saturated fat. The intake of such products has therefore been reduced by half. No account is taken of food processing modifications which could reduce their fat content. Carcass meat consumption has been reduced by approximately a third; this should be achieved by the purchase of smaller quantities of lean meat derived from leaner carcasses, not by the diversion of large quantities of surplus fat into meat products. MAFF carcass grading standards will need to be reviewed. Liver and poultry, both low in fat, have been increased. Overall, these changes will reduce the weight of meat purchased by about a third.

Fish

Partly to offset the reductions in carcass meats, and partly to increase consumption of food low in saturated fat, fish consumption has been doubled. It is important that the processing industry seeks to minimise the amount of total and saturated fat added to fish products.

Eggs

The NACNE working party made no recommendation to change cholesterol intake. Therefore, no changes have been made to egg consumption.

Fruit and Vegetables

Fresh fruit and vegetable intake has been increased. The new diet contains

2–4 potatoes per day. "Other fruit and fruit products" and "other vegetables and vegetable products" have been maintained at the 1981 level because many contain added sugar, salt, or both, which the processing industry should reduce. However, these categories also include frozen fruit and vegetables which could be increased without harm. The increase in dried beans (supplying about 1 g dietary fibre), could be achieved by increasing consumption of canned baked beans (17 g/head/day, 1981); but because sugar and salt are added to canned baked beans, it would be better to adjust cooking practices (by adding dried beans and pulses to stews, for example).

Cereals

Bread has been increased by 50% to a total of 190 g/day, or 4–7 slices, of which half is wholemeal, a quarter brown, and a quarter white. This change achieves most of the increase in cereal dietary fibre proposed by the NACNE working party. An important part of the change in bread consumption will be the nationwide provision of much better quality bread, which can be eaten with most main meals without a thick covering of fat. "Other cereals and cereal products" (including oats, breakfast

Table II – Contribution of different food groups to national nutrient intake in the 1981 NFS and new NACNE diet

	Energy:kcal(Mj)		Protein (g)		Fat (g)	
	1981	New	1981	New	1981	New
Dairy foods	420 (1·75)	311 (1·36)	16·1	16·3	31·9	21·3
Meats	362 (1·50)	267 (1·12)	22·6	21·7	28·0	18·2
Fish	26 (0·11)	52 (0·22)	3·2	6·4	1·1	2·2
Eggs	38 (0·16)	38 (0·16)	3·2	3·2	2·8	2·8
Fats, oils	232 (0·95)	154 (0·60)	..	..	25·6	19·1
Sugar, preserves	199 (0·85)	99 (0·42)	..	..	..	..
Vegetables	192 (0·81)	274 (1·15)	6·8	9·2	2·0	2·0
Fruits	63 (0·27)	88 (0·38)	0·8	1·0	0·9	0·8
Cereals	640 (2·71)	790 (3·54)	17·4	24·4	10·0	10·4
Beverages	7 (0·03)	7 (0.03)	0·4	0·4	0·1	0·1
All other foods	33 (0·14)	33 (0·14)	0·9	0·9	1·1	1·1
Total: all foods	2212 (9.29)	2113 (9·12)	71·5	83·5	103·5	78·0
% energy	100	100	12·9	15·8	42·1	32·2

A fuller version of this table giving the contributions to national nutrient intake of all the food groups in table 1 is available from the author on request.

cereals, rice, pasta, milk puddings) have been doubled. Cakes and biscuits have been reduced by a third. There is scope for the food industry to diversify into cereal products which are low in fat, sugar, and salt.

Margarines, Cooking Fats

These products provide 24·8% of total and 19·3% of saturated fat in the UK diet. They have been reduced by a third and are specified as being low in saturated fat. Thus less fried food will be eaten and the fats used for frying will be vegetable oils rather than lard or hard margarines. Small quantities of soya, sunflower, corn (maize), and olive oils and others low in saturated fats should be used. Margarine, like butter, will be spread thinner on bread, and less will be used on vegetables. For those who find it difficult to reduce the total amount of butter or margarine, low-fat spreads will be useful.

Sucrose

NFS excludes sweets and soft drinks and also does not show the contribution of different food categories to sucrose consumption. It is therefore difficult to assess the impact of the above changes on total

| Fatty acids (g) | | | | | | Carbohydrate (g) | | Dietary fibre (g) | |
| Saturated | | Mono- unsaturated | | Poly- unsaturated | | | | | |
1981	New	1981	New	1981	New	1981	New	1981	New
18·8	12·6	10·1	6·6	0·9	0·5	18·0	18·6	..	..
11·5	7·4	12·3	8·0	2·0	1·5	5·0	2·5	..	..
0·2	0·4	0·4	0·8	0·4	0·8	1·0	2·0	..	..
0·9	0·9	1·1	1·1	0·3	0·3	..	..	..	..
8·8	3·4	10·5	4·7	4·9	9·5	..	..	..	..
..	..	..	..	..	..	53·0	26·5	0·06	0·03
0·6	0·6	0·8	0·8	0·5	0·5	39·0	57·1	9·8	11·9
0·2	0·2	0·4	0·3	0·2	0·2	14·0	20·0	1·5	2·5
4·0	3·4	2·9	2·9	1·9	2·2	128·0	172·0	7·8	14·4
0·1	0·1	..	..	..	..	1·0	1·0	..	..
0·4	0·4	0·4	0·4	0·3	0·3	5·0	5·0	..	..
45·6	29·4	38·9	25·6	11·4	15·8	264·0	304·7	19·2*	29·6
18·5	*12·5*	*15·8*	*10·9*	*4·6*	*6·7*	*47·7*	*57·7*	..	..

*This is an underestimate; fibre is present in all foods to which cereals have been added but values are not always given in food tables.

sucrose consumption. Consumption level estimates will be the only indicator of national change. The food industry should explore ways of reducing the sucrose content of processed foods. This may require changes in legislation (eg, for jams). It will certainly involve changes in food texture as well as taste. The use of artificial sweeteners could provide a short-term solution to the problem of the nation's sweet tooth.

Salt

NFS data give no details about the distribution of salt in the British diet. Food cooked with less or no salt may not become acceptable overnight. Greater use of other flavourings (eg, herbs, spices, lemon juice) will be helpful. The food industry should explore ways of reducing the salt content of nearly all processed foods.

Conclusion

This analysis is only one way of correcting the British diet. There are many others. The NACNE long-term dietary goals can be achieved, and are reconcilable with British food habits. The greater part of the recommendations can be met by the relatively straightforward steps outlined above. However, both MAFF and the food industry will need to work towards agreement about compositional changes for a very large number of processed foods in order for the long-term goals to be met in full. Labelling of all processed foods will need to be greatly improved.

Department of Community Medicine,
St Bartholomew's Hospital and City and Hackney Health District,
18–21 Charterhouse Square,
London EC1

REFERENCES

1.   National Advisory Committee on Nutrition Education. Proposals for nutritional guidelines for health education in Britain. London: Health Education Council, 1983.
2.   Marr J, Morris JN. Changing the national diet to reduce coronary heart disease. *Lancet* 1982; i: 217–18.
3.   Oliver MF. Should we not forget about mass control of coronary risk factors? *Lancet* 1983; ii: 37–38.
4.   Marr JW. Putting dietary theory into practice. *British Nutrition Foundation Bulletin* May 1983: 65–72.
5.   British Nutrition Foundation. Implementation of dietary guidelines: obstacles and opportunities. London: BNF, 1982.
6.   Braudel J. Capitalism and material life, 1400–1800. London: Weidenfeld and Nicholson, 1973.

7.   Quick A. Sheiham H, Sheiham A. Sweet nothings: an analysis of the information the public receives on sugar and health. Report to the Health Education Council, 1980.

8.   Burnett J. Plenty and Want. A social history of diet in England from 1815 to the present day. London: Scolar Press, 1979.

9.   Walker CL. The national diet. *Postgrad Med J* (in press).

10. Ministry of Agriculture, Fisheries and Food. Household food consumption and expenditure 1981. London: HM Stationery Office, 1983.

11. Paul A, Southgate D. McCance and Widdowson's *The Composition of Food*. London: HM.

CHAPTER FIVE

CAMPAIGNING

———— •◦• ————

'Both scientific and public debate about the quality of human life is being
stifled for the convenience of the civil service and the food industry.'

'It still happens,' Caroline wrote in September 1985. 'I'm sitting at
my desk and the phone goes. "Er hello, I'm writing a newspaper
article about food and health, the British diet, that sort of thing. I
thought, well, that you could, er . . ." "Help?" I say. "What exactly do
you have in mind?" (the British Diet and Health being a largish subject).
"Well, what I wanted to know about is, have you heard anything about
a report, a government report, that's been suppressed?" "Ah," I say.
"You must mean NACNE or JACNE." "Yes yes, that's it," they say,
excitedly. "I want to write about it." "You do?" I say. "Yes," they say.
"An exclusive sort of article, you know."

I do indeed, and while I pause to decide whether to spend half an
hour explaining the NACNE report for the umpteenth time, or to tell
them to go away and read all about it in one of the other "exclusive"
NACNE articles, I wonder how on earth any journalist could have failed
to read about it in 1983 and 1984, so widespread was the publicity.

For almost every journalist who reached for the phone in 1983 or
1984, and for those who are catching up in 1985, NACNE was their
introduction to the seedy politics that control decisions about food and
health in this country: the two and a half year delay to publication, the
cosy relationship of the food industry with government, the distasteful
politicking and tittle tattle that goes on behind closed doors, the flagrant
disregard for public health in the face of threats to financial gain, and
the contents of the report itself. Most writers were certainly a bit
shocked by what they found.'

Caroline often worked for no payment; this feature was for *Health at*
School, a new professional journal for school teachers and nurses. The
editor who commissioned the feature liked it; but the owner refused to
publish it, even after the saucy bits above were cut out. Caroline and I
worked together, after we met in June 1983, and wrote *The Food Scandal*,

published in June 1984; so I shall use 'we' in this chapter. We joked about incessant requests for hard-hitting, ground-breaking, muck-raking, history-making features which, at the same time, must not cause any trouble with lawyers, advertisers or sponsors. In April 1986 Caroline agreed to write a feature criticising the draft Government report 'The Diets of British Schoolchildren', for *Precis*, a 'quarterly review of recent literature designed to emphasise the role of nutrition in the maintenance of health and primary prevention of disease', owned by the Unilever subsidiary Van den Berghs, or to be more precise, by the 'Flora Project for Heart Disease Prevention' through its PR agency Burson Marsteller.

In June, Julian Stainton of Burson Marsteller got a rocket. 'Dear Julian,' Caroline wrote. 'I have just had a telephone call from Liz Anfield of Education in Practice . . . . She wanted to know if I would consent to some changes which had been requested by Burson Marsteller. I said I wouldn't. What I want to know is, why does Flora censor *Precis*? . . . If all the articles come out with stuff that's kind to Flora, your readers will be very suspicious. If you try to alter articles that are a bit on the sensitive side, I cannot see the point of writing at the top of the newsletter "the views expressed in these articles are entirely those of the authors." They obviously aren't.

It won't do, Julian. Please tell your Lord and Master that I won't have my article changed. And that you shouldn't be meddling with other people's words either.' She ended with a tip to make Flora more money. 'My sister says that if there were decent oven-ready chips, lower fat than the others, polyunsaturated, no anti-oxidants, no nasties, she would buy them. I told her I had already suggested it . . . .'

Caroline and I were once asked to write a hard-hitting, ground-breaking book for a leading charitable organisation, on the great food scandals of 1983 and 1984, to 'spearhead' its new healthy food initiatives. After delivery a letter arrived from the publisher regretting that the book was '*ultra vires* our Governing Instrument'. We went to see him, and he spoke of 'imputations of state of mind', 'malicious libel', 'didn't commission a campaigning book', 'our status as a charity', 'contract null and void', and so forth. An idea then occurred to me and I asked to see the annual report; and there among many others were grateful thanks to donors Tate & Lyle, British Sugar, Berisfords, Cadbury Schweppes . . . . Just as well there's nothing about smoking in the book, given that Mr Unmentionable of Colossus Tobacco is Chairman of your Board of Trustees, eh? We laughed. We cancelled the contract. We didn't return didn't return the advance, because we hadn't been given one. (This story does not suggest bad faith on anybody's part, nor that any boss of Cosmos Weeds believes that smoking causes cancer, or puts pressure on charities, or knows anything about this story. Really. I mean it.)

Like 'activist', 'campaigner' is rather a bad word, in Britain. 'You're not really a journalist now, are you?' a features editor on *The Times* once said to me. 'You're a campaigner. Maybe you're an expert.' (Being an expert beats being a campaigner; experts can say what they like. Professors and doctors are experts, as indicated by headlines like 'Prof slams "health" foods' or 'Sugar OK, says top doc'. Be an expert, if you get the chance.) In Britain journalists, like scientists, are supposed not to have a point of view. Facts, like data, are supposed to 'speak for themselves'.

But it is people, not facts and data, who have voices, and brains. A lot of the time Caroline wasn't campaigning; she was simply speaking her mind. In response, editors talked a lot about 'balance' with her. 'We couldn't run your piece by itself,' they'd say, as if they had no choice. 'We'll have to balance it.' And so another contribution would appear, from the Cake and Biscuit Bureau, or from a scientist who says that whole food causes malnutrition, and a controversy would be fabricated.

Sometimes she would say, after reading a published version of what she had written: 'Where did all these "may"s and "some"s come from? I wrote "soft drinks are a health disaster", not "some soft drinks may be undesirable".' 'We couldn't run your piece as it stood,' editors would say. 'We had to tone it down.' And hence, the sub-editorial additives, and any controversy would be neutralised, along with her meaning.

Caroline's first successful campaign was to achieve publication of the NACNE report. At that time I was working for the *Sunday Times*. In June 1983 I was sure of my story, and went to see the News Editor, Anthony Bambridge. 'Tony,' I said, 'I've got the front-page lead news story next week, and it's about nutrition.' Bambridge continued to read proofs, and did not look up. 'I guess you think nutrition is about meals on wheels, and Asian schoolchildren with rickets,' I said. He looked up. 'Well, isn't it?' he said. 'What if I were to tell you,' I said in reply, 'that a report on food and health originally commissioned by Government has concluded that the food we typically eat in Britain is a major cause of killer diseases, starting with heart disease, and that this report has been suppressed by Government because of its implications for the food industry?'

'I think you've got the lead story,' he said, and so I had: 'Censored – a diet for life and death', was the front page headline on 3 July. Caroline told me later that a number of scientists who, like her, were outraged by the suppression of the NACNE report, had targeted me as one journalist who could be encouraged to reveal its existence, and force its publication. That is how campaigners use newspapers, but Caroline herself was never that cool or calculating. The first draft of the report, which I needed to clinch the story, was posted to me from Scotland, not from her.

For most campaigners, campaigning is a living, like being a scientist or a journalist. It wasn't like that for Caroline, either. What she did for me was to make me realise in the words of a nameless scientist quoted in my *Sunday Times* revelations, that NACNE 'is the biggest scandal in British public health since the Victorian days when officials refused to accept or act on the fact that cholera and typhoid were caused by open drains.' So I left the *Sunday Times*, joined Caroline, and became a campaigner, or maybe an expert.

Next for us was *The Food Scandal*. I wrote an introduction, translated the NACNE report from scientific into ordinary language, and wrote one other section: forty-five pages of the original hardback edition. While I groaned and moaned over this task, Caroline wrote the rest of the book, 140 pages, in three weeks, like a long letter, around 2500 words a day. 'That was the NACNE report,' she started. 'So much for theory and science. Where does it leave you the shopper, cook and consumer of three meals a day, 1095 meals a year? . . . Food is not just a physical matter. It provides entertainment, hospitality, warmth, fun and pleasure . . . . Can meals containing less fat, sugar and salt ever provide the same amount of enjoyment?'

Indeed they can, she said; and concluded by saying, 'When it's your birthday, eat whatever you like. When you have something to celebrate, be thoroughly self-indulgent. The day-to-day breakfasts, lunches and dinners are the ones that count as far as your health is concerned. If you put them in order, a plateful of chocolates once in a while will do little damage. This is how traditional societies operate. They eat healthy food day to day, and for celebrations kill the fattened pig or cow, eat expensive sweets and fry their foods in oils. What we as a nation should do is to put the celebration foods back where they belong instead of eating them every day.'

The Food Scandal was published on 11 June 1984. On 28 June it made publishing history; it is, as far as I know, the only book to be simultaneously banned and to be number one in the bestselling charts. Beecham, the drug, food, haircream and toothpaste manufacturers, secured an injunction against us and Century, our publishers. A total of three statements of claim were filed against us: two from Beecham, and one from Kelloggs, the breakfast cereal manufacturers.

Why were Beecham, Kelloggs, and other manufacturers who did not sue us, so hostile? In his thoughtful obituary of Caroline, her friend John Rivers wondered why *The Food Scandal* 'leapt to the top of the bestseller charts at the same time as the gagging writs descended from the food manufacturing industry'.

'It is difficult to escape the conclusion, in retrospect,' he went on, 'that legal action was a grotesque over-reaction, just as was the attempt to block the initial NACNE report. Far from isolating or suppressing criticism, such antics added to their news value and popular credibility. Moreover, the venom of the industry counter-attack was almost heartening, since it provided the most direct evidence that the charges were hitting home. Caroline, of course, never conceded the argument against *The Food Scandal*. "If I hadn't already been ill," she recalled "I'd have fought them all the way to the House of Lords."'

The British food manufacturing industry makes most of its products and profits out of fatty, sugary and/or salty processed food, and so does not want to be told that such food is unhealthy. What made our book vulnerable was the naming of branded names. If you are going to be rude about food, be careful before you name brands. For example, salty foods are unhealthy, and most popular breakfast cereals are salty. But if you then say (to take an imaginary example) that Korn Krunchos are a nutritional disaster, you may be in trouble; and the manufacturer has a point. Because there is probably nothing singularly terrible about Korn Krunchos. It's safer to name all brands, than one or two.

What did we say to upset Beecham, and its product Bovril? To avoid any further legal excitement, here is what our Counsel said in court when the case was settled, in September 1985. 'The Defendants regret that they included Bovril in their list of savoury products including sugar, which they did in the sincere belief that caramel (contained in Bovril) is a form of sugar. While it is also true that Bovril cubes contain sugar (as acknowledged on the label) the Defendants agree that it was Bovril paste, not Bovril cubes, to which they were referring. The Defendants have each undertaken to the Plaintiffs that they will not repeat the publication of the words complained of or any similar words claiming that Bovril paste contains sugar.'

It may be that without Caroline, the NACNE report would have been published, in some even more obscured form. (Its title, when it eventually emerged, was 'A discussion paper on proposals for nutritional guidelines for health education in Britain', and that's about as dull a title as you ever will see.) But without Caroline the good news in the report, that 'the quality of food is fundamental to good health', as she put it, would never have been heard by the nation. In his tribute to Caroline at her Thanksgiving Service, our friend Jonathan Aitken, the Conservative MP, described her as an 'evangelist', and said, 'there must be many in this congregation here present, and many hundreds of thousands in the wider world, who owe Caroline more than they will ever know, simply because their personal well-being, their vitality and their health has been enhanced by Caroline's indefatigable campaigning for better food and nutrition.'

She had a personal message for the consumer, and a political message for the citizen, which after all is the same person – you and me, and everybody who eats and votes. 'The healthiest food is whole, and fresh; heavily processed foods made of processed sugars, processed starches and processed fats are unhealthy,' she said; and at the same time, 'Food and health is back on the political agenda, which is where it should be. For what is more important to people than their state of health? . . . It is up to us: if we care about our health, and the health of the next generation, we should remember that good food is fundamental to good health.' As a campaigner she was not shy of repeating the same truths, again, and again.

On 28 June 1984 we were in Court, before Judge Israel Finestein, who in his summary said, 'In my view the matters complained of by the Plaintiffs are such that an award of damages would not in the event be likely to be sufficient. I am bound to say that I share the great doubts forensically expressed by Mr Bowcher [the QC appearing for Bovril] of the Defendants meeting damages if the Plaintiffs succeed at trial.' Good grief! we said to our solicitor (or rather, the solicitor hired by our publisher's insurance company). What might this mean? Three years' hard? Half a million pounds damages? Bankruptcy? He looked glum. 'You could appeal,' he said. 'It would cost you.' How much? 'Maybe £25,000. Maybe £50,000.'

A little over two weeks later, on 16 July, we were in the Commons, with Jonathan Aitken. 'Almost everyone who knew her has a favourite Caroline story,' he said; his story illustrated 'her formidable skills as a Parliamentary lobbyist and publicist'. The year before, as Secretary of the Coronary Prevention Group, she encouraged him to put down Parliamentary Questions. For 16 July, she proposed 'a full-scale Parliamentary Adjournment Debate on the prevention of coronary heart disease'.

'While this Debate was in preparation,' he said 'Caroline got busy making constructive mischief in her own good cause. She had leaked the NACNE report, she had hotted up various journalists, and she had even pressurised the Government into releasing, somewhat reluctantly, its own Chief Medical Officer's COMA report [on Diet and Cardiovascular Disease] a few days before the debate. And if all this scene-setting wasn't enough, she decided that an evening in Parliament needed a good few theatricals thrown in, to make it go with a swing.

'So half an hour or so before the Debate, she strode into the Palace of Westminster, wangling her way past the security guards, with a shopping bag in which there were two colourful props: a packet of pink socks, and a pound of supermarket sausages. And so it was, under Caroline's stage-directions and script, that the House of Commons was treated to the enjoyable spectacle of a Debate on the prevention of coronary heart disease whose highlight was an MP waving the socks in one hand and the sausages in the other.'

The relevant extract from the record in Hansard is as follows. 'It is a serious criticism of both the food industry and the Government that manufactured foods are not already labelled with the sort of minimum nutritional labelling that gives the public the opportunity to know which foods may increase the risk of heart disease and which foods are best for healthy eating,' said Jonathan, for of course he was the MP.

'We need a policy of full disclosure on food labelling.

To illustrate my point, I ask my Hon Friend the Parliamentary Under-Secretary to reflect for a moment on the difference in contents labelling between a pair of socks and a packet of sausages. I have here a pair of socks. They are well labelled, as the law requires . . . . They are 80 per cent cotton, 20 per cent nylon, they were made in Hong Kong, they should be washed in warm water and given a minimum spin. All information which is very helpful and informative.

I also have with me a packet of sausages, and the labelling might be described as a highly edited version of the contents. There is a long list of such contents as colour, spices, salt and so on, but there is no mention of the quantities involved. Rather puzzlingly, there is also no mention of fat, though even an O-level chemist such as myself could easily discern a large quantity of killer fat in these sausages.

I hope that my Hon Friend the Under-Secretary of State for Health and Social Security, who is to reply, will note the sharp contrast between the labelling required by law for an ordinary pair of socks and the misleading labelling of a packet of sausages and many other foodstuffs. I press my Hon Friend to tell us when and how he expects to bring in regulations that will impose adequate food labelling on the food industry.

My Hon Friend will not have an easy task, because he is sure to encounter resistance from vested interests such as some sections of the food industry, its lobbyists and its marketing organisations.'

And he ended 'Much should be done to convince the public that far too many British people are digging their graves with their teeth and needlessly increasing their risk of heart disease and heart attacks. I recognise that no government can prevent people eating foolishly if they choose to do so, but governments can ensure that those who wish to eat wisely are not made fools of either by nutritional ignorance or by misleading food labelling. The medical experts have given their judgment. COMA has reported and I hope my Hon Friend will rise to the challenge by starting the campaign for heart disease prevention.'

Characteristically, Caroline became friendly not only with Jonathan, but also with his Hon Friend, then Under-Secretary of State for Health and Social Security, John Patten MP, who remembered Caroline as 'the sock lady'. He wrote later 'I admired her very much, and gained a lot from working with her when I was at the DHSS.'

Meanwhile, outside the High Courts and the House of Commons, the word was out. 'New revelations on our diet – why change is vital,' said the *Sunday Times*. 'Health warning: the food you eat can kill,' said the *Daily Express*. 'Britain's diet "not healthy",' *The Daily Telegraph* said, cautiously. 'The food scandal. The cover-up that kills,' was one of three features I wrote for *The Times* with Caroline's guidance; extra staff were hired to handle the vast correspondence, and a total of thirty letters were printed by *The Times* over a period of two weeks under the general heading 'The food scandal'.

Caroline was photographed eating a strawberry, for a feature syndicated throughout the regional press. 'What is good for the food business is bad for our health,' she said. 'Some manufacturers start out with a healthy food which is not very profitable and turn it into an unhealthy product which is.' And, 'When people cut back on buying sugar, the manufacturers began shovelling it back into other foods. And they even disguise its use by giving it a different name on a product label, in words that the general public would not understand.'

'Danger, this food *will* damage your health,' said the *Daily Mail*. 'Scandal of Britain's food deaths cover-up,' was the *Morning Star* headline. 'Our "scandalous" diet provides food for thought,' was the *East Anglian Daily Times* headline. 'The most important book on food I've read for a long time,' said Derek Cooper in the *Listener*. 'Hard-hitting in hard covers, it anatomises the conflict which has been taking place during the last three years about the future of the nation's health.' In the *Glasgow Herald*, Ann Shaw's feature was headlined 'There's death on your plate. Keeping Britain unhealthy is big business.' John Patten said to me, 'The food industry know that the writing is on the wall.' Jonathan Aitken introduced us to his libel lawyer, Richard Sykes, who wrote, 'Can I tell you that your book has greatly influenced my eating habits. It has been avidly read by my wife and daughter and the results are beginning to manifest themselves in my diet.' Such letters made it all worth while.

Caroline was not responsible for the headlines in the newspapers, but she rode the media bronco with a skill learned from her previous campaigning work with the Child Poverty Action Group, Agricapital, and the well-named British Society for Social Responsibility in Science (BSSRS). Eventually she had the animal eating out of her hand. 'Phil thinks I've had it,' she said sadly in a letter, of Dr Philip James. 'He has gone rather quiet of late, and I think he is anxious to distance himself from the rabble-rousers of which he tells me I am now one.'

She roused more than rabble. I spent most of my time writing. She toured the country. I have a file of letters from people who asked her to give lectures. The first twenty of well over a hundred are from the Oxford Prevention of Heart Attack and Stroke Project; Winchester Health Authority; the Scottish WHO Monica Project; Argyll and Clyde Health Board; East Cumbria Health Authority; the University of Cambridge Department of Community Medicine; Sheffield Health

Authority; Charing Cross Hospital; East Suffolk Health Authority; Worcester and District Health Authority; the Institute of Biology (Scottish branch); Queen's Medical Centre, Nottingham; the London School of Hygiene and Tropical Medicine; Brent Health Authority; Cambridge and District Occupational Health Nurses Group; the Greater Glasgow Health Board; Long Ashton Research Station; North East Thames Health Authority; Eastbourne Health Authority; the National Childbirth Trust.

Sometimes Caroline didn't accept invitations, because she was too busy or not well. 'Me again!' she'd say when somebody telephoned offering travel expenses for what amounted to a day away. But she did her best. 'Tremendous enthusiasm has been engendered,' wrote Winchester Health Authority. And Caroline wrote to Worcester Health Authority, 'Thank you for sending me a copy of your sandwich spaceships. It's a nice idea, one of the best I've seen, and another triumph for the Worcester Food Policy Team.'

She wrote to food manufacturers. 'I have been shown a box of Fox's Chocolate Fruit and Nut Cookies,' one letter reads. 'How come the French ingredients on the label lists E numbers and the English list does not?' And of the trilingual label, 'I'm afraid I can't read the Arabic. Would you advise me to eat the cookies while thinking in French, English or Arabic? I'm told the cookies are very nice!'

She wrote to Trading Standards Officers. 'What about these Wotsits?' she wrote to a friendly Chief Inspector of Trading Standards. 'And how about these Burton's Jaffa Cakes, containing no orange juice but featuring the usual cut orange on the front? I know that McVitie's Jaffa Cakes have been recently ticked off for doing the same thing; orange juice has miraculously reappeared in their ingredients list . . . .'

She wrote to the Advertising Standards Authority. 'By saying that "generations of families have enjoyed the traditional British sausage", this advertisement is clearly wishing to give the impression that sausages today are the same as they always were, twenty, forty, sixty, eighty years ago. They are not, as anybody can see from the list of ingredients, and from reference to history books (e.g. *The Book of the Sausage*, by Anthony and Araminta Hippisley Cox, Pan Books, 1978).'

She kept an eye on fellow scientists. 'Dear Tom,' she wrote to Dr T.A.B. Sanders, once a fellow student. 'It is not the first time that you have asserted in public that I do not know what I am talking about, and then proceeded to mislead the audience! I suggest you check your own facts, and resist the temptation to say the first figure that comes into your head,' she wrote at the beginning of a long letter on interpretation of the official National Food Survey.

She wrote to Government. Dr David Buss of the Ministry of Agriculture responded to another long letter on the Food Survey. 'Dear Caroline. It's hard to know how to respond, for most of the things you have asked for I have been trying to get into the reports myself!'

She wrote to food manufacturers' trade associations. In a *Daily Telegraph* feature on meat in June 1985, she proposed a Harrington Medal for 'the person in the food trade who has done most to promote good health in Britain by revising current practices. Which other parts of Britain's food industry have done as much as the Meat and Livestock Commission?' She followed this up with a humorous letter to MLC Planning and Development Director, Geoff Harrington. What we need is fit animals, she said. 'My solution is the re-introduction of the wolf to the British countryside, to make the animals run about. Or all the beef cattle could be fed at the top of hills and shooed down again after they have eaten up. I hope the lean butchery campaign is going well.'

She wrote to the newspapers. 'Woodrow Wyatt is absolutely right,' she wrote to *The Times*. 'The manner in which decisions about food and health are taken within the Ministry of Agriculture and the Department of Health are fundamentally undemocratic, and favour the trade at the expense of consumers' knowledge and health. For example, the recent COMA report on 'Diet and Cardiovascular Disease' was made available in advance to relevant sections of the food industry (e.g. the Bacon and Meat Manufacturers' Association) allowing them time to gather their defence against recommendations to reduce saturated fat in the national diet. Not only consumer groups such as the Coronary Prevention Group, but also Members of Parliament were denied this privilege, giving the industry a head start . . . . Both scientific and public debate about the quality of human life is being stifled for the convenience of the civil service and the food industry.'

She gave public lectures; a transcript was made of her talk on 'Counterfeit food: additives as consumer fraud' given to a conference organised by the Food Additives Campaign Team, itself co-founded by her. 'Her technique was devastatingly simple,' Derek Cooper wrote of her. 'When invited to speak at a conference, mounting the platform with a shopping bag, she would begin to pull out the heavily-advertised rubbish that was masquerading as good food and through ridicule and laughter make the point that much of the nation's legacy of ill-health comes from these very packets and tins.'

'Here are three kinds of pot noodle,' she declared. 'Lamb and tomato, cheese and tomato, beef and tomato flavour. They contain no lamb and no beef. The cheese and tomato flavour doesn't contain any cheese – well, it contains a tiny bit of cheese powder, but it doesn't contain cheese in the sense that you and I know it. And the only bit of beef that pot contains is beef fat.

Here is a disgusting drink, laser-beam blue, and it's called Tropic Ora, Mixed Fruit Drink. Here is the list of ingredients: water, glucose syrup, apple juice, pear juice, citric acid, tropical fruit flavouring, blah blah blah, colour 133 (no E number). This thing doesn't contain any tropical fruit, only tropical fruit flavouring, and at the end of this lecture I am going to ask somebody from the audience to share with me some of this delectable drink . . . .'

And so, half an hour later, she repeated the little experiment she had tried out the day before, at the Dorchester Hotel, before an audience including industry people. 'Yesterday Paul Levy, who is a gourmet cookery writer, sampled this wonderful drink. I want some brave person from the audience to come and tell me what they think of it. Yesterday nobody from the food industry volunteered . . . .' The transcript ends: 'Volunteer: "It tastes faintly of nail varnish remover".'

Now that the food scandals of the mid-1980s have been followed by the bug scandals in 1989, everybody knows that the cheapened food supply of this country is unhealthy and unsafe. Moving towards 1992, Europe, and the next British General Election, food and health is emerging as the first environmental issue; and the first major political party clearly and convincingly committed to a healthy food and agriculture policy may well therefore form the next British Government. Talking to Derek Cooper just before she died, Caroline said, 'I think we're coming to a period which will be very exciting, and I'm sorry I won't be around to see it.

'One of the great steps forward that can now be made is to join together the aims of environmentalists, nutritionists like myself, cookery writers, scientists . . . to try to work together towards a common goal.' That goal is to create a British food supply that is fit to eat.

In 1937 John Boyd Orr wrote, 'A few years hence when the connection between the poor feeding of mothers and children and subsequent poor physique and ill-health is as clearly recognised as the connection between a contaminated water supply and cholera, the suggestion that a diet fully adequate for health should be available for everyone will be regarded as reasonable and in accordance with common sense, as is the preservation of our domestic water supply from pollution.'

A lot of aluminium, nitrates, chlorine, slurry and assorted creepy-crawlies have flowed through the reservoirs since Boyd Orr's day. His 'few years' has turned into more than half a century. But he is right. In the 1980s, among all those who have spoken for public health, Caroline's voice is the clearest. She above all convinced the British nation that good food is vital for good health, not just because of her talent, vision and energy, but because of her special quality as a human being. She always did her best to tell the truth.

In July 1986, when invited to lunch at the Food and Drink Federation by its then President, Sir Derrick Holden-Brown, we told him and his colleagues that the watchword for food manufacturers from then on, should be 'quality'; people will pay good money for good food. Sir Derrick, who is Chairman of Allied-Lyons, whose pre-tax profit in 1988–9 was £502 million, was interested; and afterwards Caroline sat down and wrote him a vast letter. This includes short-term and long-term plans for the FDF and its member companies. Caroline's proposals are as good and apt now as when she wrote them; and her lovely enthusiasm, another special quality, shines on.

'Dear Sir Derrick. Your hospitality has had a good effect . . . . Here are a few ideas that the FDF could consider supporting:

*Voluntary ban on all coal-tar dyes, at least from sweets, cakes, biscuits, soft drinks, puddings and other foods liable to be eaten by children.

*Support the Food Advisory Committee in their work on fish fingers, a staple food for youngsters. Support a 60 per cent minimum fish content.

*Voluntary ban on polyphosphates and other water-holding agents, particularly in meat and fish products. I note that some large retailers have already removed them from their bacon and fish fingers: very good news for their reputation (or it will be when I have congratulated them in my column in *The Daily Telegraph*!)

*Voluntary maximum on water level in bread. There may already be one, that I don't know about. Clearly some bread is wetter than others; why should we pay for added water?

*Support the British Dietetic Association, the Coronary Prevention Group and others in their demands for nutritional standards for school meals. These should be reinstated as soon as possible. Privatisation in the absence of standards will be a disaster for the industry. Competition for contracts will result in rubbish being produced at rock-bottom prices; this can only be bad for industry's reputation.

*Support an across-the-board reduction of sugar content in savoury foods. Total added sugar(s) content could be reduced by 2 per cent a year, and the public would not notice. Sweet foods are another problem!

*Think about the implications of raising the extraction rate of flour from 72 to 80 per cent. Or even 82 or 85. This could have a huge impact on health. What would it do to the industry?

*Fitness. A fit nation will eat more food, which can only be good for business. Could industry help to provide playgrounds in inner city areas, as I suggested at lunch? In many areas parents are afraid to let their children go out, because there are no safe playgrounds.'

And seventeen other ideas. 'I would be pleased to come and talk to you about them, as I enjoyed meeting you and your colleagues.' Towards the end of October a nice reply arrived from Sir Derrick: 'I look forward to meeting you again,' he said. But Caroline was soon to be in hospital again.

What follows is a feature, 'What we are not told about the food we eat', that she wrote for *Secrets*, the journal of the Campaign for Freedom of Information, around the time she was writing to Sir Derrick; it appeared in October 1986. She raises more campaigning issues: official secrecy; the closed circles of advisors from government, science and industry; the need for democracy in food and health policy. This was another feature Caroline wrote for no payment. Sometimes it is supposed that best-selling authors are rich. Caroline did all right. Her total tax liability for her four years as a freelance, between 1984–5 and 1987–8, was a little over £2000.

WHAT WE ARE NOT TOLD ABOUT THE FOOD WE EAT

Here are the ingredients of a packet of Six Deep Jam Tarts. Raspberry and apricot flavour; wheatflour, sugar, glucose syrup, animal and vegetable fats, apples, gelling agent (pectin), apricots, raspberries, blackcurrants, salt, citric acid, acidity regulator (E331), flavours, colours (E102, E110, E122, E123, E124, E132).

How many additives are there in these sticky snacks? There are six colours, and one acidity regulator. Total number: seven. Right? Wrong. The actual number used may be six times six. For all those flavours are likely to include an array of different substances, of which the manufacturer is not obliged to give you details. Nor is the manufacturer obliged to tell you about the additives already in some of the ingredients before they reach the mixing vat. Flour, for example, can legally contain a handful of other additives, none of which need to be declared.

'Processing aids', additives used during manufacture to smooth the passage of ingredients through machinery, also do not have to be declared, on the assumption that they are present in inconsequential amounts in the final product. But chemicals used to grease the baking tray, or to release the product from other machinery, are bound to leave traces on the food. You, however, have no right to know their identity.

What about the actual quantities of ingredients used? That, too, is a Trade Secret. The only clue is that ingredients are listed in descending order of amount. How about the jam tart's nutritional value? What is the sum total of different nutrients supplied by this concoction of twenty-plus ingredients? The manufacturer is not obliged to tell you that either, so you have no way of knowing which of several varieties of jam tart contain most fruit, least sugar, and least saturated fat.

To cap it all, one other piece of information is also missing: the date of manufacture. You know the tarts aren't immortal, because the SELL BY date is 13 September, but how old are they? The legislation does not require the manufacturer to say.

What about the safety of all the ingredients used? That, too, is a secret. To understand why the contents of a jam tart are so heavily protected from public scrutiny, let us take a trip around the Whitehall committee rooms where decisions about food and public health are made.

First stop, the Department of Health and Social Security. The Nutrition Division at DHSS, working within a paltry budget, is ostensibly responsible for overseeing the nutritional health of the nation, and for making recommendations about future food policy. The Chief Scientist at DHSS, Sir Donald Acheson, is advised by the Committee on Medical Aspects of Food Policy (COMA), of which he is chairman. COMA is a permanent committee which meets twice a year. Membership is drawn from the scientific community (10 seats), and also includes representatives of the DHSS, MAFF, the Medical Research Council, the Public Health Laboratory Service, and the Chief Medical Officers of Scotland and Wales.

Today's members of COMA sign the Official Secrets Act (OSA), as they have done since its inception in 1956. The agenda and minutes of their meetings are not available for public scrutiny.

In practice, COMA delegates much of its work to sub-committees, which are chaired by a member of main COMA, and include scientists not on main COMA. Their work too is covered by the OSA. The deliberations that led up to the 1984 COMA report on Diet and Cardiovascular Disease, and their reports on the nutritional aspects of bread and flour, nutrition of the elderly, infant foods and Asian rickets are withheld from public scrutiny.

COMA is not the only DHSS advisory committee dealing with nutrition. The Committee on Toxicity (COT), together with its sub-committees on Carcinogenicity and Mutagenicity (COC and COM), advise on the safety, or toxicity of food ingredients. Dr Erik Millstone, of the Science Policy Research Unit, University of Sussex, has spent over ten years examining the toxicity of food additives, and the way in which they are regulated by these committees. He says "It is very hard to discover very much about any of these committees because their activities are concealed behind the Official Secrets Act". One thing that is known is that membership is drawn from the medical profession, industrial employees, but no consumer organisations.

Within the DHSS there is also the COMA Panel on Novel Foods, which assesses new developments in food technology, such as the production of food from fungi and bacteria, and the advisability of bombarding your dinner with radiation as a means of prolonging shelf life.

Newcomers to the field of food and health often assume that all nutritional problems are, or should be, dealt with by the DHSS. After all, good nutrition is fundamental to good health. But in practice, how much influence does the DHSS actually have on the quality of food supplied to the UK population? Very little.

Whatever COMA or any other DHSS advisory committee may say about a particular food, an additive, or even the general health of the population, their conclusions are carefully picked over before and after publication by civil servants in a far more influential ministry, the Ministry of Agriculture, Fisheries and Food.

Their offices contain the control rooms of food policy in the UK. MAFF is primarily responsible to the needs of farmers and the food processing industry, the UK's largest overall employer. With the exception of its duty to keep food clean to minimise the risks of food poisoning, MAFF's efforts on behalf of the consumer are given very low priority. Nevertheless, MAFF actually has a much larger nutrition division than the DHSS, with a much larger budget. And its advisory committees are also much more powerful.

The Food Advisory Committee (FAC), formed in 1983 out of the merging of the Food Additives and Contaminants Committee and the Food Standards Committee (which used to assess the need for statutory minimum compositional standards for foods), is responsible to the Chief Scientist at MAFF, Dr Robert Crossett. Its 13 members are doctors and scientists, food industry scientists, a home economist, an employee of the Consumers' Association, and a Trading Standards Officer. FAC members are subject to the OSA. Duties of the FAC are wide-ranging, and include food labelling, misleading descriptions, value for money, food standards, new processing techniques and, most important of all, advising government on future food legislation.

I have said that the interests of consumers are given low priority within the decision-making process in Whitehall, which is where food legislation is created. What evidence is there for this statement, and how is it affected by secrecy?

Official policy on food and health is determined by the recommendations of government advisory committees, insofar as their recommendations are acceptable to the government of the day. They may also be delayed, rewritten, suppressed, withdrawn, or ignored. Government policy is also determined by what is *not* discussed by official advisory committees. Thus over the last three years, MPs, consumer groups, and representatives of the medical profession have repeatedly called on the Minister of Health to ask the COMA committee to review the subject of sugars and health, and to make recommendations about national sugars consumption. For without a COMA report on sugars, MAFF refuses to tackle the high level of sugar consumption in the UK, 2lb per head per week, considered by the Royal College of Physicians and the British Medical Association to be twice the amount that is good for our health.

It has taken three years for the Minister of Health to bow to this pressure. Finally in June 1986, members of main COMA were told that a COMA subcommittee would be set up to look at sugars and health. Up to then the sugar industry had evidently persuaded DHSS that an average consumption of 100lbs of sugars a year is harmless. Government advisory committees are instruments of policy. They are not accountable to MPs.

How are the agendas of these committees set? This is the job of civil servants, presumably with the chairman, who in the case of COMA is also a civil servant. In addition to servicing these committees by providing information and drafts, civil servants can, and frequently do, exert a disproportionate influence on the workings of all food and nutrition advisory committees.

Who decides which papers are submitted? Are they a fair representation of the scientific literature published world-wide? We do not know. It is an official secret.

Take the 1984 report of the COMA committee on Diet and Cardiovascular Disease. The panel was convened at the end of 1981, and met ten times. The literature reviewed included "over 600 published scientific papers" published prior to February 1984, and "over 40 working papers prepared by members of the Panel, and by experienced investigators who were not members of the Panel". The published report (32 pages total) lists just 24 of the 600-plus scientific papers reviewed. To my knowledge, DHSS has never released a full list of the 600 papers. Nor are the "over 40" working papers available for scrutiny.

Independent medical researchers in the UK, or well informed members of the public, might like to know on what basis the 1984 recommendations to prevent heart attacks were based. Without the background papers, there can be no effective discussion. Lack of information stifles debate.

Are the recommendations of advisory committees always supported by scientific evidence? No, they are not. Again, COMA 1984 serves as an example. The subcommittee examining diet and cardiovascular disease made its recommendations for the entire population, children as well as adults. But when the final report was referred back to main COMA, members of the COMA Panel on Child Nutrition insisted that children under 5 years old should not eat less fat, because they felt it might be harmful. What evidence did they have for thinking this? The answer is none. Not one shred of scientific data was put forward to support their view. Nor has it been supported with evidence in answers to Parliamentary questions on the subject. To this day the COMA Panel on Child Nutrition has not justified a statement of official government policy, which even now is causing health visitors throughout the country to encourage young children to continue eating saturated fat in large quantities. The DHSS's own way of saying that the statement was difficult to support was to set up another COMA subcommittee to examine infant feeding, announced in May 1985.

We know, too, that the main body of recommendations made by advisory committees have also been manipulated. For example, confidential minutes and background documents to the 1981 COMA Bread and Flour report show that, in draft, the report made it clear that wholemeal bread is altogether nutritionally superior to white bread. However, this key emphasis was changed and the first and foremost recommendation in the report as published is: "The consumption of bread, whether it be white, brown or wholemeal, should be promoted". One member of the committee, Professor Jerry Morris, protested, but on the strength of this recommendation the bread industry continued to promote white bread to the public, quoting the statement in advertisements. It was only after the publication of the National Advisory Committee on Nutrition Education published its guidelines on healthy nutrition (the NACNE report) that advertising of wholemeal bread was seriously undertaken.

Are members of these committees always given the common courtesy of scrutinising and commenting on research work undertaken on their behalf by MAFF and DHSS? Again, no they are not.

In April this year, the DHSS Nutrition Division published the results of its 1983 survey into the eating habits of British teenagers. This was the largest and most comprehensive survey of adolescent food habits undertaken since the war (3285 children), and it showed that they are growing up on just the sort of food that doctors the world over have condemned as unhealthy: fatty, sugary meals which contain inadequate whole, fresh foods. The survey was done to satisfy critics of the controversial abolition of statutory nutritional standards for school meals in 1980.

Main COMA members asked to see the results, but were shown only a brief summary of the final document, whose publication was delayed by over one and a half years. On at least four occasions, parliamentary questions about publication of the report were deflected, once by Mrs Thatcher herself. The document as finally published was generally reckoned to be rather a shoddy piece of writing which did not do justice to the wealth of data collected.

Many members of government advisory committees are employees of large food manufacturing companies in the UK.

Independent researchers and doctors come to these committees with their particular expertise, but as senior academics, are usually over-worked, overstretched, and do not have the time or facilities to read all the background material relevant to the discussion, particularly when it concerns industrial practice and food technology. The toxicology of just a sprinkling of additives can run to thousands of research papers. These people must rely primarily on their wit and wisdom to see them through.

Contrast this with senior scientists employed by industry. They can call on the huge national and international information services offered by their companies, and by industry as a whole. It is in their interests to do so. They can arrive at meetings extremely well briefed, backed up by voluminous, immaculately prepared papers to support their case.

How impartial is the data reviewed by government advisory committees when they draw up recommendations for future legislation? The additives in those jam tarts are a good example of how it all works. Government relies on its scientific committees for advice about which additives should be permitted, in which foods, and in what quantities. Much of the data scrutinised therefore concerns toxicity, or safety. Who provides this data, and on what basis?

The overwhelming majority of experimental data on additive toxicity is conducted, and is owned by, the food industry. Industry makes an application to use an additive. Industry conducts the safety tests, some of which are published in scientific research journals and many of which are not. Industry submits the results to whichever committee is doing the scrutiny. The data are then covered by the OSA. If you ask the DHSS or MAFF if you can see the data, you are told that it belongs to the industry. If you ask the industry, you will find it is an Official Secret.

In May 1985, in a letter to Jonathan Aitken MP(Cons) about the use of the OSA to cover the work of FAC and COMA, Junior Agriculture Minister Peggy Fenner justified this extraordinary use of the OSA as follows: "It is necessary from time to time for information on manufacturing processes or other commercial sensitive material to be placed before the members of these Committees in order that they can properly advise Ministers on matters before them. The signing of the Official Secrets Act by members of these Committees is the way of ensuring that the integrity of this information is protected from unauthorised disclosure to commercial competitors."

However, one year later, Mrs Fenner was forced to admit that she had been badly briefed. It seems that her own advisors did not know what was what in the control rooms of food and health policy. In June 1986 she wrote: "Members of COMA which is serviced by DHSS are required to sign the Official Secrets Act declaration and have done so since the Committee's inception in 1957. Members of my Ministry's Food Advisory Committee on the other hand are not required to sign the declaration. Instead they are informed at the time of their appointment that information given to them in their capacity as members of the Committee is subject to the Official Secrets Act and should not be disclosed outside the Committee".

In practice, this makes not a blind bit of difference. Whether the advisors sign or do not sign the OSA, they are subject to it. A commercial secret is an Official Secret. And that's official.

This use of the OSA works against the interests of consumers, and against the future health of the nation. It should be immediately withdrawn, and the whole structure of government advisory committees should be reviewed. In its manifesto for a new national policy on food additives, the Food Additives Campaign Team (FACT) has proposed the following: "The work of all [government advisory] committees should not be covered by the Official Secrets Act. Their setting up and meetings should be publicised, their hearings held in public and oral and written evidence published by HMSO together with their reports for all to see.

"All members of expert advisory committees to be delegated by and accountable to a full range of relevant expert bodies. These could include the Royal College of Physicians, the British Dietetic Association, the Local Authorities Co-ordinating Body on Trading Standards, the National Consumer Council, the Trades Union Congress and the Women's Institutes.

"No person employed or otherwise paid (as a consultant, for example) by firms in the food, drink, drugs or agrichemicals industry to serve on food advisory committees. However, unions, and trade associations such as the Retail Consortium of the Food and Drink Federation to be eligible to delegate members. Industry to be free to give evidence."

Government should now show a real commitment to public health. All government advisory reports on food and health should be accompanied by supplementary volumes including all background documents and written and oral evidence. This is done in the USA, where the Freedom of Information Act operates; it is done for Royal Commissions; and it is done for reports of House of Commons Select Committees.

CHAPTER SIX

HEROES

———◆———

'The Second International Congress on Essential Fatty Acids, Prostaglandins and Leukotrienes invited all the congress participants to a Cockney High Tea . . . .'

Caroline needed inspiration, too. Cardiff was a wrong turning. At 7.15am on Saturday 22 September 1979 Mrs B Jones of 54 Craig-y-Fedw, Abertridwr, weighed her breakfast plate (240g), plus toast (260g), plus Anchor butter (265g). A fortnight before, on 8 September, Olwen Evans of 185 Nantgarn Road, Caerphilly, weighed her breakfast plate (160g), plus toast (210g), plus butter – Anchor again (220g). Two weeks before that, Mrs Kathleen Sherbourne of 13 Nantgarn Road rose early, at 6.30am, and had a cup of tea, which she did not weigh. Later on, Mrs Jones had bacon and black pudding (53g, on a 162g plate), with tomatoes fried in the bacon fat (95g). Mrs Evans had fried bacon, egg and tomatoes. Mrs Sherbourne had two beefburgers, two cobs (corn on the cob?), fried onion and baps.

That's how it is for a field-working nutritionist, and Caroline did not resent the tedium of analysing the dietary intakes of the women of South Wales, as far as I know, although she would have been inclined to prefer to tell the good ladies what awful rubbish the food trade was perpetrating on them. She liked meeting people, but it was not part of her plan to measure out her life in breakfast plates. Anchor butter is not something to believe in. The work done by the MRC Epidemiology Unit in Cardiff didn't matter much one way or the other, as far as she could see. Perhaps it was not meant to matter. Among all her diaries just one, for 1978, included an epigraph: she wrote 'Wisdom comes through suffering. But to whom does it come? Happiness is only an illusion. And a turning away.' Caroline was not given to lamentation; this sadness shocked me when I read it. She felt trapped in the narrow valleys.

But there was Archie, her consolation. Professor Archie Cochrane, a founding father of the science of epidemiology, lived in retirement in Rhoose near Cardiff, when Caroline knew him. He fought in the Spanish Civil War (for the International Brigade, naturally); was imprisoned in

Crete in the 1939–1945 war for four years; and back in Wales after the war, accomplished the spectacular achievement of screening an entire population in the Rhondda, in order to understand pneumoconiosis. Archie was a rebel. He was decidedly sceptical about modern medicine, and published studies showing that the more child doctors there are in any community, the more child death. These statistics were perhaps presented as a tease, which was an additional reason why Caroline was fond of him. He certainly attacked the idea that 'every medical complaint deserved a bottle of medicine or a packet of pills, with the disastrous consequences we still face'.

He was a bit moth-eaten when Caroline knew him. In 1978 he wrote his own epitaph. 'He lived and died, a man who smoked too much, without the consolation of a wife, a religious belief or a merit award. But he didn't do so badly.' He died in the summer of 1988. Caroline liked his eccentricity, knowing for herself that remarkable people listen to an inner voice. She kept some of his papers; in a profile he was quoted as saying 'I am getting rather old and we don't seem to be producing any young heretics. Are there any coming along? I haven't come across any.'

Cardiff struck no sparks from Caroline. Her heart and soul were elsewhere. She roamed. In 1979, she thought she had been offered a job and a life in Costa Rica after meeting Professor Leonardo Mata ('The Bandit', as she described him in her diary). That year she did a lot of work for the radical food policy group Agricapital, sometimes meeting at 'Uhuru' in Oxford. She didn't take this altogether seriously; another diary entry read, 'Agricap. Utopia and how to get there!' She still saw Josy Zalman, a Romanian deserter from the Israeli army who had been her boyfriend in Amsterdam. None of this amounted to much.

Her sights were raised in Israel. In 1968, just eighteen, she went straight from Cheltenham Ladies' College to Haifa, for Voluntary Service Overseas. She taught science to Palestinian children at a school run by the nuns of the Convent of Nazareth in Abbas Street. 'I love this country and its people so much,' she wrote in her diary on 22 March 1969. 'I'll never want to go.' In Jerusalem on 2 April, the entry says, 'Saw dead soldier.' Living with the Arab people, it was evident to her then that Israel was a police state. She did not waver from this unpopular view when she returned to England.

After her first degree she went back to Israel in 1973, and was there during the war. In October she noted, 'Cemeteries: 100 − 300 bodies

thrown in huge graves each night at Haifa. 100 × 18 = 1800 (the least).'
And 'Land confiscated in Galilee for the use of roadmaking. No
compensation worth speaking of. People lay down in the fields to stop
the bulldozers – no good. Olive trees torn up – how many years of
income gone? . . . Government informers everywhere in Haifa.'

Sister Theresa Davis, a nun who knew her in Haifa at the time,
remembered her well, writing from Toronto in 1989. 'She was so full
of life, so vital, such high ideals. She attacked anything that was injustice
to little people . . . . She used to come barefoot to our house. She spoke
passionately. I loved her. Saw so much potential in her. I had no idea
she had made such a mark on England.'

In 1968 she met the first man who inspired her, Samih al-Kasim, the
Palestinian Communist revolutionary, and in 1973 she lived with him
and saw Israel as he saw it. Samih is not as ferocious as this description
sounds; although in and out of prison, he is a poet and visionary who
makes fun rather than bombs against the Israeli authorities. Caroline told
me he once embarrassed magistrates by insisting on conducting his
defence when on trial in Ancient Hebrew, which he was legally entitled
to do; he spoke the language better than most Jewish scholars.

If women were properly respected in the Near East, Caroline might
have stayed with Samih, but she left to find her own way. The last she
heard of Samih was a hilarious headline in the *Independent* in August
1988: 'Police "arrest wrong Palestinian poet".' The story said, 'The
distinguished Palestinian poet Samieh al-Quasem said yesterday that he
was held at a London police station as a suspected terrorist on Monday
evening when he was due to be reading his work at Chelsea Town Hall.'
I tried to trace him, but he had gone.

Samih and Archie were tasters, for Caroline. I think perhaps the first
man who inspired her professionally and gave her a sense of her own
mission was Dr Richard Turner. Dick Turner is a cardiologist who is
outraged by what he sees as the complacent refusal of the British medical
establishment to take the prevention of heart disease seriously. With Dr
Keith Ball, he wrote 'A counterblast to present inactivity' for the *Lancet*
in 1973; was instrumental in setting up a Royal College of Physicians'
report on 'The Prevention of Coronary Heart Disease' in 1974; and in
1979 set up the Coronary Prevention Group. He was on the look-out
for young radicals, and found Caroline, as she was moving from Cardiff
to Cambridge. Early in 1980 he made her Secretary of CPG.

Samih and Dick meant different things to Caroline but she admired them for the same reason. They had the courage of their convictions. They spoke out, nothwithstanding abuse. And they believe their cause is just. As it is written in Proverbs: 'Where there is no vision, the people perish.'

The coincidence of Phil James and her work at the Dunn, and Dick Turner and her work for CPG, galvanised Caroline. As she amassed the scientific evidence that heart attacks are preventable, Dick Turner cascaded her with plans for action. 'I suggest you take the lid off impediments to progress in coronary prevention,' he wrote in March 1980. 'They certainly include the Government and the dairy industry.' In June he reckoned that Sir George Young, then junior Health Minister, 'has to be cautious but I suspect he will be a strong ally'. In July he wrote, 'Rona needs to get a lot of files ready, such as The Dairy Industry, The Margarine Industry, Hypertension, Meat, Finance, Minutes of Meetings . . . . We want a lot of working groups, e.g. on bread, which is an interest of yours.' A week later, 'It looks as though it might have to be a fight to the finish with the butter people. Luckily *The Times* say they like my feature article.' Later the same month he devised a 'prudent diet', translating accepted American recommendations into British food. 'It should be cheaper. Use wholefood stores and market gardens and try buying in bulk . . . . Carrots and celery sticks are better than sweets for children. Potatoes baked in their skins could be popular . . . .'

Still in July, he wrote, 'Community nurses are a good group to work on . . . . What we want is snowballing.' A few days later, 'I have in mind such simple things as converting the local population, starting with young children, from white to wholemeal bread. This means education at every level in the home, schools, clubs, canteens etc . . . . Another idea is the stimulation of market gardens in every region of the UK. This could be a profitable enterprise . . . . Consumption of baked and boiled potatoes requires encouragement. One might experiment with baked potato shops of which there are now six in Edinburgh . . . . There could be prizes for success in the various areas . . . .' Three days later, 'Do you know about Sally Oppenheim and whether we can have a meeting with her . . . . I once had an encouraging letter from Renée Short. Eric Moonman was once a member of CPG. Do you know where he is? . . . I appreciate we cannot do everything at once. I think you should start writing articles yourself in various journals. Women's journals are very important indeed as they can have great influence, as doubtless you know, and you can write as Secretary of CPG . . . . We will also have to decide what to do about wickedness in high places, e.g. the Milk Marketing Board, Butter Information Council and other branches of the dairy industry. They have been sailing very near to the wind.'

What's needed, he said in October, is the 'prudent diet' advice written in ordinary language. 'I have in mind such headings as Evolving Man; The Formidable Facts; The Fat Story – and so on. Later on, when it is thoroughly established and I am too old, you might take on the scientific work. I will contribute last thoughts on my death-bed – if there's time!' Two days later, 'Would not wholemeal bread including its pricing be a good subject for the 'Food Programme' on Radio 4 at 12.30 on Sundays?' Next month, 'Do you think you could master the sources of official data such as the Registrar General's Report, WHO reports and such statistics?' And, 'I have got a counterblast to almost everyone who doesn't agree with us, having been at it for so many years . . . . I have nearly got my complementary paper to that of Barry Lewis finished, but it's fairly tricky to convince all the doctors, and I want to add the EFA and cholesterol stories, together with platelet function and the importance of fatty acid composition of adipose tissue . . . .'

Enthusiasts are valued in America, where public health reformers with half Dick Turner's energy, vision and goodwill orchestrate masses of resources, for the general good, and are recognised and honoured. In Britain the few people like Dick Turner are disliked, as busybodies, ridiculed, as dreamers, rejected, as heretics; and eventually they become old, or tired, or ill. Shame on us. Shame, not that the campaign to prevent heart disease in Britain can be said to have begun with a correspondence between one old man and one young woman in 1980, for there is some glory in that; but shame, that despite heroic work done by the few who care about public health, Britain's rate of premature death from heart attacks is comparatively worse now than then, and has become just about the worst in the world.

Why? On 20 July 1989 *The Daily Telegraph* reported that 'MPs condemn failure to tackle heart disease'. The story covered a report by the Parliamentary Public Accounts Committee. 'The Government's failure to follow the lead of other countries in mounting a concerted drive to reduce high levels of heart disease, the largest single cause of death in Britain, was condemned by an all-party group of MPs yesterday.'

During the 1980s Caroline, and those who worked like her, made some of Dick Turner's colossal sketches into blueprints, models for the policy of a future government. I didn't know much about these early influences when Caroline was alive. In the mid-1980s I corresponded with Dick Turner, unaware of Caroline's earlier correspondence, which in time became sporadic. And I know more now than I did, about Samih and Archie. Caroline was not sentimental.

As she wrote and studied more, great men emerged for her out of the past. From the nineteenth century, she celebrated Frederick Accum and his 'Treatise on Adulterations of Food and Culinary Poisons', and Dr Arthur Hassall and Dr Thomas Wakley, who together exposed the tricks of the food manufacturing trade in the *Lancet* between 1851 and 1854, which led to the first Food Act. Their work was not mere social history to her. She saw the parallels, and the perversions of the Food Act that make much modern food what she termed 'legalised consumer fraud'. She also noted Accum's ostracism; John Burnett, author of *A Social History of Diet*, reckons that 'there existed a deliberate conspiracy of vested interests determined to discredit and silence Accum'.

From the time of the beginnings of the science of nutrition, she learned from the men of vision, who in total contrast to virtually all scientists living today, were well educated, wrote good English that any thoughtful reader might understand, read widely, put their work in a cultural perspective, and were guided by a sense of social responsibility. Herself not a scholar, she recognised her own human qualities in others: the evangelism of McCarrison, the zeal of Cleave, the audacity of Boyd Orr. Modern scientific writing is rinsed of any such savour, which is why, like technological food, it has a plastic quality.

Caroline's contemporaries have moved into industry, where most of the jobs are, or else, most of the rest of them, smoothly through academia towards professorships, consultancies, membership of expert advisory committees, and the international lecture circuit. Caroline was not inclined to be a martyr or a fanatic. So why not her too? She became a campaigner and therefore a heretic for a number of reasons, I sense.

She knew that the scientific case against British food is proven beyond reasonable doubt. Possessed of this knowledge, she felt bound to speak out. And she was moved by those who, like her, had convictions and courage. Sometimes she felt alone, but she was encouraged by a number of scientists of an older generation, like Dr Hugh Sinclair, Sir Francis Avery Jones, and Dr Denis Burkitt, who admired her.

And Sister Theresa is right: injustice gave her an angry energy. She told me one evening that an old lady had come to be screened that day in the Hackney Healthmobile. The old dear was very shy, and Caroline had to coax her gently, to expose her arm so her blood pressure could be taken. But she was deformed; so much so that the cuff could not be wrapped round her arm, and so she went away disappointed. She didn't want to see anybody else. Before she went, she explained that she had always been that way, although it had got worse of course, because of inherited syphilis. Caroline was so angry. 'Nobody ever helped her,' she said. That was a reason why Caroline was a campaigner.

She became a heretic because science now seems to have no values, and she did not believe in nothing. A passage from *Pilgrim's Progress*, in which Pilgrim's friends warn him of the ways of the world, is apt.

'They also told me that this way was full of deceivers, and of persons that laid await there to turn good men out of the path. They told me that Mr Worldly-Wiseman did lie there in wait to deceive. They also told me there was Formality and Hypocrisy continually on the road, and that the Flatterer would catch me in his net. But none of these things discouraged me. They seemed but as so many nothings. I still believed what Mr Tell-True had said, and that carried me beyond them all.'

What follows was written as two features for *New Health* magazine in 1985 and 1986, which I have made into one. Caroline tells all you need to know about good and bad meat, poultry, game, fish and shellfish; tricks of the trade; and why some fats are positively good for you. The features are also fan-letters to two of her Tell-Trues: Dr Hugh Sinclair and Professor Michael Crawford, great scientists and great characters, who are two of Caroline's heroes. The admiration was mutual.

FAT THAT'S GOOD FOR YOU

On 25 March 1985, a splendid tea party was held at the Museum of London. The organising committee of the Second International Congress on Essential Fatty Acids, Prostaglandins and Leukotrienes invited all the congress participants to a Cockney High Tea, where they were welcomed by Tubby Isaacs, Pearly Kings and Queens (two of each) and a master of ceremonies. Tubby dispensed his cockles, whelks, shrimps and jellied eels in the entrance hall, while the Pearly Kings and Queens explained to mystified foreign scientists that their costumes weigh about half a hundredweight each, with several thousand buttons apiece – and the Isle of Dogs Pearly King sews on *all* his own buttons, with his calloused fingers.

Then downstairs to the Lord Mayor's coach, surrounded by fish dishes ancient and modern, starting with Roman soused fish and poached mussels with a liquamen dip. On to Black and White medieval fish pie, John Farley's fillets of pickled mackerel (Tudor and Stuart), a Georgian pupton of spinach and sole, and mackerel in gooseberry sauce, Victorian cockle tarts and Arnold Bennett omelette on oatcakes, whole dressed crabs, cod's roe paté and fish soup. And there was more . . .

Professor Michael Crawford, who organised this magnificent feast, is keen on fish, and in his book *What We Eat Today* he explains why: 'Examine the fat of brain, liver, kidney, lung, heart, spleen, testes and muscles and you find . . . a complex of fat components, many of which animals cannot make themselves but must find in their food . . . On a dry weight basis, about 60 per cent of the brain is fat.' The vital organs of the body contain a high proportion of essential fatty acids, and a rich dietary source of these is fish.

In 1956 Dr Hugh Sinclair proposed that degenerative diseases which are common in westernised countries are caused by lack of essential fats. Much scientific evidence has now been accumulated to support his theory: our food contains only small amounts of essential fats compared with that of traditional hunters and gatherers, and with pastoralists and agriculturalists who do not have access to modern methods of animal husbandry and food processing. And we eat abnormally large quantities of non-essential saturated fats which harm the basic structure of cellular material, and hence harm our essential organs. Furthermore, the artificial hardening (hydrogenation) of marine and vegetable oils produces by-products (trans fats) which are antagonistic to essential fats in the body, blocking their proper metabolism.

Most of the polyunsaturated fats in the British diet come from oils and margarines, which are increasingly of the 'high in polyunsaturated fats' variety. These products are mostly made from seed oils which are high in linoleic acid – an essential polyunsaturated fat. There is, however, another essential fat called linolenic acid, which is found in green leafy vegetables. In the human body, linolenic acid is converted into eicosapentaneoic acid (EPA) and docosahexaenoic acid, which, along with the derivatives of linoleic acid, are used for the growth and maintenance of the brain, nerves, reproductive organs, blood vessels and other vital organs. They are also used for the manufacture of all-important prostaglandins, which regulate the body on a second by second basis.

The importance of fish fat is that it contains large quantities of EPA and docosahexaenoic acid; so if you don't like green vegetables, you should head for the fishmongers without delay.

These essential structural fats (so called because they are needed for the growth and maintenance of vital organs) are now an expanding research area, thirty years after Dr Sinclair indicated just how important they might be. At the International Congress on Essential Fatty Acids in March, just about every disease you could think of was being linked with them, or with a shortage of them in the diet. Multiple sclerosis, cystic fibrosis and rheumatoid arthritis are all depressing disorders in which patients have been shown to respond to added essential fats in the diet.

Marine animals can be divided into those which are fatty (including mackerel, sardines, herrings, sprats, salmon, seal and whale) and those whose flesh is virtually fat-free (all white fish and shellfish). Fatty fish have been of particular interest to scientists because of their ability to lower blood cholesterol and other blood fats and prevent blood clotting, prolonging bleeding time, thus making the circulatory system less prone to blockages, or thrombosis and heart attacks. Fish fat is a chemical Dyno-Rod.

Fish are cold blooded, and adopt the temperature of their environment, that is the sea. Sea water, and particularly the North Sea, tends to be a bit chilly, so the fish swimming in it are cold inside. What would happen if, like butter, the fat inside the muscle of fish was solid at North Sea temperatures? Herring might have a bit of trouble swimming along with a tail of freezing, lard-like consistency. Fish fat is so high in polyunsaturates that it stays liquid, even at North Sea temperatures. It is very different from meat fat. And this sort of fat is very beneficial to health.

The effect of fish fat on the circulatory system has been studied in the few remaining Eskimo in Greenland, who ate about a pound of fish a day before Western trading posts came along. And Hugh Sinclair himself ate nothing but seal's meat for a hundred days in order to investigate the effects on his own body. In recent years there have been numerous studies on volunteers fed fish fat.

While the effect of fish fat is similar to that of polyunsaturated vegetable oils (such as corn, sunflower, safflower and soya), its action is more potent.

And it is not only fatty fish which are good for you. The Japanese, who eat an average of 95 grams or roughly four ounces of mostly fresh fish a day outlive the rest of the world. Much of their fish is very low in fat.

A study just completed and reported recently in the New England Journal of Medicine looked at the effect of fish consumption on health in a group of men in the Netherlands. The authors of the study looked at 872 men of 40 to 59 years and measured their food intake. Those who ate more fish of all types had a lower rate of death from heart attacks after 20 years than those who ate a little. 'We conclude that the consumption of as little as one or two fish dishes per week may be of preventive value in relation to coronary heart disease,' the authors say. The fish eaten by these men was one-third fatty, and about two-thirds white.

Why should white fish, which has very little fat, be protective against heart attacks? It must be partly to do with the replacement value – if you are eating fish, then you are unlikely to be eating a hunk of marbled meat with its saturated fat at the same meal. But the nutritional value of white fish is not yet well understood.

The other great nutritional plus about fish is that seafood is now the only major part of our diet which has to be hunted, and animals which live free and are fit are likely to be healthy to eat.

Yet we only eat just under five ounces of fish per person per week in this country, and only one ounce of that is fresh. All the rest is bought frozen or processed (mostly canned). For health we should probably eat at least twice that amount per week, and to make sure you get the full nutritional benefit from fish, buy it fresh. There are good reasons for avoiding most processed fish.

Some very peculiar things have been going on in the fish processing industry in the last few years. In 1984, a report published by the Institute of Trading Standards Administration, entitled *Fish Technology – Its Uses and Abuses* by Shropshire County Council's David Walker, described how the quality of frozen fish and fish products has deteriorated over the years.

The cod war and the extension of national fishing limits to 200 miles effectively wrecked the UK deep sea trawling industry, and we now import about 65 per cent of all the cod we eat. Much of this fish arrives in Britain in the form of fish blocks which are later carved up to create fish fingers and other kinds of fish products.

How does white fish come to be squeezed and moulded into a standard size block? The fish are filleted, by hand or machine, packed into a mould and frozen. Freezing causes fish to expand and thus to fill the mould. But the temptation to add a little something to spin out an expensive raw material is sometimes just too great. Spray or dip fish into polyphosphate solution, or put the two together into what looks like a builder's concrete mixer for a little tumble, and out comes a nicely-expanded fish.

The fish skeletons and odd bits and pieces left after the fish has been filleted are fed into a bone separating machine to produce fish mince. As with the modern sausage, the aim to use all edible parts of an animal rather than waste them is admirable, but this process is not without its problems. First, fish mince tastes funny. A fish mince block is to fish as chipboard is to wood, and the similarity does not end there, because fish mince can taste like cardboard.

It is also tough. The disintegration of tissues releases substances which speed up rancidity, so storage life is reduced. Minced bones make it taste gritty, and the more bone, blood and entrail present the greyer the final product. And last, but by no means least, fish mince is the dried pork rind of the industry – it sucks up water.

Fish mince is often used in block manufacture, either by itself or with fish fillets. These blocks are then used for fish fingers and other coated products.

Before the 1970s fish fingers were normally made of filleted fish, according to the original American recipe of the 1950s. Invented in the USA in 1952, they were an instant success, as they were on introduction to the UK in 1955. Given that they are almost universally popular with children, and that we spend £100 million pounds buying 40,000 tonnes of the things each year, what of their quality today?

The quantity and proportion of fish in a fish finger is a frequent subject of discussion between trading standards officers and the manufacturers. There are no compositional regulations for the minimum fish content of a fish finger (nor, for that matter, are there any for any other breaded or battered fish products), so the consumer is not protected.

How is a fish finger made? Fish blocks are sawn into finger shapes, coated in batter, and covered with breadcrumbs. The finger is partially fried and frozen. Now if you were a fish finger manufacturer and had costs on your mind, you might do what some UK manufacturers have been up to since the early 1970s: choose a cheaper fish block, cut the fingers thinner, spread the batter thicker, add more breadcrumbs. The ratio of fish to coating is an all-important sum which you would be keen to do at frequent intervals. For a thick fish finger has proportionately less batter and crumbs, and more fish than a thin one. The thinner the finger, the greater the weight of cheap batter you can sell to your unsuspecting customer.

Trading standards officers stated in 1983 that the lean fish content of fish fingers had fallen from 80 per cent in the 1960s, to a present average level of 56 per cent, with a substantial proportion of them also containing added water. Their 1983 analyses of 475 samples (involving 6,500 fish fingers) showed that the lowest quantity of fish was 33.7 per cent, and 13 per cent of fish fingers contained less than half lean fish. Ten per cent of the samples contained more than a fifth added water. Three-quarters contained more than a tenth added water. The average was 13.8 per cent. The trading standards officers considered that legislation is urgently needed to control both quality and labelling of these products.

The industry, for their part, maintains that variations in fish content are due to variations in the quality of raw materials, the inadequacy of the chemical test for 'fish', the extra water is in the batter, not the fish, the quality of starting materials is kept at a premium, and, perhaps most important of all, fish fingers have never had a fish content of 80 per cent, so how could it have decreased to the extent maintained by the trading standards officers?

The enforcement officers have conducted many analyses of fish fingers over the years, and while some argument about the methods of analysis may be justified, there can be no doubt that at the lower end of the market, a very poor quality product is being sold, and that overall, the amount of fish has gone down, and the amount of water and batter, up.

The fish finger of the 1980s is pointing firmly downwards, towards the general debasement of a popular food. It is time that the Ministry of Agriculture's Food Advisory Committee sat down to look at the problem.

Apart from the battering on the outside, there is ample evidence that a lot of coated fish products have been well and truly battered on the inside. 'Reformed' fish, in other words unrecognisable bits of fish stuck together with a liberal dose of polyphosphates, and moulded with great artistry into fillet shapes, are covered with breadcrumbs or batter. Some manufacturers even have the nerve to call these things fish 'fillets'.

Of course, some manufacturers and retailers take great care to ensure that their products are what they say on the label. But once a leading retailer places an enormous order with a manufacturer whose standards are not of the highest quality, it forces others to debase their product in order to compete with a lower price. And with only a handful of supermarkets now accounting for three quarters of the UK grocery trade, competition for these bulk orders is obviously fierce.

Second cousin to the reformed joint of ham, scampi has not escaped the water-holding agents either. Much loved by the catering trade for its ease of preparation, and by the public for its connections with high society, the watered down, reformed, heavily breaded scampi is a well-researched animal.

It starts its life as a nice little lobster, whose tail is much in demand. Chopped off, the tail is iced and frozen, whereupon the meat inside expands and cracks the shell. After thawing and shelling, the tails more often than not come to rest in a tankful of polyphosphate solution (what would the food industry do without this helpful chemical?).

Now any idea you might have had about scampi being a plain ordinary fat shellfish surrounded only by tasty breadcrumbs is quite wrong. For the majority of scampi caught nowadays are miserable little lobsters, netted before they have fully grown. But the bigger the tails, the higher the price. The imaginative manufacturer is not deterred by such a trivial problem as miniscule scampi. The answer is simply to bung them all into a mincer or chopper, mash them together with a good dose of polyphosphates, squeeze it all through a nozzle, and out comes a whopping great scampi.

Then there's the prawn. Beware the double glazing salesman and above all beware the double glazed prawn.

Most of the prawns eaten in the UK are imported, although some are caught in the North Sea. Many are bought into the UK in bulk, and then packed for distribution. The prawn is cooked, deshelled, washed, soaked in brine, frozen and glazed with a very thin coating of ice, which protects it during storage. The weight of the glaze comes to about a tenth of the final weight of the prawn, if the process is done with care. However, unscrupulous processors manage to add up to a third by weight of ice, and worse still, import ready-glazed prawns and give them another going over before packing and sealing – hence the double glazed prawn!

Faced with these problems, the answer for consumers is to buy fresh wherever possible.

And next time you meet a crafty Cockney, remember that they are a living example of what Granny always said; fish are good for the brain.

And now for something equally delicious and good for you: game. If everyone in Britain decided to join the huntin' and shootin' fraternity on August 12 (when the first grouse from Scotland plummet onto the dinner table) and eat their way through their fair share, or one fifty-five-millionth, of all the designated game animals and birds in Britain, what would happen? I reckon there would be just about one and a half or two meals per person before the last rabbit curled up its tootsies in protest at the loss of all its pals.

Having added up all the ducks, geese, pigeons, deer, pheasants, hares, rabbits and other game species – among them 852,650 wild game fowl, 860,000 deer and between three and five million pairs of pigeon, I have to tell you that there aren't enough to go round.

The scarcity of game, which is reflected by its cost, means that it has to be an occasional treat. But it's a treat we can all learn from, for its taste and nutritional value are far superior to those of intensively reared animals. The Ministry of Agriculture, Fisheries and Food would do well to set its animal research departments to work to discover how modern farming practices can produce meat closer in quality to that of wild animals and birds.

In days gone by, of course, humans were outnumbered by wild game, rather than the other way around. Wild animals and birds were an important part of the national food supply for rich and poor alike. The aristocracy chased and pointed guns at anything large that moved (good sport, fair game and all that), while lesser mortals relied on poaching smaller fry.

A banquet for Charles I in 1634 included storks, herons, ruffs, reeves, redshanks, dotterels, godwits, curlews, swans, bitterns, mallards, peewits and dozens of other birds, some now extinct in Britain. A trip to London's National Gallery will leave you in no doubt that the tables of our wealthier ancestors were groaning with meats. Yet historical records suggest that heart attacks, which are today associated with fatty meaty meals, were rare. Why?

Game animals are very different from domesticated beasts. First of all, they look different. The meat is dark red, the muscles are taut. The flesh feels firm: a wild duck carcass is sinewy and can't be pulled about. By contrast, domesticated duck are flabby and fat. In short, the difference between them is that wild birds and animals are strong and fit. Domesticated beasts are fat and unfit. Selected over centuries for fatness and fleshiness, today's pigs, cows and chickens take next to no exercise. The modern pig spends its day confined to a concrete pen, with nowhere to go and nothing to do.

Leanness alone, though, is not everything. They taste different too. Why? Fit muscles are a different thing altogether from feeble, weak ones. The fibres contain more pigment which affects the taste. Have you ever wondered why chicken legs are pinkish, while the breast and wings are white? The leg muscles are the only ones a modern chicken uses, standing in its cage or taking a stroll around the sights of a broiler house. Because the bird doesn't fly, the rest degenerate. They lose their structure and are prized for their tenderness. Battery farming is not a twentieth century invention; in Elizabethan times poultry, pigs and game birds were often fattened in confinement, the object being to cram them with food, and so soften and whiten the meat.

There is another reason why the taste is different, and that has to do with what they eat. Wild birds and animals thrive on variety (or they did until EEC farming policies had the effect of turning huge areas of Britain into prairies). Animals are just as affected by the contents of their meals as we are. Feed them polyunsaturated fats and oils and their flesh will change. As long as wild animals eat a wide variety of herbs, seeds, grasses, leaves and flowers, their flesh will taste different from an animal fed on Mr Fat'n'Fill's instant pig mix.

The nutritional difference between game and confined animals is that game contains less fat, the fat is less saturated and more polyunsaturated, and the water content is lower. Standard textbooks have little to say about these differences. That's because any scientist who suggested polyunsaturated fats might be beneficial was until recently regarded as a bit of a nutter.

Like fish, game contains large quantities of 'essential' polyunsaturated fats, essential because the body cannot make them and so has to be supplied with them in food. These essential fats make up a large part of the fatty material in the brain and nervous tissues. They are also important in other vital organs of the body: heart, liver, kidneys, spleen. Indeed, no cell in the human body can function without a good supply of essential fats, and that supply must come from food.

Fish fat lowers blood cholesterol and makes obstructions less likely to develop on the arterial walls. It also makes the blood 'thinner' and less likely to clot. But fish aren't the only source of essential oils. Game animals and birds, too, contain them in good quantities, and so do the vital organs of all creatures, even those that are domesticated.

The origin of all essential fats is plants. Green leaves and seeds supply them to animals, such as humans, and we concentrate them in areas of the body which most need them. During early life, large amounts of essential polyunsaturated fats are deposited in the brain and nervous tissues. They 'create' intelligence. The growth of the brain is complete in the first three years of life, so it is no surprise to find that human breast milk contains lots of essential fats, as long as the mother eats healthy food and as long as her fat stores are not full of processed, saturated fats.

Mother's milk depends on mother's food. Cows' milk, on the other hand, is designed for calves, whose brains are less demanding. Born at a later stage of maturity, with brain, nerves and vital organs intact, the calves' first priority is to get moving (or was until man decided their legs were redundant). Cows' milk is highly saturated – a good energy supply, but no good for building brain scaffolding.

Because we eat so much milk fat in this country, we get through a large pile of saturated fat. But milk fat isn't the only problem. Cows and sheep are ruminants, which store vast armies of bacteria in their stomachs. These convert the polyunsaturated fats of plants into saturated fats, which are then deposited in the flesh. Because they take little exercise and are bred to be efficient converters of food, twentieth century beef and lamb are fatty meats. They are nowhere near the quality of wild pigeon, partridge or hare.

Can intensively reared animals ever be as delicious and nutritious as game? Farmers and animal research stations have a lot to learn from wild animals. Uniformity of diet produces dull and boring taste. Lack of exercise produces obese and flabby animals. Leanness produced by growth hormones is not the same as leanness produced by exercise. The animals we now eat daily are the result of a national 'cheap food' policy, which has produced quantity at the expense of quality. Fitter, healthier meat can be produced, but it will cost more. Are you prepared to pay for it?

CHAPTER SEVEN

ADVICE

———•◆•———

'For the price of artificially coloured and flavoured fizz, you can have a small bag of tangerines, apples or bananas. And what's wrong with water?'

'One of my fundamental objections to the way in which decisions are made about food in this country, in Whitehall, is that far too many of the decisions are made by middle-class, middle-aged men who don't cook, and who don't go shopping,' said Caroline to Derek Cooper, in her last interview in August 1988. 'Think of Whitehall. There's not a shop to be seen in it. When do the civil servants there go shopping? Their wives do it! – because it's predominantly men who work in Whitehall.' What's needed is more women to be involved in food policy; and more appreciation of food as one of the delights of life.

'We've taken the excitement out of food and turned it into sets of scientific nutrition tables. We've rather encouraged people to think of food in terms of nutrients . . . If you talk about food as a nutritionist and a scientist, you're considered to be emotional and unscientific and to have taken an easy road. Whereas you're considered to be scientific and a clever person, if you talk about the amount of cholesterol in food, or the amount of vitamin B.'

What scientists have done, she said, is to medicalise food.

'When I've been to lecture at conferences, I always go with sackfuls of food. And at the end of the conference, I guarantee that some man is going to come up to me, and say: "It's fascinating. Where did you get this stuff?" I can't believe it! I say "Where do you think I got it. In the shops!". They've got no idea what's on sale, half of them. I think it's pathetic.'

The first time I saw Caroline's picture in the paper was eight days before I met her. On 14 June 1983 *The Times* ran a full-page story on prevention of heart disease, tied to a new BBC TV series, 'Plague of Hearts'. The feature divided into two parts. On top, Professor Geoffrey Rose of the London School of Hygiene and Tropical Medicine was photographed peering at the reader over his half-moons, explaining the recommendations of the 1982 World Health Organisation committee of which he was Chairman. 'The WHO recommends a diet with only 10 per cent of saturated fat and at least 3 per cent polyunsaturated fat. For countries such as Britain where obesity is common the total fat should be restricted to 30 per cent. Yet 38–42 per cent of the energy in our diet is derived from fat.'

'Be of good heart . . .' was the title of this main feature. Below, the subsidiary story was '. . . and this is the way to do it.' Caroline was photographed with a big grin.

> She was asked by the television series to devise a healthy diet based on the WHO recommendations for preventing coronary heart disease. She adapted the average weekly shopping list for a family of four as compiled by the Ministry of Agriculture's National Food Survey . . .
>
> She advises smaller quantities of lean meat, particularly of lamb and beef, and more chicken and fish. (Even oily fish are safe as they are low in saturated fats). She increased by half the fibre foods – fruit, vegetables, cereals (but watch out for the sugar-coated ones) and bread. She thinks that the quality of the average loaf must improve before people will adopt the continental habit of eating bread with each meal without adding butter; and that it is time people realised that bread, potatoes, rice, noodles and spaghetti are good for you and not particularly fattening if eaten without much fat.
>
> She cuts down on sugar and jams and on cakes and biscuits; some cake and biscuit manufacturers use the cheapest palm, coconut or blended oils, which may contain high amounts of saturated fats. She reduces sausages and meat pies, as many of these also have a high saturated fat content; the manufacturers are not required by law to show the fat content on the label.'

And so forth, and so on. (I hear Caroline's voice saying, 'Here we go again. Where did this word "particularly" come from? Starchy foods by themselves are not fattening. And what is this "some", "may" and "many"? All the big manufacturers use cheap oils. They're all saturated. All sausages and meat pies are stuffed with saturated fat. Show me one that isn't!' But that's by the way.)

Right from the start of her work with the Coronary Prevention Group in 1980, Caroline insisted that its advice to the public should be about food, not just nutrients. What, after all, does 38–42 per cent of fat look like? She was not just an attractive face, to television producers, although they were desperate for women to appear with the middle-aged, middle-class men on healthy living programmes. Indeed, without Caroline some of these programmes would never have been made, not because she had the most authoritative voice, but simply because an all-male cast on any television programme whose interested audience is mostly women, simply doesn't work.

Caroline's added attraction, is that she spoke good, plain language ('bog-standard', she called it), and talked straight. When she hit a stride as a writer, later in her life, she was the only one of two British scientists in her field under the age of 60 with any feeling for language, any evident ability to write good English with vivid images, clear examples, and with a sense of style and the meaning of words. (Professor John Garrow is the other.) As a speaker, once she learned the tricks of the trade on a lecture platform, and in a radio and television studio, she was an organiser's and a producer's dream. She was also quite self-critical. In an early letter, she wrote to me 'Tomorrow I'm doing "Ear to Ground" following "Womans Hour". Christopher said I said um all the time and did it badly. (He on the other hand . . .). Everyone else said it was OK. He's horrid. Did I really do it badly? Yours in a decline . . .' (Christopher was right about the ums, I told her. Over the years we checked the recordings of her television and radio appearances, and gradually the um-count dropped).

The Coronary Prevention Group, television, and Caroline, was a potent combination. Her first published booklet of advice was a CPG/Granada production with Christopher Robbins in August 1981, which 'Reports Action' called *Junk The Junk Food* (big letters, graffiti-style) and 'A simple guide to healthier eating' (small letters). 'A very important message is that healthier eating can be very enjoyable, and can cost less, and that healthy food does not necessarily take longer to prepare' they wrote. And, in those days when wholegrain bread was not nationally available in Britain, they gave an example. 'Good bread is difficult to buy but very easy to bake at home. No magic and special skills are required and without much effort it can become the most enjoyable cooking of the week. The smell of fresh-baked bread is part of the pleasure.'

Junk The Junk Food was requested by 20,000 viewers and later reprinted by CPG minus Granada TV's cheeky title. For the 1983 *Sunday Times* National Fun Run, Caroline, Christopher and CPG produced 'The Healthy Heart Guide': a poster for any changing-room wall. By this time Caroline had encouraged CPG to use a cartoon by Mel Calman as a symbol; one of Mel's rueful little men, holding a heart, with the line 'I'll take care of you'. The little heart was repeated by the lines of advice 'Eat more bread (especially wholemeal), potatoes, fresh vegetables, fresh fruit, poultry and fish'.

Underneath, Caroline added a project idea for kids. 'Start a collection of food labels and make a league table of the additives (including salt, sugar etc) that you most often see in the list of contents. Remember, the nearer the top of the contents list things like sugar come, the more has been added!'

In 1984 and 1985 Caroline worked with the CPG team, producing booklets on *Blood Pressure and Your Heart*, *You and Your Heart*, *Healthier Eating; a Good Foods Guide*, and *Healthier Eating and Your Heart*. Each of these had a circulation of around 10,000. Caroline put some cheek in them, and was very pleased with the Larry cartoons on their covers; *Healthier Eating and Your Heart* has a woman looking like she might be in town for the Annual General Meeting of the Women's Institutes, on her knees with an aerosol, spraying 'Down with saturated fat' on a brick wall, watched by a bemused copper.

Her last work for CPG was, with Dr Michael Rayner, the introduction for the book *Eating for a Healthy Heart*, published by Ebury Press in 1988. This ends 'The writing is on the wall for the dominance of food issues by civil servants, government committees, and the food industry. Increasingly, consumers are demanding and winning a say. Food and health are rapidly becoming vote-catching issues. But if we are to ensure that the present progress towards the production and availability of healthy foods continues, it is essential that our MPs and MEPs are left in no doubt of what you, the public, want.'

Some of the CPG booklets were published with the Health Education Council (HEC), whose then Director-General, Dr David Player, was doing his best to get the healthy eating message across. (In 1987 Dr Player was sacked by the Department of Health and Social Security, or as wags called it, the Department of Stealth and Total Obscurity, by means of the complicated expedient of abolishing the HEC under him).

Caroline bombarded Dr Player with ideas. On 17 July 1984, the day after Jonathan Aitken's socks'n'sausages Commons Adjournment Debate, she wrote from City and Hackney Health Authority:

'Dear David. Here I go again! Last week COMA arrives on your desk, so you get through two days' breathing space before this turns up! My question is, of course, when do we all get a bagful of leaflets and booklets about healthy eating? I need them badly for my cardiovascular prevention programme in Hackney; and many, many others round the country also want up-to-date materials. I could of course tell them to read my own book, injunctions permitting, but it would be nice to know that HEC advice was just around the corner.'

How about (1) Leaflet on healthy eating – no words . . . This is important because many people, as you know, cannot read English, or are illiterate. (2) Leaflet on healthy eating – with words . . . (3) Leaflet on slimming . . . (4) Booklet on healthy eating . . . I am thinking of something like the CPG booklet (which you are funding – thank you) . . . (5) Training manuals . . . Lest you think I am making this request for altruistic purposes, let me tell you that this is essential for my own sanity, never mind the nation's health. For I am getting tired of giving the same lecture and answering the same questions about what to tell the Great British Public. No doubt the Health Visitors too are getting tired of listening to me. (6) Eating for children – leaflet . . . (7) Healthy food on a low income . . . . (8) Food labels. I left the nasty one (from your point of view) until last. What we need is a little booklet which explains exactly what food labels mean; what is the difference between glucose, fructose, sucrose (if any); what different fats are, etc. But maybe it is a little premature for the HEC to do this. I have it on good authority that some retailers and manufacturers are so keen to do something that they might beat you to it . . .

I am sorry to be so persistent about these leaflets [no she wasn't] but I know my questions are repeated by many others around the country. It is also important that HEC is seen to take a lead, because others (such as the Butter Information Council) are busy cashing in on the widespread interest in food and health. With best wishes, Caroline.'

'We are proceeding as fast as we can on a leaflet on healthy eating' replied Dr Player. Accordingly in September 1985 Caroline was sent the draft of a booklet eventually called *Guide to Healthy Eating*, published in June 1986, for her comments. She had plenty of advice to give about the HEC advice. She had detailed points to make about all 24 pages. Here are some.

'Page 6. "You don't get any fibre at all in animal products . . . like meat". So what are Eskimo turds made of? Hugh Sinclair tells me that traditionally the Eskimos did not eat nuts and berries (as the fibre men would have us believe) but only ate meat (raw). So meat-diets still contain fibre, and it is quite reasonable to suppose that some of the meat we eat finds its way into the top of our colons. It's always best to be honest.' (Caroline is probably wrong, here. Eskimos ate sinew and skin and hair, which acts like fibre. We don't eat such bits of meat).

Page 12. "Tips: Drinks". Do you really want to encourage people to drink low-calorie rubbish? Why not suggest pure fruit juice instead? I know it's expensive, but tins of soft drinks aren't exactly cheap. For the price of a can of artificially coloured and flavoured fizz, you can have a small bag of tangerines, apples or bananas. And what's wrong with water? I think you should say somewhere that babies won't die if they're given water, or fruit juice half diluted with water. Nor will the rest of the population.

Page 12. "General". I still think you should talk about sugars. (Do you know that Tate & Lyle's lawyers are having some cosy little chats with Tesco about their healthy eating leaflets? Next one out is all about sugar, and my guess is that the subject under discussion is the *legal* meaning of sugar, which is sucrose – one very good reason why you might like to talk about sugars instead).

Page 12. Para 3. "Sugar promotes tooth decay". I still think you should say "causes".

Page 16. "Made-up products like pies, burgers and sausages . . . Some are excellent . . ." I have yet to come across an "excellent" meat burger or sausage, but I live in hope.

Page 24. "Books". I'm going to say it again. So what's wrong with *The Food Scandal* by Caroline Walker and Geoffrey Cannon? Everyone else gets their books plugged, including those that rewrote *The Food Scandal* in boring language for the Great Unwashed. You can't say we didn't explain healthy eating, because two-thirds of our book is devoted to advice for the individual. All right. I'll shut up about it now.'

How come you're wheeling in people from the food industry-funded British Nutrition Foundation, to give 'independent' expert advice about food and health? Caroline demanded, of one or two radio producers, in the early 1980s. 'Sorry' said one reply from the Radio 4 'Today' show. 'In our innocence we clearly boobed'. Caroline became a regular radio broadcaster, starting in 1979, and notably for Vanessa Harrison on 'Woman's Hour' and then 'The Food Programme', and all the national talk networks – Jimmy Young and John Dunn, as well as Radio 4 from dawn to dusk – 'Today', 'Morning Call', 'You and Yours', 'The World at One', 'PM', and any news programme after she herself had made some news.

After a couple of national tours for *The Food Scandal* (hardback in 1984, paperback in 1985) she reckoned that the most challenging and rewarding radio, 'The Food Programme' aside, was made outside London. In Glasgow she could stretch a live interview with Jimmy Mack from the scheduled six minutes to fifteen, with her vivacity. And Nick Meanwell on BRMB, Birmingham, gave you two hours of live phone-in, between ads and discs. Caroline socked it to them.

Caroline made what Dr David Player called 'the new public health' meaningful to everybody who listened. And she did more than that.

For four years, between 1983 and 1987, she personally inspired hundreds of professional teams – scientific research units, health districts, voluntary associations, industry research and development departments, legislators and their advisors, food and health forums, television and radio production teams, newspaper and magazine feature departments – to get the message about food and health. With others, she created a new rhetoric to make the message meaningful. In time the advice became more and more simple and clear. 'I've got it!' she said one day. 'Here it is, in four words:

EAT WHOLE, FRESH FOOD.

Simple as that,' she said enthusiastically for a period, when journalists telephoned. 'Four words, seventeen characters.' 'We can't make a story out of that,' they said. 'Why not? Print it in nice great big words all over the page?' 'We'll have to spin it out a bit if we're going to write another book,' I said.

Filing cabinets multiplied in our home. After reading thousands of scientific studies, hundreds of expert reports, and countless specialist journals, together with shelves full of books on nutrition, we devised an even more elegant message: four words, pared down to fifteen characters, inspired by some thoughts of the great American nutritionist Elmer McCollum:

GOOD FOOD GOES BAD.

One professional team inspired by Caroline worked for BBC TV Continuing Education: executives Peter Riding and David Hargreaves, and producers David Cordingley and Jenny Stevens, and others who are not forgotten. Starting in 1983, for two years they planned a season of several series of programmes, with the general heading 'The Food and Health Campaign'. In 1985 they were ready. Will you do it? Caroline was asked. The Controllers of BBC1 and BBC2 had agreed 'O'Donnell Investigates the Food Connection', a four part series starting in September on BBC2, repeated on BBC1; 'The Taste of Health', an eight-part series on BBC2; a repeat of the 1983 'Plague of Hearts' five-part series on BBC1; 'You Are What You Eat', a six-parter on BBC1 starting in January 1986; 'O'Donnell Investigates the Food Business', a six-part series on BBC2 starting in April; and 'Go For It', a thirteen-parter on BBC1 also starting in April.

The BBC Food and Health Campaign was not Caroline's idea. But there is no way it could have been mounted, without the climate of national opinion she above anybody else had created, as David Cordingley, Jenny Stevens, and others from the BBC told us. Did viewers really want that much? Yes, we were told: the audience research had been done. (And on transmission, many of the programmes broke audience records). Would the BBC hierarchy accept a Campaign? Listen, we were told, this is a really important issue, we're talking about the nation's health. (After transmission, there were recriminations, and one series has never been repeated, after representations from the sugar trade).

Caroline advised four of the 'Food and Health Campaign' series, telling the production teams what to read, who to see, where to film. Scripts piled up at home. The telephone bill rocketed. Motorcycle messengers triple-parked outside the house. Producers, directors, editors, interviewers, and sound, lighting and cameramen set up shop inside the house, and Caroline advised on scripts, interviews and locations

And that wasn't all! She wrote and contributed to four of the booklets published to accompany the various series. First, she wrote *Eat Your Way*

To Health, to accompany the first O'Donnell series in September 1985. This was requested by 100,000 viewers. In January *You Are What You Eat* was published; we wrote about half of this, and it was requested by 250,000 viewers. In the spring of 1986, *Food: Go For Health*, and *Alcohol: Friend or Foe* were sent out to another 120,000 viewers. 'People don't want to be told what they should and shouldn't eat' say government and industry representatives. Oh yes they do.

In the week starting 7 October 1985, Caroline was too busy even to watch the television programmes she was advising. On the Monday Granada TV broadcast a 'World in Action' special on 'The Great Food Scandal', telling the story of the suppression of the NACNE report. The account given in *The Food Scandal* was confirmed by the scientists who were the key players at the time: Dr Derek Shrimpton, ex-Director General of the British Nutrition Foundation; Professor Jerry Morris, ex-Chairman of the main NACNE committee; and Professor Philip James himself. The programme started with three tipper trucks off-loading 420 pounds of fat, then 420 pounds of sugar, then 45 pounds of salt: the amounts that an average family gets through in a year. The data came from Caroline, of course.

And 'The Great Food Scandal' made history by filming mechanically recovered meat being made. Next day the manufacturers of the Great British Sausage were very sad men indeed: by amazing coincidence, 'Good Enough To Eat?', a two-part series made by Thames TV, was broadcast, also nationally, on the Tuesday and Wednesday; and there, again, was mechanically recovered meat being made. Thames published more advice from Caroline: she co-wrote a booklet on chemical additives, requested by another 60,000 viewers. In April the next year, Granada TV broadcast a second 'World In Action' special, 'The Threatened Generation', on the suppression of the Department of Health report 'The Diets of British Schoolchildren'. Caroline set up, advised and appeared in all these programmes.

While all this was going on, Felicity Lawrence, then editor of *New Health* magazine, devised a series of features on the use and abuse of chemical food additives. Caroline did another one of her Orson Welles acts: with others, she devised, wrote, and edited the series, and starred too, as it turned out: the Food Additives Campaign Team, which grew out of the *New Health* series, was launched in the Houses of Parliament on 12 December, and Caroline marched over to 10 Downing Street to present the hamper of Christmas goodies with added chemical value, to

Mrs Thatcher, as described in Chapter 3.

In 1986 the *New Health* series was the Periodical Publishers Association Campaign of the Year. Caroline's last interview with Derek Cooper was made into a 'Food Programme' which won the Glenfiddich Award as radio programme of the year, in April 1989. And in June 1989 Caroline was posthumously given the Rosemary Delbridge Award, for the person who has done most to influence Government and Parliament to act in the public interest; and a Winston Churchill Memorial Fellowship.

What follows is the advice Caroline gave to 16–19 year-olds about their food and health, for a Health Education Authority 'Action Pack' published by the National Extension College in the autumn of 1987. Of all the advice she gave, this is the last, and I think the best.

I asked many of her friends to say what they thought about Caroline, for this book. In May 1989 Dr Claudia Sanchez-Castillo, who now works for her country in Mexico as a food policy planner, said this.

'Caroline was a key person in my development when I first came to Cambridge, not just because of her knowledge in the field of nutrition, but also because of her enormous capacity for love and for understanding people's needs. She approached me and offered her warmth, love and understanding. She was very patient and when she asked me to give her some physiology lessons she used to listen with great attention to my torpid and badly spoken English, as if I was giving the most important lecture in the world.

She was a person whose presence was about always. She made herself beloved and needful, caring for children, adults and old people, caring for her people, the nation and the developing world . . . I will make sure that what she did for me reflects in my country in her name and spirit.

I cry so much for my dear friend.'

FOOD AND HEALTH: ADVICE FOR EVERYBODY

In the last 25 years, more than 50 independent medical reports have been published by different government and medical committees around the world which have studied the links between food and disease.

Many of the earlier reports were concerned only with the prevention of coronary heart disease (heart attacks), which has become the Number 1 killer in the Western world. However, many of these 50 reports have also considered the prevention of diseases and disorders other than heart disease, such as:

tooth decay	overweight
diverticular disease	piles (haemorrhoids)
constipation	diabetes
colon cancer, stomach cancer	gallstones
breast cancer	strokes

Indeed, more than 70 different diseases and disorders have now been linked with food: eg. asthma, migraine, skin disorders, inflammatory diseases of the intestine (Crohn's disease, ulcerative colitis), arthritis, hiatus hernia, osteoporosis, kidney stones.

We all die sometime!

Why should we be concerned with these illnesses? All of us have to die sometime. Surely illness is part of life? Doctors and governments have become concerned because these illnesses are a common cause of death and disability in young people and in the middle-aged. Early death of a man or woman leaves behind a dependent family. Unfit people cannot live life to the full. Investment in training is often wasted.

Premature heart disease, overweight and other chronic conditions are common in Westernised, or industrialised, countries. They are rare in peasant communities and the Third World. All communities which change their lifestyle to a 'Western' way, develop these diseases. Premature death and disability become common. This is as true of urban communities in the Third World, as it is of the richer, Western world.

Industrialisation

Industrialisation brings many changes, including changes in food. Technology brings new foods: fish fingers, oven-ready chips, instant puddings, quick noodles, space-age snacks, imitation cream. Scientists invent new ways of making the expensive bits of the recipe go further: soya instead of meat, artificial flavours and colours instead of fruit, flavour enhancers, artificial cheese, imitation milk powder.

How do we know that it is the change of food that is responsible for the development of early illness, and not other things? Environmental pollution, smoking, lack of regular activity and exercise, dependence on machinery, overcrowding, noise, breakdown of traditional family and community life: these are all common features of an industrialised community. Sorting out the cause of a common disease is difficult and time consuming.

The ideal experiment would be to take at least 500,000 babies at birth, and randomly allocate them to two groups: one to eat one sort of food, the other to eat another; for the whole of their lives. *All other things* (smoking, jobs, activity, etc.) *would have to be kept the same.* At the end of their lives, all the causes of death would be added up and compared. Of course, such an experiment can never be done! But those who criticise the evidence linking food with disease must be aware that 'proof' is impossible to achieve. We cannot control human behaviour in this way, so the evidence used in medical studies must be of a deductive sort, the kind used in a criminal court.

Detective work, the linking of different sorts of evidence, is a regular feature of medical studies. It was detective work which led to the linking of lung cancer with smoking. Most doctors and the public accept the validity of this link, despite the fact that it has never been 'proved'. The links between food and health are of similar uncertainty, and always will be. Scientific proof is never absolute.

UK Reports on Food and Health
The Royal College of Physicians (RCP), the Department of Health and Social Security (DHSS) and the British Medical Association (BMA) have all produced reports on the links between food and health. Taken together with the reports of the World Health Organisation, they say that if we in the UK ate 'healthier' food, our chance of developing illnesses early in life could be greatly reduced. Particular problems in the UK food supply are large amounts of saturated fat, processed sugars and processed starches. The UK food supply is, as a result of historical, EEC and climatic factors, weighted towards fatty, sugary foods.

The main changes in British food since the nineteenth century

What have been the main changes in British food since the nineteenth century?

Britain's sweet tooth
The fast expanding cities of the nineteenth century were overcrowded and dirty, the people poor, and weakened by inadequate food. They died from infectious diseases. British meals were transformed by ever-increasing quantities of imported foods. Sugar was the biggest change. Before colonisation in the Caribbean, sugar was a luxury few could afford. Sugar cane plantations changed all that. The cheaper sugar became, the more the British ate.

Sugar consumption in the UK is 46kg. per head per year, or 2lb per person per week. Of this, 38kg. is sucrose, 8kg. is glucose, 0.4kg. is honey. One third of sugar eaten is purchased as bags of sugar. The rest is in manufactured foods (eg. biscuits, cakes, soft drinks, jams, puddings, sweetened breakfast cereals, sweets, chocolates). Sugar has changed our food and our health.

The constipation of a nation

The processing of cereals also affects our health. Flour milling was mechanised in the nineteenth century, producing refined, white flour instead of brown. What does this do to our health? Two fifths of British adults say they are constipated and one fifth take laxatives. The amount of dietary fibre we eat in the UK is small by comparison with countries where rates of intestinal diseases are low.

Fat food

With industrialisation, the quality of fats has also changed. Cakes, biscuits, sauces, pies, puddings, soup mixes, margarines, cooking fats – these are made with processed or hardened ('hydrogenated') fats. When plant oils are hardened, polyunsaturated fats which are essential to health are destroyed. Polyunsaturated fats do not keep; they go rancid and are no good to a manufacturer looking for a product with long shelf life and reliable quality. Saturated fats, on the other hand, keep very well.

Intensively reared animals which take little exercise and eat concentrated feed produce fatty meat, which is highly saturated. We eat a lot of saturated meat fat, especially in pies, pates, liver sausage, processed meats. (The Meat and Livestock Commission is trying to make animals leaner, however.) Dairy fat is also saturated. Our ancestors ate butter and drank milk, but not in the quantities we do now. Saturated fats are harmful when eaten in large quantities.

Food processing

Four-fifths of the food we eat has been processed, and an increasing amount nowadays is highly processed. Highly processed foods are usually of poor nutritional value. Most cakes, biscuits, ice creams, sauces, snacks, soft drinks and many breakfast cereals consist of processed starches, processed (saturated) fats, processed sugars, colours, flavours and other additives to stick them all together and make the mixture 'keep'. They contain only very little, or none, of the essential oils, vitamins, minerals and fibre that are in the plants from which they derive. They supply calories and not much more.

Additives – the 'E' numbers

The estimated consumption of additives in the UK is 7–16lbs per person per year. Although the number of additives used comes to over 6000, the number of additives regulated by government is less than 300.

All foods made after 1 January 1986 must have the 'E' number, or the name of any additive used, in the list of ingredients. Some additives have a number, but no 'E' prefix; these additives are permitted in the UK but not in other EEC countries.

In general, the more 'E' numbers in the list of ingredients, the more highly processed a food is, and the more lacking in essential ingredients.

Flavourings

The vast majority of additives are cosmetic. Flavourings account for over 95% of all additives used. There are more than 6000 of them, and they do not have 'E' numbers; they are listed simply as 'flavouring'. And, except for a handful of flavours which are banned in the UK, manufacturers can use any flavour they like, provided they satisfy themselves that it is 'safe and necessary'.

About half of these flavours are 'natural', or copies of natural flavours. The rest are new inventions of flavour technologists. Flavourings are the big secret in food processing.

Colours E100–E200

Again, cosmetic. Manufacturers say they colour food because we like it. But there is another side to it. Why use expensive egg if you can replace it with cheaper yellow colouring and artificial thickening agents; or, real raspberries rather than a splash of red colour and a sprinkle of artificial flavour?

The most common colour is caramel (E150), found in cola drinks, soups, gravies, sauces, biscuits, meat products and beer. It makes food brown and appealing. We eat a pound of caramel per person per year in the UK and the safety of industrially prepared caramel has been questioned.

Next, in terms of quantity, are the coal tar dyes, made from petroleum by-products. There are 17 of them permitted in the UK (compared with just seven in the USA), and as a group, they have come under suspicion. Many cause allergic reactions in vulnerable people, particularly children. Skin disorders, migraine, fits, hyperactivity – these are some of the symptoms reported in medical journals.

Coal tar dyes have been voluntarily withdrawn from baby food by manufacturers. But what about the rest of us? They are very difficult to avoid, as anyone who has tried will know.

Preservatives and Anti-oxidants

Preservatives prevent food going mouldy, and stop dangerous food poisoning bacteria like botulinum growing. Only a very small number of additives are preservatives. Anti-oxidants stop food going 'off', and give long shelf life. Biscuits can stand on a shop shelf (or on a shelf in your kitchen) for weeks, even months, without going bad.

Many preservatives and anti-oxidants are of questionable safety. Some retailers have asked their manufacturers to find safe alternatives.

Processing aids
Many additives help in manufacture: emulsifiers, stabilisers, firming agents, gelling agents, aerating agents, raising agents, anti-caking agents, texture improvers, thickeners, thinners, binders, buffers. On the whole, they are of more benefit to manufacturers than to consumers.

Are all additives harmful?
No. Some additives, like vitamin C and E, and natural plant colours, are quite safe. But a healthy diet means cutting down the quantity of additives consumed.

Irradiation
In 1986, a DHSS advisory committee recommended that manufacturers should be allowed to irradiate foods in order to prolong their shelf life, and reduce the number of food poisoning bacteria. Irradiation is used in several countries in a limited number of foods (e.g. to stop sprouting in potatoes, keep strawberries 'fresh' looking), but no country has yet allowed irradiation of all foods. Supporters of irradiation, including the DHSS advisory committee, say it is not harmful, and will benefit society. Opponents say it reduces the level of vitamins, many of which are already in short supply in the average UK diet (eg. vitamin C, folic acid, vitamin E), and damages polyunsaturated fats. The long term effects of eating irradiated foods are not known. Consumer groups, and government advisory committees, have said that irrradiated foods should always be labelled as such.

Food and ill health

Tooth decay (dental caries)
Ninety five percent of adults in Britain have tooth decay. Each year over 30 million teeth are filled, and 5 million teeth extracted at a cost of over £400 million. Today 700,000 teenagers have had, between them, a total of 55 million cavities in their first 15 years of life.

Dental health is improving. Fluoridation of water and toothpaste has helped, but it cannot stop the actual cause of dental caries, which dentists agree is sugar in food, particularly, sucrose added to foods.

All countries with low levels of sugar consumption have low rates of tooth decay. When consumption of sugars fell in the second world war in Europe and the UK, rates of dental caries also fell. Dentists' children have remarkably healthy teeth; they eat less sugar and clean their teeth regularly. Children who for medical reasons cannot eat sugars, have very little dental decay.

Overweight and obesity

Official records of food consumption show that in the UK we are eating less today than in the 1950s. Average energy consumption is about 300 calories less today than in the early 1950s. Yet as a population, more of us are overweight. Why?

We are less active in everyday life. We drive cars and use public transport, and have labour-saving devices in our homes. We sit down most of the day. Fewer and fewer people are involved in active work. Lack of regular activity must be the main cause of overweight.

Studies of life insurance records show that increasing weight is associated with increasing risk of disease. An overweight smoker has twice the risk of death as an overweight non-smoker.

Surveys in the UK show that 15% of 15–19 year olds are overweight. The number increases throughout life; by 60–65 years, 54% of men and 50% of women are overweight.

Overweight increases the risk of heart attacks, gallstones, high blood pressure, diabetes, cancer of the reproductive organs (breasts, cervix, uterus), arthritis, respiratory problems.

Any slimmer above a certain age will remember being told that carbohydrates are 'bad'. This was wrong advice, and encouraging people to think in terms of carbohydrates has proved unhelpful. In fact, whole, starchy foods like wholemeal bread and cereals are the staff of life; whereas processed, sugary foods are a disaster. Bread and potatoes in whole form are excellent foods for everybody, including slimmers. But white bread spread with fat and sugary jams, and potatoes turned into chips and crisps, are fattening and unhealthy.

Foods high in fats and sugars are considered by the DHSS and the RCP to lead to overweight. So does inactivity.

Heart attacks

The UK has the highest rate of death and illness from premature heart disease (before 65 years) in the world. Worst affected areas are Northern Ireland, Scotland, South Wales and the North of England. Poor people, and unskilled workers and their families, are at much higher risk than professional people and their families.

Coronary heart disease causes the annual loss of a quarter of a million years of "working life", with nearly 30,000 deaths in men under 65 years and around 10,000 deaths in women under 65 years. In 1984, coronary heart disease accounted for 31% of all deaths in men and 24% of deaths in women. One in four men will have a heart attack before 65 years of age.

Heart disease is 'multifactorial' – several factors combine to cause a heart attack. The World Health Organisation, the DHSS, RCP and BMA and more than fifty expert committees around the world, are all satisfied that food which is high in saturated fats is the main underlying cause of heart disease. Smoking also causes heart attacks. Lack of regular activity is a contributory factor. So is stress.

Saturated fats in food raise blood cholesterol and other blood fats, encourage blood to clot more easily and to be more 'sticky'. Polyunsaturated fats, on the other hand, make blood thinner, clot less easily, and lower blood fats.

Most of the cholesterol in blood is manufactured by the body (the liver). The rate of manufacture is increased by saturated fats provided by food. Cholesterol in food (found mainly in eggs, cream, meat) make blood cholesterol go up, but it is not as important a cause of high blood cholesterol as saturated fat.

Sugars in foods increase blood fats in about 20% of people. Much more research on sugars and heart attacks is needed. This has been a neglected area. In the Caribbean where sugar consumption is high, and fat consumption quite low, rates of heart attack are high.

Strokes and blood pressure
High blood pressure (hypertension) causes strokes. Reducing the level of blood pressure can dramatically reduce the risk of stroke.

What causes high blood pressure? Medical research has not yet discovered the exact cause, and studies have produced conflicting results. All societies which eat a lot of salt have raised blood pressure, but reducing salt in food does not always lower it. The following factors seem to be important:

SALT   (sodium chloride and other sodium salts) may raise blood pressure.

POTASSIUM   may lower blood pressure. Fresh, whole foods are rich in potassium and low in salt (fruit, vegetables, cereals, meats, fish).

WEIGHT   overweight increases blood pressure.

FATS   saturated fats may raise blood pressure and polyunsaturated fats may lower it.

EXERCISE   regular activity may reduce blood pressure.
STRESS   relaxation lessons helps to lower blood pressure in people
             with hypertension.

Intestinal problems

Constipation, and probably piles, are caused by insufficient fibre in food. Colonic diverticulae (abnormal little 'pockets' in the large bowel) are present in 20% of 50–60 year olds in Western countries. Large bowel cancer accounts for 12.5% of all cancer deaths in England and Wales. After heart attacks and lung cancer (caused by smoking), colon cancer is one of the biggest causes of death in the UK.

Colon cancer is thought to be caused by fatty food which is low in fibre. Societies which eat large amounts of cereal food (rice, potatoes, maize, bread, etc.), fruits and vegetables, and little fats and processed foods, have low rates of colon cancer.

Other intestinal problems such as ulcerative colitis, Crohn's disease, may also be caused by low-fibre food, although the evidence is not as strong as for colon cancer.

Stomach cancer used to be very common in Britain. The rates have dropped through the twentieth century. Salty, and heavily pickled foods, may be one cause. So too, may nitrates in food. And a number of other things are also suspected: smoked foods, low vitamin C levels in food.

Diabetes

Middle aged diabetes (as opposed to juvenile diabetes) is common in the UK. It is most common in overweight people, and increases the risk of heart attack.

What causes diabetes? Diabetes is common in countries where sugar consumption is high, and it is possible that continual heavy sugar consumption puts a strain on the pancreas so that it no longer works properly. However, the medical profession have not reached agreement on the exact cause, even though most doctors would probably agree that typical Western food plays a large part.

Allergies, migraines, skin problems, psychiatric problems

It is now recognised that all of these conditions can be caused by food. A small number of people are allergic to specific foods (strawberries, wheat, milk, etc.).

Some food additives, in particular colours and anti-oxidants, also cause problems in sensitive people.

Much more work in this area is needed to find out the real size of the problem. At the moment, we really have no idea how many people may be affected.

Anorexia nervosa

Compulsive slimming, leading to chronic underweight, is quite common in teenagers, especially girls. One in 100 girls over 16 years had severe anorexia nervosa in one study, and more may be affected by severe slimming, bingeing and vomiting.

Is anorexia a psychiatric disorder, or is it caused by a nutritional imbalance which leads to loss of appetite? Whatever the starting cause, both nutritional imbalance and psychiatric problems develop. Nutritional deficiencies (eg. zinc, some vitamins) can cause loss of appetite.

Weight-conscious teenagers need to understand that regular activity, and good food, are needed for good health. Activity in everyday life, and taking part in sports, are the best ways to stay slim.

Food and specific groups

Ethnic minorities

Britain's different ethnic groups have much to teach us about healthy food. Traditional Italian, Greek, Chinese, Asian, Turkish meals are often healthier than typical British ones.

Black communities tend to have higher blood pressure than whites. Asians tend to have higher rates of heart attack; typically, Asians living in the UK eat more fatty, sugary foods than in their parent countries.

Pregnant women

The quality of a woman's food prior to conception is important. Low levels of B vitamins (particularly folic acid) and minerals (particularly zinc) have been linked with neural tube defects (eg. spina bifida). These congenital malformations develop in the first weeks after conception, often before a woman realises she is pregnant.

During pregnancy, a woman does not need to 'eat for two', but it is important to eat high quality food. Fresh fruit and vegetables, whole grain cereals, fish, lean meats, beans and low-fat dairy foods are all important. Vegetarian mothers and their babies remain quite healthy as long as the mother keeps a healthy balance in her meals.

Babies and young children

Breast feeding is the healthiest way of feeding a baby. Breast milk has the right balance of all nutrients, but it is important to realise that its final quality depends on the quality of the mother's food: if it is low in essential polyunsaturated fats, zinc, folic acid and other minerals and vitamins, the milk will also be low in these nutrients.

Breast feeding should be continued as long as possible (in Third World countries it is natural to breast feed babies until about 2 years, as a supplement to other food). Most babies need extra foods after 3–6 months. In the UK, only 23% of babies are still breast fed at 6 months.

Small children should not be given sugary drinks and sweet foods. Their teeth are very susceptible to damage, and sugars are unnecessary. Babies and children will get all the nourishment they need without added sugars in food.

Vegetarians, vegans

Vegetarians (who eat no meat or fish) and vegans (who eat no milk, eggs, or any animal foods) are quite healthy if they follow the correct principles. Indeed, they have lower rates of many illnesses than meat eaters. Vegans occasionally develop vitamin deficiencies (eg. B_{12}); some take B_{12} supplements. Children brought up as vegetarians and vegans are perfectly healthy, but may be lighter than other children (this is usually not a problem: many UK children are overweight).

Many teenage girls, in particular, decide to become vegetarians, but do not eat healthy meals. They are overdependent on sweet, fatty snacks and eat insufficient amounts of fresh fruit, green vegetables, beans and cereal foods.

Can the nation's food be improved?

With information, we can choose healthy and delicious food. But government, too, and manufacturers and retailers, have to help. The Ministry of Agriculture controls what goes into food through legislation. Manufacturers invent recipes. Retailers choose what they put in their shops. Advertising persuades us. Taxes and subsidies come and go. Should health be ignored in all of this?

We all eat, at least twice a day. Schools, hospitals, workers' canteens, restaurants, cafes, catering companies, employers and government all provide food for people. Many of these services are now trying to make their meals healthier. Should they pay more attention to health?

Food purchases are affected by dozens of different factors, and the politics of food are as complex as those of defence or the motor industry. Here are a few of the major determinants of choice.

Price

The poorer you are, the more important the price of food is. Many cheap, convenience foods are of remarkably poor nutritional quality.

Advertising

The food industry spent £483 million on advertising, and £2340 million on packaging in 1985. Least healthy foods tend to be most heavily advertised: sweets, chocolates, sugary breakfast cereals, soft drinks, biscuits, etc.

Legislation

Legislation controls what is put into food eg. white bread contains 72% extraction flour, by law; sausages and other meat products contain a minimum amount of meat etc. Legislation is recommended by civil servants in consultation with government advisory committees. Consumer representation is minimal; the manufacturers of highly processed foods have a bigger say in future policy than representatives of the ordinary consumer. Is this right? These committees also meet under the protection of the Official Secrets Act, so that widespread debate about legislation is effectively stifled.

EEC/Government support

The EEC and the UK government give grants, subsidies, loans, and minimum price guarantees to farmers for different crops. The price of milk is controlled by the Milk Marketing Board. Government sponsors research into plant and animal breeding and husbandry. The price of basic foodstuffs is not determined by a free market. Does the EEC/government have the right priorities when fixing prices? Should health be part of the equation?

Third World

Agricultural workers earn unacceptably low salaries compared to westerners. Are we prepared to pay higher prices for tea, coffee, sugar, vegetable oils etc? If we did, what would that do to our consumption of products such as these?

Availability

Three retailers now control nearly half of all purchases of packet grocery goods in the UK. Hypermarkets replace many small shops. Should town planners allow small shops to go to the wall? What effect does this have on community life? The elderly? The sick? People with no car?

What can we do for ourselves?

Although government, manufacturers and retailers have a major role to play, there is still much we can do for ourselves. Anyone who wants to eat a healthier diet can do so now by starting with these six "dos" and "don'ts".

Healthy food: six 'do's'

As a basic principle choose whole, fresh food, and preferably food of vegetable origin.

1. BREAD
Eat lots more good quality wholemeal bread. Eat bread at all main meals. Eat sandwiches, not greasy pies/rolls for lunch. Good bread needs less butter and margarine.

2. POTATOES, PASTA, RICE
Like bread these are not fattening in themselves. Eat lots of potatoes, preferably whole. Go easy on fried potatoes and chips. Eat more rice, pasta, noodles. Brown rice is easier to cook.

3. VEGETABLES, FRUIT
Eat lots more, and plenty of variety. Cook green vegetables lightly, with less water and salt. Eat fresh and dried fruit instead of sugary or fatty/sugary snacks. Try beans and pulses.

4. FISH, MEAT
Choose lean meats. Use more vegetables in meat dishes. Eat more fresh fish. Fatty fish (mackerel, herrings, sardines) are good for you. Free range chickens and meat taste best.

5. DAIRY, EGGS
Have fresh skimmed or semi-skimmed milk. Have yoghurt rather than cream. Buy better quality mature cheeses with more flavour. Three or four eggs a week is about right. Many cooks think free range taste best.

6. FATS, OILS
Choose oils that are 'high in polyunsaturates': sunflower, soya, corn, safflower, sesame, walnut, and olive. Use a heavy frying pan, and less oil. Choose 'polyunsaturated' margarines and fats.

Six 'don'ts'

As a basic principle, avoid saturated fats, added sugars and highly processed foods.

1. SUGARS
Added, processed sugars have no place in healthy food. Sucrose, glucose, fructose, dextrose, sugar, syrup – watch for them on labels. Sugars occurring naturally in fruit are fine. Have fewer sweets and soft drinks.

2. FATS
Avoid fatty meats, pies and sausages. Avoid all margarines and oils

without the 'high in polyunsaturates' label. Watch for 'hydrogenated' fats and oils in cakes, biscuits, puddings, sauces, snacks, sweets.

3. DRINKS

Soft drinks and colas, and 'health' fruit drinks, are chiefly made of sugars and water, with additives. Whole fruit and unsweetened fruit juices are healthier. Alcohol has no health value.

4. SNACKS

Avoid highly processed sugary, fatty, salty snacks. Have fruit and nuts instead. Fruit cake, scones, tea cake, sandwiches, currant buns, fruit are healthier alternatives.

5. SALT

Whole, fresh foods contain the right balance of salt and minerals. Highly processed foods are usually salty. Use less salt in cooking and at the table. Use more herbs and spices instead.

6. ADDITIVES

The more additives on the label, the more highly processed the food, and the lower the nutritional value. Some people are very sensitive to additives.

FRESH FOOD IS BEST!

Reading

Official reports
DHSS: *Diet and Cardiovascular Disease.* HMSO, 1984.
Royal College of Physicians: *Obesity Report*, 1983.
Health Education Council: *NACNE*, 1983.
British Medical Association: *Diet, Nutrition and Health*, 1986.
MAFF: *Manual of Nutrition.* HMSO.
DHSS/MAFF: *Report on the Safety and Wholesomeness of Irradiated Foods.* HMSO.

Lay guides to good food and health
Burnett, John *Plenty and Want: A social History of diet in England from 1815 to the present day* Methuen. (Written by the Professor of Social History at Brunel University, this book is a source of useful historical data, particularly pre-1945.)
Cannon, Geoffrey *Fat to Fit* Pan Books. (How to eat healthy food, be fitter and control body weight without dieting.)
Erlichman, James *Gluttons for Punishment* Penguin. (Pesticide residues in food, and growth-promoting drugs in animals. Discussion about safety, regulation, quantities used.)
Graham, Louise *A Good Start* Penguin. (Nutrition for parents of small children – also useful for older age groups.)
Mulcahey, Risteard *Beat Heart Disease* Dunitz. (Useful statistics and explanations about heart disease and its causes.)

Hobhouse, Henry *Seeds of Change: five plants that changed mankind* Sidgwick and Jackson. (World history of sugar, tea, potato, cotton, quinine. Very readable, very useful.)

Lawrence, Felicity *Additives: Your Complete Survival Guide* Century Hutchinson. (Comprehensive guide to all additives – their safety, where found, legislation, functions, etc.)

Millstone, Erik *Food Additives* Penguin. (Discussion of safety of additives, government regulations, methods of testing.)

Hanssen, Maurice *E for Additives* Thorsons. (Catalogue of E-numbered additives, brief summary about each.)

Pelham, Rambletree *Open University Guide to Healthy Eating* (A mixture of medical background, practical advice and ideas about food and health.)

Walker, Caroline and Cannon, Geoffrey *The Food Scandal* Century Hutchinson. (Two thirds of the book is advice for the individual, and explains how industry works; one third explains the medical background.)

Webb, Tony and Henderson, Angela *Food Irradiation: Who Wants It?* The London Foo Commission, P.O. Box 291, London N5 1DU.

CHAPTER EIGHT

COURAGE

———— ◆ ————

'Being a semi-colon is bad enough, but I don't relish the thought of going a stage further and turning into a comma, let alone a full stop. . . .'

'Can you get to the meeting at the Royal College of Physicians on the use of British Heart Foundation funds and, despite the short time for discussion, get up and say something without indicating that we are acquainted? Professor Oliver and Dr Somerville have fixed a meeting and apparently intend to defend the British Heart Foundation.'

Caroline received this note from Dr Richard Turner, co-founder of the Coronary Prevention Group, in June 1980. The British Heart Foundation is a pillar of the medical establishment. Its patron in 1980 was (and is in 1989) HRH The Prince Philip KG KT; its President The Rt Hon Viscount De L'Isle VC KG PC GCMG GCVO; its Chairman Sir Ronald Bodley Scott GCVO MA DM FRCP. Not people to mess with; after all, the initials GCMG are in a well-known joke held to stand for 'God Calls Me God'.

Nevertheless Caroline turned up at the Royal College for the Foundation's Annual General Meeting on 17 July. After the speeches she stood up and asked why the many millions of pounds collected for the Foundation, much by people standing in streets with collecting boxes, was spent on diagnosis and treatment of heart disease, with a negligible amount devoted to prevention? How much was spent on prevention? she asked. And what percentage was this of the Foundation's income? In response, the Chairman regretted that there was no time for questions, and declared the Annual General Meeting closed.

In her diary for that day Caroline noted, 'Herewith begins the correspondence with Michael Oliver on diet and decision-making on national policy.' She followed through, and developed a bond of mutual respect with Professor Oliver, a man of great influence in national policy-making who holds a Chair funded by the British Heart Foundation and who, in the 1980s, has become convinced that good food is vital to cardiovascular health. And in her work for the Coronary Prevention Group she opened up diplomatic lines with the British Heart

Foundation. After her death the new Medical Director of the Foundation, Professor Desmond Julian, wrote, 'All of us at the BHF were well aware of Caroline's constant efforts to educate the public in caring about what we eat. Her work, as we know, was of tremendous importance.'

Caroline mastered an art, vital for any campaigner, which can be called 'making yourself unpopular without making yourself unpopular'. The follow-through took a lot of energy. The initial confrontation took a lot of guts. I first met her in the summer of 1983, oddly enough in the same room at the Royal College of Physicians, at another annual conference, this time held by the British Nutrition Foundation.

One of the issues being debated that day was 'Who should be entrusted with the responsibility for setting standards for food and public health?' The room was packed and the air was charged. Here is how Caroline told the story, in the interview she gave Derek Cooper for 'The Food Programme' just before she died. 'I had stood up and made a statement about the BNF, saying that because it was sponsored by the food industry entirely – all its money comes from there – it was not a suitable body to give nutrition education to the public. This is what the entire conference was geared towards. They wanted the government to donate to them the whole field of education on food and health. They actually were within a pretty good grasp of getting it.

So I took the opportunity at this conference to stand up and refute what they were suggesting, and say this was not a good idea. And the chairman of the conference was very shocked, and he suggested that what I had said was a libellous statement, and he asked if I would withdraw it. I said no, I wouldn't. Because I stood by it; and perhaps somebody else in the audience would care to support me.'

I was sitting next to Caroline; or rather, she was sitting next to me, because she had targeted me, then working for the *Sunday Times*, as a journalist who just might take a sustained interest in the cause of food and public health. As she stood her ground I looked up at her, young and golden-haired, and saw that she was trembling. Then, in her words:

'Now in the audience I knew were a really good handful of people who supported me completely behind closed doors: people from charitable organisations; universities; scientists who I thought had got a very clear message about the connection between what they did and their duty to the public, to tell the truth. And not one of them stood up. And to be quite honest, I thought: what a load of wimps. I was shocked that these people could be so wet in public. I was just about to sit down when Aubrey Sheiham, who is now Professor of Community Dental Health at the University of London, stood up and said, "I will support you".'

And in the final words of that interview, her last public statement, Caroline said, 'He was the only one.'

This pressure was almost as nothing compared with what Caroline felt in the summer of the next year, 1984. We had published our book *The Food Scandal* and were sued, twice by Beechams, once by Kelloggs. 'The first thing that really shocked me,' said Caroline, 'was the isolation that Geoffrey and I found ourselves in as soon as word got around that we'd been sued. It was really quite frightening how many people totally abandoned us. I can remember that for a while the telephone stopped ringing. And people who had previously been very friendly on a work basis suddenly shied away.' And talking to me, remembering the implications of being at the mercy of the law and lawyers, she said, 'There's always a frightening side to being a pioneer, to being the first. The fact that all our possessions were at risk – our total security . . . .'

Those who believe that stress is a cause of disease will think that the fear and trembling Caroline suffered was a cause of her cancer. She thought so too. Would she be alive now if she had kept quiet then? Perhaps. If she had not merited obituaries there might have been no need of them.

'When I turned up at the hospital with an obstructed gut aged thirty-four and they operated, they couldn't believe their eyes,' she told Derek Cooper. 'Here's this young woman, a nutritionist of all things, stuffing herself with wholemeal bread and the right kind of goodies, and she goes and gets her gut ruined!' But 'it's never shaken my belief that cancers are preventable and that cancer of the large intestine is primarily of nutritional origin. It's very likely to be, isn't it? What goes through the gut? Food.'

So why her? Yes, stress for one thing. And 'the earlier prevention starts, the better. I didn't grow up eating all the foods I advocate. It didn't sink into me about food and health until I was in my twenties. My ideas built up gradually. It wasn't until I was about twenty-seven that I took them on board myself.' And, she recalled, 'seven years at boarding school with disgusting food – lack of fresh food, lack of whole food – sticky buns, sweets, white bread and hard margarine.'

As she lay dying, Caroline knew, I think, that people would remember her, and remember her death; and the strength of her voice as she spoke to Derek Cooper, propped up on pillows, supported by 500mg of pethidine and 50mg of methotrimeprazine driven into her every day, was remarkable. She wanted the facts of her life and death, and her views, on record. 'I had some other problems which I believe were related, and not properly attended to by the medical profession,' she said.

In her early twenties she reacted to the contraceptive pill with headaches, nausea, fainting, cramps, high blood pressure and piles; but was argued out of other methods of contraception by a succession of male doctors, who as so often in those days and these days, think that women make too much fuss about such 'minor and transient' ill-effects. ('They should try it,' I hear Caroline say). From her mid twenties she suffered acute and sometimes excruciating pain above her rectum, on what turned out to be the site of the cancer that obstructed her in 1985; but successive doctors found nothing and so said there was nothing; nothing serious, anyway. Indeed, we were both told that cancer of the colon is occult; it doesn't cause pain. ('They better write my case into the textbooks, and change their minds,' said Caroline).

My own view is that the original cause of Caroline's cancer was part bad luck, part ignorance. She was dreadfully ill throughout 1976 with what her family called 'Caroline's mystery illness'. She was sick, faint, weak, depressed, and sometimes prostrated. There's evidence that she had more than one illness, bacterial and/or viral infections, picked up probably in Amsterdam and/or Israel. They were never diagnosed confidently. Brucellosis was suggested, and she was experimentally prescribed septrin, a broad-spectrum antibiotic, for several months, sometimes in double doses. This may have killed the bugs that made her ill. It is also true that the adverse effects of septrin include headache, faintness and weakness, and anaemia. And like anybody treated with long courses of powerful antibiotics, Caroline would have been left without vitality, the 'friendly flora', the bugs in the colon vital for gut health and general health, wiped out. In those days nobody was warned about the after-effects of antibiotics, or advised how to build up gut health. Caroline certainly wasn't. And she was never the same again. When I knew her, she usually faded in mid-evening.

In the many letters she wrote in and out of hospital, she has a lot to say about health and illness; life and death; hospitals, surgeons, doctors and nurses. And she always thought of others as well as herself. On the ward, she saw a young woman with advanced cancer switched from intravenous feeding to meat pies from one day to the next: result, of course, convulsive sickness. She saw old women go mad from the shock of surgery. So she started to sketch out a manual of nutritional support for surgical patients: good food before admission, supplementation before surgery, instructions for loved ones to bring in whole fresh food, recommendations to convert unused rooms into kitchens in which to make soothing soups and nourishing stews. 'There's a book there,' she said. There is, too.

How about controlled trials of zinc and associated nutrients for surgical wound-healing? she asked. What about a return to the old system where sisters ruled the ward, and spaced-out housemen were not allowed to wander round the ward shooting off their mouths to terrified patients? Let's have a pilot study of the possible benefits of gentle methods such as aromatherapy; after all, it's lovely being pampered. Why use naso-gastric tubes when the pain of the tube is greater than the pain of being sick? 'Within days of major surgery, she was discovering for herself the inadequacies of hospital food and the nutritional ignorance of surgeons,' wrote Philip James in his *Guardian* obituary for Caroline, 'and vowed to write a book on hospitals.' What's needed too, is a reincarnation of Caroline; someone with the charm and cheek she used on the British Heart Foundation, who will get nutrition not only on the national agenda, but also on the medical and surgical agenda.

Caroline's cancer was discovered in January 1985: an adenocarcinoma contained within the bowel, not expected to recur. But in January 1987 she had a second, massive operation; a pelvic clearance with a colostomy. This operation went wrong, and she immediately had a third operation to stop haemorrhage, which took 34 units of blood. This caused a crisis in West London's transfusion service, and she had to be given some units of blood of the wrong type; and others long past their 'best-by' date, which amused her. She had hoped so much that the second operation would be conservative, but it was not; and after intensive care and in great pain, she asked me, 'Would it be easier for you to tell me what they've taken out, or what they've left in?'

In the spring and summer of 1987 she regained her old love of nature, in Scotland and in our garden. Around the time of our marriage in September the cancer had grown back and intermittently obstructed her, and she asked for a further operation in December. The surgical team led by Mr Geoffrey Glazer couldn't tell at the time whether the procedure, to by-pass the blockage, had worked; if it had, they thought Caroline would live for a few weeks, if not, for a few days; and in either case would die in great pain. But she delighted Geoffrey Glazer, who became a friend; she lived, took her life in her own hands, embraced naturopathy, aromatherapy, homeopathy, reflex zone therapy, Chinese herbal medicine, the Gerson therapy, acupuncture, infusion with vitamins and minerals, healing; inspired her GP; found Dr Anne Naysmith, consultant at the local community hospital, who relieved all pain, and after a lovely holiday in June and July on Jura, came home, opened our house and her garden to all our families and friends, and transformed her dying into a festival of love and light.

What follows are some of her letters to Mr Glazer, his colleague Mr Mason, and to her dear friends Phil and Jean James in Aberdeen, starting just before her second, big operation in 1987, and ending six weeks before she died. The theme of these letters is partnership. She fought for mutual trust and respect, and won it, because although she was afraid, she stood up and stood her ground. 'Come on,' I hear her say. 'I was in a bed most of the time!' True, but her light shone, and shines on; for her ideas and her integrity matter as much to us as they did to her.

I STILL HAVE A LIFE TO LEAD

Letter to a consultant surgeon

Friday 9 January 1987

Dear Mr Glazer. Thank you for your help and support on Wednesday. After seeing you I realised that in my general panic about the ?uterus lump, I did not really concentrate properly on other things that might be related.

It may be nothing, or it may be something – from time to time I have had a slight ache in my back – on the left side of the pelvis. Nothing agonising, just a small ache. Should I have it X-rayed? After seeing you on Wednesday, I have noticed it again, which may be a sign of my excellent imagination . . . .

The problem with things like this is that part of me just doesn't want to know. Why invite you to find something wrong? Also, one cannot attribute every twinge to horrible malignant growths. Apart from anything else, it takes up too much time. I've spent quite a while in the last two days making mental arrangements for my last days on earth.

I am having the scan on Monday 19th, 10.00am. I couldn't see Mr Mason until 18 February, and my appointment with you is on 25 February.

I will be away next week, sampling the delights of an Austrian health spa (just what I need?) which is so attentive to the needs of its vastly rich patrons that even the varnish on the furniture comes from lovingly nurtured organic trees, and the whole place is insulated against electromagnetic waves from the lighting system. It's all in the brochure, and all I have to do is write 800 words. One of the perks of Fleet Street. You see – now I've written, the ache has quite vanished.

With all good wishes
Caroline Walker. Hosp Number 049497

Letter to another consultant surgeon

Sunday 25 January 1987

Dear Mr Mason. I recognise that the abdominal mass that has been discovered in me, may be a cancer, or else pre-cancerous. I greatly appreciate the time and care you and Dr Hamilton-Fairley have taken, in discussing my case. Geoffrey Cannon (who is my next-of-kin) and I have had the opportunity to think out, in consultation not only with you but also with friends who have expert knowledge, as clinicians or scientists, how I would like you to proceed.

This note is written before my consultation with you tomorrow, and of course I may want to revise what is in this note as a result of our consultation, in which case I shall alter this note or else write an extra note on my consent form, to which this note should be attached.

I recognise that five possible diagnoses have been identified:

1. A secondary cancer from the colon which may have spread towards or into the ovary.
2. A primary cancer of the ovary which may have spread towards or into the colon and if so, may have spread further into the rectum.
3. Cysts from the ovary (which may be pre-cancerous).
4. Fibroids from the uterus.
5. Something else, or some combination of the above.

In general, bearing in mind my age, my general good health, the fact that

I have expert knowledge and resources that other patients do not have, and my strong personal feelings, confirmed after consultation, I want the surgical procedure to be as conservative as is consistent with recognised surgical practice. Specifically:

After taking a biopsy and doing a frozen section, you will come to one of three conclusions: not malignant, possibly malignant, or malignant.

1. Not malignant. Please remove the mass and leave the surrounding tissue and organs functionally intact unless this is technically not possible. For example, if the mass is cysts or fibroids, please leave the ovary or uterus intact. I recognise that if the mass is too entangled this may not be possible.

2. Possibly malignant. Please be conservative. If the diagnosis on frozen section is equivocal, please remove the mass only (as above). I recognise that if further histological examination does show malignancy I shall have to have another operation. Because of my previous history you may feel it best to remove surrounding tissue just in case. But if this would mean removal of both ovaries, or the uterus, or pieces of small intestine or colon, or other functional organs, please do not do so at this stage and, instead, wait for the exact histology.

3. Malignant. Again, please be conservative. In particular:

a. If there is a cancer of the colon sited around the previous surgical suture, which has spread into one ovary, please remove that ovary only. I recognise that this may increase the risk of further surgery should there be later evidence of further spread of the cancer.

b. If there is a cancer of the colon which has spread down towards the rectum and the sphincter area, do not consider surgery which endangers the sphincter mechanism and thus involves possible or certain permanent colostomy unless there is unequivocal evidence of cancer in the sphincter area itself. I recognise that this too may increase the risk of further surgery.

c. If there is a cancer of one ovary, please remove that ovary only, leaving the other ovary and the uterus intact, unless there is clear evidence of cancer in the second ovary or the uterus, or unless the cancer is unequivocally identified as a type reliably known to be likely to have travelled to the other ovary by the time it reaches the stage evident on your examination.

d. If the cancer has spread to other sites, so that you have to consider a pelvic clearance, please do not consider involving a permanent colostomy unless there is clear evidence of deep cancerous infiltration into the pelvis that can only be cleared by removal of the rectal stump.

I recognise that in the event of a pelvic clearance a temporary colostomy may be necessary.

e. If there is malignancy, I do not want to be given chemotherapy or any other anti-cancer drug therapy, unless I specifically consent to this in writing after the operation. (I do remember that we have already discussed this point.)

4. General. The last days have been a very anxious time for me, and in all the circumstances I do want to be just as clear as possible about what I want done – and not done. I have deliberately looked at the 'worst case' possibilities because I have decided to take a special responsibility for my case, not having been able to do so two years ago. Once again, I recognise that in so doing, I am accepting a possible higher risk of further cancer and further surgery. I accept that risk after careful thought and consultation. If you feel there might be difficulties in following this note, then I also recognise the possibility of delaying the operation while a further opinion is taken.

I hope, though, that you will find what is here helpful, as a statement of a responsibility shared with you. Obviously you know that I want as little surgery as possible; I want to keep my reproductive organs functionally intact; and I want to avoid a colostomy. But I feel that anybody would say as much, and that it's better to be more precise.

I do feel I am in good hands.
Caroline Walker

Letter to friends in Aberdeen

Friday 18 September 1987

Dear Phil and Jean. Quite an exciting week – married on Saturday, opened presents half of Sunday, persuaded Jasper Carrott to help CPG on Tuesday, had aromatherapy on Wednesday, got a blocked gut on Wed. night, visited Chinese doctor on Thursday and drank his repulsive herbs on Friday.

Felicity Lawrence decided to give me a massage for a present, so along comes this spiritual lady with a bagful of oil of basil, chamomile, lavender, frankincense, and turns me into a jar of pesto, fit to flavour a bowl of pasta at fifty yards. She gave me reflexology too – the foot bit – and said I needed to visit Mr Lee in Maida Vale, for revitalising herbs. So after my intestine yet again went on strike on Wed. night, I made an appointment to see Mr Lee. At Mr Lee's, you must take off your shoes at the door, whereupon you are ushered into a drawing room full of

Chinese dragons, porcelain vases, buddhas and Mr Lee's family photographs, and on to a pale blue Chinese carpet about two inches high and covered in exquisite dragon and floral designs.

Mr Lee conducts all his case histories in public, and everyone is asked to stick out their tongue. Then you get your ten pulses felt. Then after some quite reasonable, and some quite extraordinary questions, he says, 'Come with me, plees,' and takes you to have some acupuncture. I got needles in my hands and legs, to stimulate the gut. My legs felt as if they were moving in mid-air. Then Mr Lee goes away and comes back with two bags of magic (all the way from China of course) – chunks of tree bark, roots, big black fungi, and great pieces of flattened goodness-knows-what – for my breakfast. 'Boil one hour, one pint water, drain off liquid, plees drink one mugful. Very bitter.' You're telling me! It is the most repulsive thing I've ever drunk – makes your face curl up in revulsion after one mouthful. Still, if it tastes vile it must be good for me . . . .

I've also been to a homoeopath who taxied some potions round to me on Wednesday night when I started to block up again – it worked! Within half an hour of taking them, all the pains stopped and my guts began moving again. The interesting thing is that both the homoeopath and Mr Lee say the same thing, that it is a nervous problem, unlikely to be scar tissue. The homoeopathic remedy was specifically for intestinal nerves, which I didn't know 'til I spoke to her today, and not for scar tissue. All very interesting, and if it keeps me away from Mr Glazer's knives, then I'll keep trying it. Next stop is a cranial osteopath who swivels your brains through 360°.

I'm so pleased you were both at our wedding, and we are delighted with your kind present. We've had rather a glut of glass bowls, and it is lovely to have something practical! Also, we were delighted with your splendid speech, Phil. Thank you so much for your kind thoughts, and we loved the bit about Cannonisation. I do hope you enjoyed the reception; I hardly spoke to anyone for more than half a minute – and I hardly got any of that wonderful food because every time I found a plate it was empty. Tomorrow we are going to someone else's wedding so I shall just sit quietly and enjoy it.

G. has a new campaign starting in the *Sunday Telegraph* mag. this weekend – aluminium in water. The food industry will rejoice. Did you see the cartoon about the BNF in today's *Guardian* (Fri)? That should keep Conning busy for a bit.

Love to you both
Caroline xx

Letter to friends in Aberdeen

Tuesday 20 October 1987

Dear Phil and Jean and Claudia. Bring me Dynorod! All these weird remedies are losing their appeal; hospitals lost theirs long ago, and what I need is a plumber. Just got over the 8th blockage – I'm getting used to them now – griping pains, sleepless nights, wake up Geoffrey, fetch bucket, be sick, do lots of groaning, clutch abdomen for twenty-four hours, fall asleep, hey presto! The bag starts working again, I change colour (according to Juliet) and all the world looks nice again.

Next week I am being put through the CAT scanner (horrors) and Mr Glazer's pompous little registrar is itching to get his knives out. They refused to send me to a gastroenterologist – so I telephoned Francis Avery Jones and he said I must see a Mr Baron (just 'very slightly better than Geoff Walker' according to Avery, and the next President of the gut men). How do other people manage without an address-book-full of the top boffins in medicine? Mr Glazer's registrar told me to mind my own business when I asked him how he intended to sew me up again, given that my abdomen is full of man-made shrapnel (scar tissue) from two operations – it feels like conkers – 'Just leave that to us; that's our job, not yours,' and he wouldn't tell me! Disgraceful.

He also suggested that my terror of CAT scanners would be quietly dealt with by the administration of an armful 'of a little sedative to quieten you down.' My notes must be full of 'troublesome patient, impossible husband'. They can't tell the difference between someone who wants to be involved in the decision-making, and someone who is very tiresome and impossible to deal with. Just wait till I write my book . . .! (And there will be a whole chapter on hospital blankets – why is it they are always too small and full of holes? The nurse tells you to take off your clothes and lie on the couch, whereupon the registrar takes one hour to come and see you. Meanwhile the blanket covers half of you, and if you haven't come in an overcoat you freeze with cold and apprehension. No wonder people go private – at least you get a warm blanket and the surgeon runs up the bill by spending half an hour explaining what he's going to do . . . .)

We spent Thursday night under a hail of treetrunks and branches. Bits of black poplar hurtled through the air at 100 miles an hour from a garden three houses away, and landed in our garden and on the roof. (Nobody else's garden or roof – just ours and our next door neighbours at no. 8!) We have a badly damaged roof, and on Friday the garden was submerged under a six-foot blanket of branches and treetrunk. We all consider ourselves lucky not to have been woken up by a twenty-foot missile through the window – some of them blew right over the roof and down the other side. Now it's hunt-the-roof-tile game . . . . Some smart fellows have bought them all up.

We've got lots of lovely photos of the wedding. Do come and visit when you're next here. Chinese herbs for dinner . . . .

Much love
Caroline x

Letter to a consultant surgeon

Monday 23 November 1987

Dear Mr Glazer. Thank you very much for arranging my admission at such speed to St Mary's. I read in the Sunday papers that you have no free beds, so I am expecting to spend my days in the laundry cupboard . . . .

The position at the moment is that I am partially blocked up most of the time. Since 12th Nov. I have only had about three days free of trouble. However, the colostomy has worked nearly every day. My gut is also a good deal noisier than before, and anything, apart from liquid, goes down sounding like a gurgling volcano. I am not surprised that my haemoglobin is low – over the last three months I must have starved on about twenty days, and eaten little on many others. Prior to all these obstructions, I was taking mineral/vitamin supplements (I have to put my training to some use!), but I stopped, being nervous of eating anything solid.

You know that I am very un-keen to be cut open yet again, but now there seems no alternative. I am tired, bored and irritated by living like this. I am, to all intents and purposes, housebound, can't get down to any work, and can't make any plans, even to go out in the evenings. I used to say that I knew what it was like to be geriatric, but now I feel disabled.

So I understand that I am to have a bit of blood (I read that there's none of that either – and it's probably full of chips and hamburgers . . .) and then what? Do you operate straight away, or let me sit in bed for a few days first? If so, I'd rather do the sitting here at home. I can live on liquid meals.

When it comes to the operation, I want someone to fix my vagina at the same time. Could you ask Mr Mason? Also, as you know, the hernia needs sewing up, again. Please find a champion stitcher, or do it yourself, so it stands a better chance of staying together. Last time I felt it was not stitched well at the top (there was a tiny bulge right after the operation), and it broke within weeks.

I am of course aware that you may cut me open and find more cancer(s). This makes me very nervous. So what I would like is to talk to you, with Geoffrey, so that I can think about the possibilities. Last time, I felt panicked by the hurry and rush, and exhausted, and unable to think. This was thoroughly bad news for me, and for Geoffrey. Even though I have had the possibility of another operation looming for the last two months, I haven't been able to think through the likely outcome because I need to talk to you first. Being a semi-colon is bad enough, but I don't relish the thought of going a stage further and turning into a comma, let alone a full stop . . . .

You will also need to check my stoma too – last time I was in hospital, the doctors said the small lump under it is the abdominal muscle. Is it?

I know you are a busy fellow, but I'm not getting on the trolley until I've seen you.

All best wishes. Yours sincerely
Caroline Walker. Hosp Number 093133

Note to herself

January 1988?

Glazer said he did a side to side join up to the large bowel, and joined a loop of small bowel into the middle of the transverse colon.

Mr Stone (GP) saw Clifford, who obviously explained to him that what they did was a desperate measure – the intestine had several dilated loops of small bowel, so they found the end of the dilated bit, and joined it into the colon.

Glazer says he hopes it doesn't cause too much malabsorption, but I don't think he really knows.

Letter to a consultant surgeon

Tuesday 26 July 1988

Dear Mr Glazer. Thank you once again for rescuing me – this time in advance. Do you know this is the first time I have actually walked into St Mary's, instead of coming in half-dead on a stretcher? (I thought – wouldn't it be a dreadful irony if I went out on one . . . .)

I'm sorry if you think I'm being tiresome about my treatment, asking for added opinions and experience. But I feel justified. Why?

(A) In December, when you did the third operation and saved me from death by bust gut, you were yourself uncertain about the result. I remember sitting up in Lillian Holland after three days, drinking soup and eating bread. 'Look!' I said as you came past one day. 'It's worked! I'm eating!' 'That's excellent,' you said. 'I wasn't sure it would. I hope it won't cause you too many problems with malabsorption. We'll have to wait and see.' I pondered this, and asked weakly of someone later, 'Why not give me a barium swallow to see how much gut I've got working?' To me it seemed eminently sensible, but my idea was dismissed. 'It would be impossible to interpret. Too much debris and scar tissue – it's difficult to measure at the best of times, but this would be very difficult.'

Well, I've since talked to several people specialising in short bowels, as you know. I am told that while you might indeed be correct, if an experienced gastroenterologist watched the stuff going down, he would be unlikely to be totally defeated. And the proof of their diagnosis lies to some extent in the doses of nutrients required to achieve balance. But they all agree – an inexperienced eye would probably fail.

(B) When I left St Mary's in December after the operation, I was given not one word of advice about the care of a short bowel. I accept that you did not know its length, but it is a good bet that removal of several loops of ileum is going to lead to at least one or two problems. And the non-function of almost the whole colon certainly causes problems, e.g. vitamin K deficiency. My GP too, is clueless about preventive action, and cheerfully admits as much. I can see that you might all have thought – this woman is littered with cancer and can't live long: why bother her with pots of pills, X-rays etc? Well, I can assure you that the hideous calcium deficiency I developed was far, far more troublesome and exhausting than swallowing a handful of pills twice a day. Supplementation with nutrients is extremely unlikely to be harmful, and in anyone with some items missing, is likely to improve the quality of their life!

(C) Having developed rampant calcium deficiency (which felt like being mentally imprisoned in a body which was at first clumsy, then exhausted, then twitchy, then full of pins and needles, then spasmodic, and finally paralysed – and, something I've not read about in medical descriptions, it was preceded by poor adaptation to changes in light – I would get residual brightness in my eyes on moving from light of different intensity. I think itching may have had something to do with it – or were these things due to other deficiencies?) I came in here to be repleted.

The result was almost miraculous! Within twelve hours, most of the symptoms vanished. And after a week, all my energy, and more, returned. Geoffrey couldn't believe the difference, and we both realised that I must have been suffering from it for some time.

(D) On leaving hospital, the only advice I was given was 'take these calcium and vitamin D pills, and get yourself a multimineral supplement'. Now, that reveals a supreme ignorance about the treatment for short bowel syndrome. The fact is that, by this stage, it should have become obvious that if I had become so low in Ca, then vague supplementation would not be enough.

To return to the individuals I have already mentioned: they monitor at first by monthly intervals, and they certainly do not dish up what is found in health food shops. Your team may take refuge in the fact that I am a nutritionist. But I am no clinician, and my knowledge about normal nutrient requirements is practically worthless when it comes to malabsorption. You may consider yourself to know about the correct treatment, but, believe me, your team does not. I have yet to see the evidence. I'm not criticising them as doctors. They're fine fellows, all of them (a pity you don't have more women: I always think the general level of sensitivity in your team is higher with a woman on board, however junior), but they cannot know everything. This is one area where they are all at sea, and resort to the pharmacology manuals, instead of consulting those who have treated others like me.

For example, I asked about B12 injections. 'Let's have a look at the blood results.' (This was a few weeks post-hospital-drips.) 'They look all right, no sign of great deficiency here. B12 injections aren't necessary – wait until your levels drop.' But what's the point of that? Why wait until I become exhausted and need another blood transfusion, because merely stuffing in some B12 late in the day won't solve the problem? There's iron and folate and a dozen others to think about by that stage.

(E) I now know enough about the problem to see that I need massive doses of many nutrients merely to achieve balance, let alone increase blood levels. And once down, some nutrients are almost impossible to correct with oral supplements alone. Magnesium, for example. Yet I had to remind your team about it, only to be told, 'It's difficult to get for intravenous injection. We may not be able to.' (This yesterday.) But, again as I have learned, calcium deficiency is invariably accompanied by magnesium deficiency, and the two need pushing up together.

(F) Your team knows nothing about the various preparations for short bowels. I even had to explain to one of them what medium chain triglycerides are. They certainly don't know how to use them. Nor do I, at least not to the extent a specialised dietitian does. I have never been sent to a dietitian. Again, you may think it unnecessary as I'm a nutritionist, but the two are very different.

The result of all this is that I have sought alternative advice, which is always tiresome for the doctor in charge. And patients who ask endless questions, interfere in their treatment, and are prone to be sceptical are, I know, inclined to be a pain! But I know I have not yet got it right. With over six foot of small bowel, oral supplementation should, if it is correct, do the trick most of the time. It may be that the disease process itself makes it all the more difficult to achieve balance.

To my mind, you have an ethical problem. In the creation of a modern medical monster, which is what I am, dependent on unnatural interventions for survival, it is not enough to send me off home and hope I'll manage. Over the last twenty years a huge amount has been learned about treating increasingly short guts. It is no longer merely experimental. Therefore you surely have a duty to send me to see someone who knows how to treat it, rather than repeatedly let me slide downhill and pick me up again, none of which is necessary. Could you not share my monitoring and treatment with another physician? Send me to Graham Neale and John Cummings in Cambridge if you like, or at least to someone in London who is equally good. My GP too, is desperate for advice.

It's really very difficult to criticise – you have done so much to keep me going, and have scraped me off the floor on so many occasions – one at least of my own doing when I practically killed myself on Gerson, through salt deficiency. (Mind you, if I had known then how short my gut was, I doubt that I'd have done it.)

I must say, as well, that having reached this stage in my illness, I sometimes feel uncertain about the attitude of your team. I remember thinking, when I was twitching all over with calcium deficiency, that they probably weren't that bothered about what happened, because I'm a terminal patient. 'Just keep her comfortable. We'll push up the odd nutrient, but not interfere too much.' I lay and panicked, thinking that my value as a medical specimen had worn off and I was of no interest any more. But maybe I was wrong, because the physical effect was dramatic, and vastly improved my life (and Geoffrey's).

So can we please organise something better? I know I may only live weeks, but I have been almost dead so many times. My GP faithfully comes round to see me off when I ring in desperation with a rumbling gut and threats of blockage, only to see me walk into the surgery days later. As long as I'm alive, I want to live decently with the maximum energy.

It's a treat to be consigned in immortality to the ward wall – my mother will purr with pride. You have all done a splendid job with the new wing, and it is a pleasure to sit in it, especially in this lovely little room. I must get out the paintbox and draw the view out of the window.

I haven't forgotten the painting you are due . . . .

With kind thoughts as always
Caroline x

Letter to a consultant surgeon

Wednesday 27 July 1988

Dear Mr Glazer. This is in danger of turning into a book.

I wrote the attached on Monday and yesterday, frustrated by dithering from your team, all reluctant to do what you suggested; namely, stuff the goodies in, and hang the biochemistry.

I got nothing in the way of drips until Tuesday evening, and then only because I made a scene.

When I was here last time, both you and Paul Sauven agreed that I was deficient in calcium and probably several other things. You very kindly proposed that I should come in again when I was ready, before gross deficiency signs, to be replenished.

On Saturday when you saw me, you said it would be sensible to take an early blood sample, but proceed with supplementation immediately. But nothing happened until the results came back on Tuesday, when there was general questioning of whether I actually needed the stuff at all! Nobody mentioned the effect of dehydration: my GP and I have been caught out before when I've been dehydrated, making my Hb and Na look all right, only to find they were rock bottom on rehydration. I was dehydrated when the blood was taken, having had a bad night and lost a lot of fluid in the bag.

The general message I got was that they all think I'm a bit neurotic and interfering, but finally they might as well shove it in to keep me quiet (while questioning if I have any signs of any deficiency, or even have had them in the past). Hamish professes to be sceptical about my previous Ca deficiency or whether an Hb of 7.6 needs a transfusion.

Why do I have to sit here and fight to get what you admitted me for? Why can't your team simply get on with it? Am I neurotic (because I say what I think)? Am I interfering (because I'm interested in my own life)? Or obstinate (just wait until they get ill!)? I may be terminal, but so what? I still have a life to lead.

I have always valued your own support, and I still do. I know I would be in a box without it. It is wonderful to be able to come in here, with all the kind nurses who are so friendly. But I feel nervous when I make a fuss – it puts one's future on the line.

All I want is to be able to continue as best I can, at home, with the maximum amount of energy. I don't feel guilty about consulting my friends about short guts – I don't think it is wrong, do you? If I have pals in the business, I'll ask them!

I won't write any more letters at the moment . . .

Best wishes
Caroline x

Letter from a consultant surgeon

Monday 26 September 1988

Dear Geoffrey. I am so sorry to hear of Caroline's death. I don't need to say how fond I was of her and how brave she was. I will never forget her.

Yours
Geoffrey

AFTERWORD

In our work, Caroline and I found that much of the most interesting information we came across was secret, or so it was claimed: 'off the record', 'members only', 'private and confidential', or Officially Secret. We usually decided that publication of such information, when it was valuable, was in the public interest; and I think we were usually right. As a scientist Caroline was sometimes accused in effect of 'not playing the game'; and indeed, she did not join the game in which scientists combine with people from government and industry, to keep the public in the dark. Caroline would not and did not keep quiet.

Privacy does have its place, though, as I found out in the last four years of Caroline's life – most of the time I knew her. At first it seemed that little could or should be said. Cancer was an unnameable. And I still don't know what to say about some of the circumstances of her suffering; these still seem unspeakable, and not for this book.

Originally I had thought to write about Caroline's work and not her life. But as with any singular person, her work and her self cannot really be separated. It wasn't just what she said; it was the way she said it. 'What struck me most about her, was her fearlessness, the clarity of her thinking and, when she gave a formal lecture, the colour and impact of her slides,' says Dr Kenneth Heaton, a friend who succeeded Sir Francis Avery Jones as Chairman of the Royal Society of Medicine Forum on Food and Health in 1985. 'There was never any question of someone going to sleep when she was speaking; on the contrary, I think most of us were on the edge of our seats!'

Many of the letters I received after Caroline died, eloquently encouraged me to write about her personally. 'The strength of mind and of purpose in one so apparently delicate had an immediate and powerful effect on all of us,' wrote Michael Meadowcroft, a Liberal MP when Caroline knew him. 'The combination of intellectual confidence and physical vulnerability added an unusual dimension to her remarkable gifts of communication.'

Colin Spencer, Chairman of the Guild of Food Writers, who knew Caroline before I did, wrote, 'I knew the first minute I met Caroline how remarkable she was. Luminous. A quality that grew in her illness. How magnificent it is that her death has been a learning experience.'

Eventually, Caroline's approach to her work, to her life, and to her death, became integrated, and this process enlightened those close to her, because she did not keep it dark. She let us understand. I used to think that we in the West live thin, pale lives because we know nothing of death, and knowledge of our mortality is what gives our lives meaning. Now, thanks to Caroline, I don't think so, I know so.

Vanessa Harrison, producer of 'The Food Programme', wrote a loving letter the day after Caroline died. 'All of us marvelled at her courage in deciding to give us her final interview when she was so ill. But it was typical of her spirit,' she said.

> 'And curiously, in spite of her physical weakness, it was tremendously heartening to see how she sustained her beliefs in the principles for which she had fought so hard. And she managed to be funny about it, too! It was both a privilege and a treat to have known her, and to have watched and listened to her being clever and funny and passionate and witty about a subject which cries out for such treatment, but never before had received it.
>
> She was both illuminating and entertaining; a rare combination, and one which she carried off with great style. We shall miss her terribly, both as a broadcaster and a friend.
>
> But Caroline hasn't really gone, she's still here, in her achievements, and in you, and in all our memories, and in the Trust. None of us will ever forget her.'

Many more people wrote in, after 'The Food Programme' celebrating Caroline, with her last interview, was broadcast the next month. 'I must admit I'd never heard of her, but what a beautiful person she must have been,' wrote Mick Penning, from Stoke. 'No sentimental delivery, just plain straightforward concern for the welfare of mankind, spoken with natural warmth, softening the hardest heart.'

Caroline did not and would not keep quiet about death, the big secret, and she was right. Afterwards, friends asked me, 'Why is Caroline buried in Scotland?'; so I wrote the account that follows, as an explanation, and as a celebration of the value of ceremony, which are reasons to publish one story not by Caroline, but of her meaning to me.

WE CAN CONTINUE OUR COMMUNION

We gathered together at the Chapel of Garioch, by Bennachie 'as a family, as a circle of friends' in the words of the Minister, Eric Milton. How was it? And why is Caroline buried by the hill of Bennachie?

Our dear friends Phil and Jean James brought us to Bennachie. It all started in January of 1987. I was at home; Caroline was in hospital for her second operation. I telephoned every hour on the hour and eventually spoke to Caroline's surgeon Geoffrey Glazer, who told me what he had found and what he had done. I knew Phil was in London; I telephoned him and he came to me, and we went to Caroline in hospital.

Phil takes up the story, in his address for Caroline at the Chapel of Garioch. 'There I found her in a state of profound shock, and within hours of a third emergency operation which went on through the night,' he said. 'I flew back to Aberdeen in great trouble. And with Jean I walked that weekend on Bennachie.'

The hill of Bennachie is a familiar friend to everybody in the lowlands around Aberdeen. Like the tor at Glastonbury, it is visible from many miles away and from the sea, and has been a place of gathering and worship for many thousand years. 'When we see it,' said Eric Milton, 'we say "och, we're almost home".' Phil, who as Professor Philip James is successor to John Boyd Orr as Director of the Rowett Research Institute, fifteen miles away from Bennachie, has made the hill part of his own life as a place for reflection and comtemplation.

'And following that walk Jean painted a picture of Bennachie, which she sent to her. And this became an inspiration to her,' said Phil. As indeed eventually it did. Phil and Jean opened their home and their hearts to us after Caroline left hospital, a month after her operations; and she healed in Aberdeen. We stayed at Wardenhill, the grand granite house designed by Boyd Orr on the Rowett estate, for two months; and one clear day, we too walked on Bennachie. This done, Caroline was ready for our tour of the Highlands and Islands, and for her ascent of Ben Nevis. We were told in Fort William to allow eight hours for the climb up and down. Caroline took a little over five hours.

We were on our way to be married in Skye. We had traced our

journey with old maps in the house of Dr Michael Lean at Dunecht, by Bennachie; and Caroline had made arrangements with Mr Jock McSween, the Registrar at Portree, on Skye. On arrival, speeded by MacBrayne's bonny boat, we found that the place for the civil solemnisation of marriage was a mile up the Dunvegan Road, next to a wrecking yard, in a back room of Jock's Shop, whose main business is the retail sale of big ends, tyre pressure gauges, noddy toys with tartan trews, and other car spare parts, accessories and impedimenta. 'You'll be the witnesses,' Mr McSween told us when he opened his door to us at the appointed hour. No, we said; and we weren't the bride and groom either; not yet, anyway. Mr McSween kept his pork pie hat on, and we left, on the road that led to our marriage in Marylebone Parish Church, in September. But the Scottish sojourn, our longest holiday together, remained bright in our minds.

In December Caroline chose to have a fourth operation. We knew it could only make her life easier; which it did. In the spring, sensing she was near death, Caroline called for Richard McLaren, our friend who had married us, and asked him to conduct her funeral service. She wished to be buried in the countryside, she said. But where? He asked us if there was a place special to us both. As for many busy London people, the glum answer at the time seemed to be 'no'.

We did not then believe that Caroline would see the summer. But with all the loving kindness of our families and friends, she did: and in June, on her birthday, we travelled to Aberdeen again, to join in the celebration of the seventy-fifth birthday of the Rowett which, in Phil's words 'over the years has developed and built a heritage of social commitment aimed at improving the life and lot of every person'.

'Caroline in her own writings was similarly committed,' Phil went on to say, 'and in her recent visit when we renewed our commitment to the future of the Rowett, she joined with us, having given so much of her own spirit in her writings, which we know so well.'

Caroline stayed on in Scotland, for her last holiday, with Lesley Morrison and Joe Wilton and their little boy 'Neeps' on Jura. Her spirit now was given to nature; and later in London, as she lay dying, she wrote a verse to him:

> I've been to stay on Jura Isle
> With Lesley, Joe and Neeps.
> It's full of birds and bees and ducks,
> And buttercups and sheep.
>
> Neeps' house is grey and blue and white,
> With shells along the front,

Which Joe collected on a walk,
When he went on a hunt.

The fires are made of coal and peat,
And wood that's got the rots;
And Neeps likes nothing better than to
Poke the grate a lot.

And she remembered the bluebell woods she loved as a little girl, and the green fields, our precious heritage, which she fought for. Both of us thought of high ground, but did not speak of it.

Whatever happened to me later, I wanted a place where I would walk and be with Caroline, after she died; and a place where friends could come, too. And in August, as I said to Caroline, 'the place that comes to my mind is the little mountain by Aberdeen that Jean painted and where we walked'. Bennachie beckoned. We were almost home. For two weeks before she died, Caroline told me and our dear friend Sandy Hunt that she wanted to go on her final journey, after she died, to be buried by Bennachie. As with so many of Caroline's inspirations, we knew she had found the right way.

At the Chapel of Garioch, Eric Milton, the minister, saw Caroline as sharing the spirit of the mountain and of the Scots who have lived there down the centuries: 'a very independent, tenacious spirit. An independent spirit; a free spirit.' And speaking of the summit of Bennachie, he said 'now Mither Tap welcomes her as a daughter'.

Mr Milton, a man of remarkable kindness, had already told the story of 'the sheer courage and tenacity of this lassie' to a group of young people in the community whose vocation is to protect the heritage of the mountain; and they asked if they could look after Caroline's grave. And so, as Mr Milton said, 'this church and this community has now taken unto itself the memory of another soul, to share with all those of independent spirit, all those who have made their mark, wherever they may have been . . . . We consider it a privilege to welcome Caroline to be laid to her rest here.'

This is how Caroline came to be buried in the Chapel of Garioch, by Bennachie.

How was the day? Sunny, in the early morning. Chris and Margaret, Caroline's parents, went with her sister Juliet to the Chapel of Garioch, where Caroline was ahead of us, in her coffin in the church. (The Chapel of Garioch is not itself a church but a small community founded round a chapel dedicated by the sister of Robert the Bruce. Or so it is said.)

The previous evening, after supper, I had gone with the undertaker, Eric Massie, to collect Caroline from the airport. As we waited he told me of his early life as a joiner, working in the great country houses around Inverurie, by Garioch, and of a friend, recently killed in an accident, whose memorial is an avenue of trees a mile long, which make the drive up to Keith Hall, a grand fortified home of local nobility, a fine aspect.

Caroline was carried to and from Heathrow, and to Aberdeen, with respect. Flowers remained on top of her coffin; even the single rose I had given to her with my little message of congratulation. It was good to be with her. (Mr Massie talked of 'the remains', but it didn't seem that way to me.) We carried Caroline into his plain van ('passengers don't like to see hearses,' he had explained) and drove to Wardenhill. Inside, he had a wee dram (or as we English would say, an octuple Scotch); and then, with many fresh flowers that had been delivered to the house, went with Caroline to his workshop.

To my mind, wherever Scottish and English customs differ, the Scottish way is better. In the matter of burial, the English nowadays 'leave it to the experts'. As with doctors, lawyers and other professionals, we in effect ask undertakers to take our decisions for us. In Scotland, by contrast, as in England in time now gone by, the men who are closest to who has died expect to bear the coffin and to lower it into the grave. Explaining this, Mr Massie said he therefore must make changes to the outside of Caroline's coffin, through which he would pass cords.

The old ways, from when death was familiar in any family, are right. In her time of dying, Caroline was at home. When she died, she was laid out by a nurse who is also our friend, with simple formality, a posy of flowers in her hands. She lay at home for a day. ('Quite right,' said Mr Viner, the undertaker from Kent. 'Respectful, that is.' We were well served by undertakers.) In the morning after her death the first visitors were Lesley, and Neeps who, dressed in the kilt he'd worn with his friend Caroline on Jura, came in and placed his bunch of wild flowers by her. In the afternoon Mr Viner and his son placed her in her coffin, very gently; and we surrounded her with mementoes of life and love, including pictures that her little friends had drawn to tell her they love her. Then we lay bunches and sprays of flowers from our family and friends on her, in abundance.

Neeps put me in my place. When he came into the house I said to him foolishly, 'you know Caroline's asleep, don't you.' 'No she's not,' he said. 'She's dead.' This from a little boy just before his third birthday.

And so I was sure that the Scottish ritual is right, and another reason why it was good to bring Caroline to Scotland to be buried. In the morning while Chris, Margaret and Juliet were with Caroline, I sat in the conservatory at Wardenhill where Caroline and I, with Phil and Jean, had enjoyed many meals in sunny light; and I brought those and many other happy times to mind. Vans arrived every twenty minutes or so, with flowers, so carefully selected, from so many people who were thinking of us that day. I arranged the flowers in the grand reception room with its marble fireplace brought back from the mines in Italy by Boyd Orr. The old-fashioned custom of viewing the flowers, also seemed right to me; they were beautiful, all sent with love, and a lovely way to be with Caroline in mind and heart.

Mr Milton kindly came to pay his respects, to welcome us, and to consider the nuances of what he would say, as thoughtful preachers do. Richard McLaren arrived at midday; he had asked, as a friend, to share the service and to conduct Caroline's burial, and Mr Milton had kindly agreed. And so to a lunch of delicious fresh food made by Jean, maybe the only wife of a professor of nutrition who sprouts beans. And then the little journey to be with Caroline, at her service at two o'clock.

Gusts and flurries of wind and rain came from a bright sky as we drove to church. Weathers in Aberdeen are often evanescent; five a day, sometimes. Every mile towards Inverurie and Garioch gave a sense of arrival. We crossed a river with swans paddling against the wavelets like small white moored craft. The fields are small here: and I remembered one of the first times I felt Caroline's anger as five years before we'd driven through straw burning in East Anglian prairies. Mither Tap was on the horizon now, majestic for such a small mountain, in its pastoral landscape. Two miles on an older side road, and we were arrived at the little community of the Chapel of Garioch, and the community of people from the Rowett who, together with friends and relations from Scotland, had come to say goodbye to Caroline. There were about thirty of us in the church which, in contrast to the urban brilliance of Marylebone, smelled of new wood, in harmony with Caroline's coffin, made from solid Kentish oak blown down in the storm the year before.

This was the occasion for Psalm 121, which Margaret told me was read in the Walker family when a member was going on a journey: 'I shall lift up mine eyes unto the hills, from whence cometh my help.' Mr Milton welcomed us and Caroline, with great courtesy, and Phil, in his address, quoted from the Quaker *Faith and Practice*, in celebration of Caroline. 'Only such writings as spring from the living experience will reach into the life of others; and only those which embody genuine thought in clear and effective form will minister to the needs of the human mind . . . . It is no disrespect to truth, to present it in forms that will be readily understood.'

And finally, Phil said, 'In bringing Caroline here, and burying her here, we can continue our communion one with another.'

We walked out of the church into a squall, with wind and rain seeming to originate in the air. Outside, Mr Massie arranged the men around Caroline: Chris and Phil in front; me and my son Ben behind. We bore the coffin on staves held by our sides, unrehearsed and cautious, across the churchyard and into the field of new lairs (which is the Scots word for graves). Richard McLaren awaited us by the graveside, resplendent in white.

Here Caroline's friends and colleagues Dr Keith Ball and Dr Michael Lean joined us. We took the cords, and lowered Caroline into her grave. I do not know quite why, but this being with her in such a literal way, this physical holding and handling, was uplifting and strengthening; and the good feelings were somehow enhanced by the skittish mischief of the weather, whose mood matched Caroline's own sense of fun.

This being with Caroline had the effect of arranging us, with our families, around her grave in a decorous way. Chris stepped back to be with Margaret, and Juliet held her umbrella over them. Keith stood with Phil and Jean; Michael with the people from the Rowett. Ben was by me.

Richard read the awesome words that I had dreaded hearing for so long; but now, at the right time and in the right place, were lovely. 'For He knoweth whereof we are made: He remembereth that we are but dust. The days of man are but as grass: for He flourisheth as a flower of the field.

For as soon as the wind goeth over it . . . .' As Richard spoke the word, the wet wind scurried around us, scattering a swirl of newly fallen leaves through us, and shifting all the flowers placed in front of Caroline's grave. A couple of bunches were borne up in the air, and Neeps started to chase after them. '. . . And the place thereof shall know it no more.'

The words and the wind and the rain all stopped, together, and after a singing silence I said that Caroline would like us all to throw our flowers on her. Neeps was first; he tossed his posy into the grave. 'For Cawoline,' he said aloud. We all followed him. In the morning Webster's terrible, wonderful epitaph had rung in my head. 'Cover her face. Mine eyes dazell. She di'd young.' With many other thoughts and words, these followed Caroline into her grave. And yet her long journey, so long, was complete.

Mr Milton walked back to the manse. Phil, Keith and I walked in the churchyard, and looked up to Mither Tap, which is indeed in the line of sight from Caroline's lair. The gravediggers did their work.

'And though with great difficulty I am got hither, yet now I do not repent me of all the trouble I have been at to arrive where I am.' Mr Valiant-for-Truth's words from Pilgrim's Progress, which I had read the day before in church at Marylebone, were also bright in my mind. And so many people have chosen to be with Caroline on her long road.

We gathered together again, at Wardenhill, for tea, and I began to reflect on the wonders of the day and the week and the months before. After guests had gone, later in the afternoon, Ben, who with my other son Matt and my daughter Lou has given me and Caroline so much love, walked out with me on the west road. By our right side we saw a complete, perfect rainbow, both ends touching the countryside; and once again, we were with Caroline.

That is how it was, for me; and that is why Caroline is buried by Bennachie.

THE LIFE OF
CAROLINE WALKER

Dates don't do Caroline justice. Certainly, many of the events listed here do give a sense of her work, but can only touch on her life. In her twenties she spent much of her time travelling, even wandering, and it was only as she approached thirty that she gained a sense of public purpose. At that time her spirit is mostly evident in private letters to family and friends. Already she had the seeds of illness in her.

Between 1980 and publication of *The Food Scandal* in the summer of 1984, her accumulated knowledge and experience, together with her sense of justice, became articulated into her mission. She wrote the best part of *The Food Scandal* in three weeks. Yet at the same time she was working in the community, first in Cambridge and then in Hackney, and much of her energy was given to others, which is a reason why her vision is brighter now than when she was alive.

In less than a year, between July 1985 and April 1986, the enlarged edition of *The Food Scandal* was published; she was advisor to the BBC TV Food and Health campaign, and also to Granada TV and Thames TV, for a total of over thirty nationally networked programmes; wrote or co-wrote six booklets most of which accompanied television series, requested by a total of half a million viewers; was a Woman of the Year; advised and guided the Coronary Prevention Group, the London Food Commission, and New Health magazine; co-founded the Food Additives Campaign Team, wrote a chapter for *Additives: Your Complete Survival Guide*, and shared the Periodical Publishers' Association prize for Campaign of the Year.

Yet she also lectured up and down the country, often to small groups, and wrote many letters of encouragement to people who heard her and asked her for advice. A letter sent after Caroline's death speaks for the millions of people that she touched. Natalie Cormack wrote from Eigg ('pop: 65', as she said). 'Even my children, ages 7 and 5½ years, are fully aware of Caroline's work and her life and death,' she wrote. 'They, our future, fully appreciate the worth of sensible eating, living and husbandry, and of sticking to one's principles.'

Caroline wanted to change the world she touched, and this she did achieve. She also wanted a home in the country, children, and a quiet private life with no call for obituaries, and was so sad to be without these ordinary joys. Eventually, her message transcended her work in public health. In the last two years of her life, so soon after her blaze of achievement, as she saw her death approaching she found her way on a new path.

Caroline did not like being alone. Most of her work was collaborative, as a member of a research, campaign or production team, and as a writer working with a partner. She gave her work a sense of family. And eventually she was not alone, because she showed those who loved her how to be with her, and become a family. And those who love her are not alone, because she found a love that does not die.

1950 *12 June*
Born Liss, Hampshire

1961 *to 1968*
Educated Cheltenham Ladies College
A Levels Biology, Chemistry, Art

1968 *September*; *to August 1969*
Voluntary Service Overseas, Convent of Nazareth, Haifa, Israel

1969 *October*; *to 1972*
Undergraduate, Queen Elizabeth College, London
BSc in Biology: Second Class (Upper)

1972 *August-November*
Unemployed

December; *to July 1973*
Editor, Elsevier Scientific Publishing, Amsterdam, Holland

1973 *July–November*
Travelling in Israel during the second war

1974 *January*; *to September 1975*
Returned to Elsevier. Staff; then freelance editing

1975 *September*; *to April 1978*
Graduate student, London School of Hygiene and Tropical Medicine;
Human Nutrition

1976 *January to December*
Ill. Prescribed broad-spectrum antibiotics for months. Illness never
confidently diagnosed

1977 *and 1978*
MSc Theses 'Single-parent families and social insecurity', and 'Vitamin
D – Asians and elderly'

1978
Clerical assistant, London School of Hygiene and Tropical Medicine
First published journalism: 'What is good food?' (*Nursing Times*)

June, July
MSc in Human Nutrition: First Class with Distinction

June, July
Unemployed
First published scientific work: 'Poverty by Administration' (*Journal of
Human Nutrition*)
First published campaign (with others): 'Our Daily Bread: Who Makes
the Dough?' (Agricapital)

and 1979
Voluntary work: Agricapital, and Child Poverty Action Group (nutrition
advisor)

July; *to May 1980*
Nutritionist, Medical Research Council Epidemiology Unit, Cardiff,
working to Dr Peter Elwood

1979 *September*
First conference: Child Poverty Action Group/Advisory Centre for
Education, on School Meals
First national television appearance: BBC TV 'Nationwide', following
CPAG/ACE conference

1980 *4 January*
First national newspaper feature (and leader): 'Short fat kids of tomorrow' (*Daily Express*)

May; *to May 1982*
Nutritionist, Medical Research Council Dunn Clinical Nutrition Centre, Cambridge, working to Dr (later Professor) Philip James

May; *to 1981*
At the Dunn, research scientist on salt and high blood pressure (the March study)

May
At the Dunn, researcher for EEC-funded project on disease patterns in Europe

17 July
First conference intervention: British Heart Foundation AGM

29 September – 2 October
First academic conference presentation: 'Dietary variations and ischaemic heart disease in Britain': EEC Colloquium on Preventive Medicine, Strasbourg

November; *to 1984*
Secretary, Coronary Prevention Group (CPG)

1981 *9–11 January*
Secretary, National Advisory Committee on Nutrition Education (NACNE) sub-committee, at invitation of Dr James. Weekend meeting.

March
At the Dunn, researcher on diet and colon cancer in Europe

August
First guide to food and health: Granada TV 'Reports Action' booklet *Junk the Junk Food* with Christopher Robbins and CPG. Requested by 20,000 viewers

1982 *March*
Advisor, Brent Health District: 'Food and Health Policy for Brent', based on NACNE draft, with Christopher Robbins

May–September
Unemployed

September; to June 1986
Nutritionist, City and Hackney Health Authority, working to Dr Ken Grant

October
CPG booklet *A Simple Guide to Healthier Eating*, based on *Junk The Junk Food*, with Christopher Robbins

1983 *June*
First work for BBC TV Continuing Education: advisor, interviewed for 'Plague of Hearts' series

22 June
Conference intervention: British Nutrition Foundation conference on dietary guidelines

August; to August 1986
Consultant, *New Health* magazine

September
NACNE report published

28–30 September
Participant, workship conference on 'How to Prevent Heart Disease' (the 'Canterbury Conference')

December
Paper, 'The NACNE Report. The New British Diet' (*Lancet*)

1984 *January*
Proposal for Health Education Council funding for nutrition education in City and Hackney

4 April
Speaker, Mersey Health Promotion Conference, Warrington

May
Director, City and Hackney Stroke Prevention Project, and 'Have a Heart for Hackney'

11 June
Book, *The Food Scandal* with Geoffrey Cannon, accompanied by three full-page features in *The Times*, national press coverage, and publicity tour

21, 28 June, 5 July
Writ served by Beecham (Bovril) against *The Food Scandal*. Injunction granted. Another writ by Beecham (Ribena, Lucozade) served (later dropped). Writ by Kelloggs (Corn Flakes, All Bran) served. (Outstanding cases eventually settled out of court)

5 July
The Food Scandal number one bestseller in *Bookseller* charts. Later also number one in the *Sunday Times* charts

12 July
DHSS COMA report on Diet and Cardiovascular Disease published. Evidence submitted with Christopher Robbins

16 July
Adjournment debate in House of Commons on prevention of heart disease. Briefed Jonathan Aitken MP on his 'socks and sausages' speech

7 November
CPG booklets *You And Your Heart* and *Blood Pressure and Your Heart*, written with others, published to accompany CPG conference

1985 *21 January – 6 February*
Ill. Emergency admission to St Mary's Hospital, Paddington. Operation, colon cancer found

27 January, 3 February
'Review Front' features 'Shock Report: Just How Well do We Eat?' with Geoffrey Cannon (*Observer*)

February
CPG booklet, *Healthier Eating: A Good Foods Guide*

23 April
Founder Council member, London Food Commission, launched this day

21 May
Geoffrey Taylor Memorial Lecture to McCarrison Society on 'legalised consumer fraud'

4 June
Chairman, CPG conference on Nutrition in Pregnancy and Early Childhood

1 July
The Food Scandal enlarged and revised paperback edition published.

August
Secretary, CPG Nutrition Advisory Committee

August
CPG booklet *Healthier Eating and Your Heart* published with Health Education Council

August; *to April 1986*
Advisor, BBC TV Food and Health Campaign

2, 3, 4, 5 September
Advisor, interviewed for BBC TV 'O'Donnell Investigates the Food Connection' four-part series

September
BBC TV booklet *Eat Your Way To Health* to accompany O'Donnell series. Requested by 100,000 viewers

7 October
Advisor, interviewed for Granada TV 'World in Action', 'The Great Food Scandal'

8, 9 October
Advisor, interviewed for Thames TV 'Good Enough To Eat?' two-part series

October
Thames TV booklet *Good Enough To Eat?*, written with others. Requested by 60,000 viewers

28 October
A Woman Of The Year: Savoy luncheon

November
Advisor, BBC TV 'Food and Drink Programme', with CPG

4 November
Elected member of the Royal Society of Medicine Forum on Food and Health Steering Committee

12 December
Founder member, Food Additives Campaign Team (FACT), launched

1986 *January*
Advisor, BBC TV 'You Are What You Eat' six-part series

January
BBC TV booklet *You Are What You Eat* to accompany TV series, written with others. Requested by 250,000 viewers

8, 15, 22, 29 April
Advisor, BBC TV 'O'Donnell Investigates The Food Business' four-part series. Advisor, BBC TV 'Go For It' thirteen-part series

April
BBC TV booklets *Food: Go For Health* and *Alcohol* to accompany the TV series. Requested by 120,000 viewers

14 April
Advisor, interviewed for Granada TV World In Action, 'The Threatened Generation'

29 April
Periodical Publishers' Association Campaign of the Year for series on additives in *New Health*, joint winner with others

May – December
Columnist for *The Daily Telegraph*

21 May
Book, *Additives: Your Complete Survival Guide*, co-written with others

3 September
Debate on additives at the British Association for the Advancement of Science annual meeting

28, 29, 30 October
Speaker, International and FACT Conferences on Food Additives

1987 *27 January – 26 February*
Second operation for colon and abdominal cancer

January
Awarded Winston Churchill Travelling Scholarship

February – May
Convalescent. Holiday in Scotland

August – December
Intermittent obstructions

12 September
Married to Geoffrey Cannon
Paper for National Extension College/Health Education Authority
'Health Action Pack' for 16–19 year olds

4–11 December
Final operation to relieve obstruction

1988
Book, CPG *Eating for a Healthy Heart*, introduction co-written with others

March, May
In hospital

June, July
Holiday in Scotland

July
Final stay in hospital

1 August
At home

31 August
Recorded BBC Radio 4 'Food Programme'

22 September
Died. Obituaries in the *Guardian*, *The Daily Telegraph*, the *Independent*, and
the *Listener*

28, 29 September
Funeral. Burial in Aberdeen, by Bennachie

21 October
BBC Radio 'Food Programme' on Caroline Walker. Awarded Glenfiddich Prize for Radio Programme of the Year in April 1989

1989 *2 June*
Awarded Winston Churchill Fellowship

15 June
Awarded Rosemary Delbridge Prize

11 October
First annual celebration of the life and work of Caroline Walker, at the
Royal Society of Arts, London

THE WORK OF
CAROLINE WALKER

———◆———

This is a list of Caroline's work, beginning with her MSc thesis in 1977, and ending with tributes to her in 1988 and 1989. Fifty of her outstanding accomplishments – books and journalism, television and radio programmes, guides to healthy eating, scientific papers and lectures, correspondence and other writing – are listed in **bold type**. Some of the writing by others about her or her work is listed in *italic type*. Private letters, including some quoted in the book, are not listed, nor is committee work done notably for the Coronary Prevention Group. Some of her most characteristic work especially lectures and radio programmes, was not recorded, and some work listed here is shown as unpublished. Most of her work was done while she was working at first full-time, then part-time, for City and Hackney Health Authority.

'Single-parent families and social insecurity'. Thesis for M.Sc. in Human Nutrition. London School of Hygiene and Tropical Medicine, 1977. Unpublished

'Vitamin D – Asians and elderly'. Thesis for MSc in Human Nutrition. London School of Hygiene and Tropical Medicine, 1977. Unpublished

'Israel'. Proposal for study of nutrition and food policy, March 1978. Unpublished

'What is "good food"?' *Nursing Times*, 4 May 1978

'Edible worms'. BBC World Service 'Outlook'. Interview, 8 June 1978

(With Dr Michael Church) 'Poverty by administration: a review of supplementary benefits, nutrition and scale rates'. *J Hum Nutr* **1978; 32: 5–18**

(With others) 'Our Daily Bread: Who Makes The Dough?' London: British Society for Social Responsibility in Science (BSSRS), September 1978

(With Dr Michael Burr and Dr Peter Elwood) 'Cereal fibre and heart disease'. Proposal for a randomised controlled trial. Cardiff: MRC Epidemiology Unit, October 1978. Unpublished

'Transit time and colon cancer'. Research proposal. Cardiff: MRC Epidemiology Unit, March 1979

'School meals'. BBC TV 'Nationwide'. Interview, 17 September 1979

Mrs G George and others. 'A TV slur on our school meals'. Letters. South Wales Echo, 24 September 1979

'TV discussion was no slur'. Letter. South Wales Echo, 27 September 1979

'Poverty by administration'. Correspondence with Margaret Wynn, September–November 1979. Unpublished

'Children and nutrition. Child health, school meals, and the poverty line'. Advisory Centre for Education Conference, October 1979

'Dyeing: not the way to health'. Letter. South Wales Echo, 11 October 1979

'The British diet'. BBC TV Wales 'Meet For Lunch'. Interview, 29 October 1979

(With others) Education Bill: Second Reading. Briefing for Child Poverty Action Group, November 1979

'How LEAs will be free to demolish school meals service'. Where, 154, January 1980

Bruce Kemble. 'Short fat kids of tomorrow'. Interview. Daily Express, 4 January 1980

Anon. 'It's the parents' job'. Leader. Daily Express, 4 January 1980

'Prevention of heart disease'. Correspondence with Dr Richard Turner, February 1980–August 1988. Unpublished

'Food and health'. Tyne Tees Television. Interview, 6 March 1980

'Bread, Allied Bakeries'. Complaint to The Advertising Standards Authority, March–April 1980. Unpublished

'Hiatus hernia and Lord Goodman'. Letter. Private Eye, April 1980

'Analysis of diet records'. Report for MRC Dunn Clinical Nutrition Centre, Cambridge, May 1980. Unpublished

(With others) 'Diet for a healthy heart'. Report for Coronary Prevention Group, 1980. Unpublished

'Prevention of heart disease'. Correspondence with Professor Michael Oliver, July–August 1980. Unpublished

'School meals'. BBC Radio Scotland 'The Jimmy Mack Show'. Interview, 29 August 1980

'Dietary variations and ischaemic heart disease in Great Britain'. Paper presented to European Colloquium on Preventive Medicine, Strasbourg, October 1980. Unpublished

'Patterns of diet and disease in Europe'. Letter to M Schneider of the Comité National de Prévention Médicale, Neuilly, France, October 1980. Unpublished

(With Hannah Wright) 'The Cordon Bleu chimp who came to dinner'. New Statesman, 19–26 December 1980

'The collection of 24-hour urines'. Guide for workers. MRC Dunn Clinical Nutrition Centre, Cambridge, March 1981

'Diet, adenomatous polyps and colon cancer'. Report on proposed case-control study at IARC Epidemiology Unit, Lyons. MRC Dunn Clinical Nutrition Centre, Cambridge, March 1981

'History of fruit and vegetables'. A directory, 1981. Unpublished

(With Christopher Robbins) 'Junk the junk food: a simple guide to healthier eating'. Manchester: Granada Television/ London: Coronary Prevention Group, August 1981

Brent Health District. 'Food and health policy for Brent'. Report of an ad hoc working group. Advisor. London: Central Middlesex Hospital, March 1982

(With Professor John Goodwin and others) 'Prevention of coronary heart disease in the United Kingdom'. *Lancet*, 1982; I: 846–847

(With Christopher Robbins) 'A simple guide to healthy eating'. London: Coronary Prevention Group, 1982

'Sausages'. BBC TV Norwich. Interview, 23 April 1982

'Dietary guidelines for district food and health policy'. Background paper for District Food Policy Workshop, NHS training, Harrogate, October 1982. Unpublished

'National food policy. An outline of the scientific background'. March 1983. Unpublished

'Heart attacks'. Lectures to women's and pensioners' groups in Haringey, April–May 1983

'Heart disease'. BBC TV Continuing Education 'Plague of Hearts'. Interview, advisor, 12, 19, 26 June, 2 July 1983

'Healthy food for a family'. Advice sheet. Published to accompany 'Plague of Hearts'. BBC TV, June 1983

Peta Levi. 'Be of good heart . . . and this is the way to do it'. Interview. The Times, *14 June 1983*

'The national diet'. Lecture to the Coronary Prevention Group (CPG) conference on 'Recent Trends in Coronary Mortality: Are We Winning or Losing?', 30 June 1983

Geoffrey Cannon. 'Censored – a diet for life and death'. Advisor. The Sunday Times, *3 July 1983*

Geoffrey Cannon. 'Battle for the British diet'. Advisor. The Sunday Times, *3 July 1983*

David Walker. 'Nutritionists attack diet habits'. The Times, *4 July 1983*

Andrew Veitch. 'Shelved report on British diet can be published'. The Guardian, *4 July 1983*

James Allan. ' "Healthier diet" advice held up by Ministry'. The Daily Telegraph, *4 July 1983*

Anon. 'Food hazard "cover-up" questions for Thatcher'. The Scotsman, *4 July 1983*

Tim Beardsley. 'Government chokes on report'. Nature, *14 July 1983*

(With Dr Ken Grant) 'Heart disease and stroke prevention programme for the City and Hackney Health District'. Draft proposals, July 1983

(With Christopher Robbins) 'Achieving a healthier UK diet'. Paper for the DHSS COMA panel on diet and cardiovascular disease. April, August 1983. Unpublished

Vegetarian Cookery. Advisor. London: BBC Books, 1983

'Diet and disease'. BBC Radio 'Woman's Hour', Interview, 11 August 1983

'Diet and disease'. BBC Radio 'Woman's Hour', Interview, 15 August 1983

'British Nutrition Foundation'. Letter to BBC Radio 4 'Today' programme (Julian Holland), September 1983. Unpublished

Anon. 'Are "wholesome" food and water good enough?' Leader. Lancet, *1983; II: 715–716*

National Advisory Committee for Nutrition Education. 'Nutrition: the changing scene'. Extracts from NACNE report. Lancet, *1983; II: 719–721, 782–784, 835–838, 902–905*

National Advisory Committee on Nutrition Education. A discussion paper on proposals for nutritional guidelines for health education in Britain (the NACNE report). Secretary of

working party. London: Health Education Council, September 1983

'The nation's diet'. Guide for the Liverpool Garden Festival, October 1983. Unpublished

'Health Education'. Correspondence with Health Education Council (Dr David Player), October 1983–1986. Unpublished

Margaret Sanderson, Jack Winkler. 'Chewing over a healthy diet'. The Health Services, 21 October 1983

Christopher Robbins. 'Nutrition: the changing scene'. Implementing the NACNE report. '1. National dietary goals: a confused debate'. Lancet, 1983; II: 1351–1353

Maggie Sanderson and Jack Winkler. 'Nutrition: the changing scene'. Implementing the NACNE report. '2. Strategies for implementing NACNE recommendations'. Lancet, 1983; II: 1353–1354

'Nutrition: the changing scene'. Implementing the NACNE report. '3. The new British diet'. Lancet, 1983; II: 1354–1358

'What exactly is a good diet?' New Health, November 1983

'Diabetic diet'. Answer to reader's letter. New Health, November 1983

'101 diet tips'. Woman, 19 November 1983

'Eating for two?' Answer to reader's letter. New Health, November 1983

Olwyn Glynn Owen. 'Disease that's eating its way into our health'. GP, 2 December 1983

'The national diet'. Postgrad Med J, 1984; 60: 26–33

Braidwood P. 'The de-coke diet'. Advisor. Woman's Own, 7 January 1984

'History of fruit and vegetables'. A direc-

tory (Update), January 1984. Unpublished

Yvonne Roberts. 'Is the British diet good enough?' Company, January 1984

(With Kathy Elliott, Dr Ken Grant and Maggie Sanderson) 'Proposal to prepare, pre-test and evaluate a nutrition education booklet in City and Hackney Health District'. Presented to Health Education Council, January 1984. Unpublished

'Meals'. Answer to reader's letter. New Health, February 1984

'Food for health'. Advice sheet for BBC Radio 4 'Tuesday Call', February 1984

'Phileas Fogg Tortilla Chips'. Correspondence with Derwent Valley Foods, February 1984. Unpublished

'Heart disease'. Granada Television 'World in Action, Countdown to Coronary'. Advisor. Two-part series: 13, 20 February 1984

'The national diet'. Thames Television 'Afternoon Plus'. Interview, February 1984

'Healthy food for a family'. Leaflet for Thames Television 'Afternoon Plus', March 1984

'The nation's diet'. Mersey Region Health Promotion Conference. Lecture, 4 April 1984. Unpublished

'Food for the 1980s'. Lecture to Institute of Biology (Scotland), 7 April 1984

'Heart disease'. Health Education Council, 'Coronary Heart Disease: Plans for Action. (The Canterbury Report)', Participant. Tunbridge Wells: Pitman, April 1984

Jeanette Arnold. 'About our advisor: Caroline Walker'. New Health, May 1984

'The banger exploded'. New Health, May 1984

'Food and health: the nation's diet'.

Exhibition for the Liverpool Garden Festival, May 1984

'Butter Information Council'. Letter to Society of Health Education Officers (Lesley Jones), 23 May 1984. Unpublished

'Nutrition'. Lecture at London School of Hygiene and Tropical Medicine, 25 May 1984

'National Food Survey'. Correspondence with Ministry of Agriculture, Fisheries and Food (Dr David Buss), June 1984. Unpublished

Anne Woodham. 'The food scandal'. *The Sunday Times, 3 June 1984*

'Have a Heart for Hackney'. Lecture to Association of Community Health Councils, 6 June 1984

'The Food Scandal'. Woman's Hour, Interview, 7 June1984

(With Geoffrey Cannon) *The Food Scandal.* **London: Century, 1984**

Geoffrey Cannon. 'The food scandal. Food, treacherous food'. The Times, *11 June 1984*

Anon. 'Britain's diet "not healthy".' The Daily Telegraph, *11 June 1984*

Robert Millar. 'Health warning: the food you eat can kill'. Daily Express, *11 June 1984*

Geoffrey Cannon. 'The Food Scandal. The cover-up that kills'. The Times, *12 June 1984*

Shirley Davenport. 'Unsavoury facts about our food'. Liverpool Echo, *Interview, 12 June 1984.*

Similar features in Colchester Evening Gazette, Belfast News Letter, West Lancashire Evening Gazette, Portsmouth News (11 June), Northampton Chronicle and Echo (14 June), Leicester Mercury (15 June), Yorkshire Post (16 June), Lancashire Evening Post (17 July), Sheffield Morning Telegraph (4 August)

Geoffrey Cannon. 'The food scandal. So you think you eat healthily?' The Times, *13 June 1984*

Brian James. 'Danger, this food will damage your health'. Daily Mail, *13 June 1984*

Professor Raymond Hoffenberg, Brian Edsall. 'Differing views on food and health'. Letters. The Times, *15 June 1984*

David Whitfield. 'Scandal of Britain's food deaths cover-up'. The Morning Star, *16 June 1984*

Sally Brampton. 'Body beautiful'. The Observer, *17 June 1984*

Anon. 'Why average diet is a killer'. Sunday News, *Belfast, 17 June 1984*

Cathy Brown. 'Our "scandalous" diet provides food for thought'. Interview. East Anglian Daily Times, *18 June 1984*

John Kitchen, Dr James le Fanu, Dorothy Dennis, Barbara Wooldridge, Joanna Jenkins, TFR Jones, Dr John Taverner. 'Talkback: the food scandal'. Letters. The Times, *19 June 1984*

Sir Francis Avery Jones, Professor Jerry Morris, Lord Young of Dartington. 'Talkback: the food scandal'. Letters. The Times, *20 June 1984*

'Fats'. Lecture to Brent Health Authority, 20 June 1984

Derek Cooper. 'The food scandal'. The Listener, *21 June 1984*

Marsh Midda, Dr Alexander Macnair, Professor Thomas McKeown, Hope Page, Trevor Mann, Dr ECH Huddy, Anthony Oliver, ADM Greenfield, Frank Adey. 'Talkback: the food scandal'. Letters. The Times, *22 June 1984*

Anon. 'A hard-hitting look at the way we shouldn't be eating'. Interview. Ipswich Evening Star, *25 June 1984*

Sir Alan Marre. 'Falsities on food'. Letter. The Times, *26 June 1984*

Fay Maschler. 'Not easy, breaking the bad habits'. *The London* Standard, *26 June 1984*

Jane Flatt. 'Exposed! The great British food scandal'. Interview. Eastern Evening News, Norwich, *28 June 1984*

Mrs JM Hammond, Professor John Yudkin, MR Walker, RA Wilson, Mrs Sally Brown. 'Talkback: the food scandal'. Letters. The Times, *29 June 1984*

'Salt and high blood pressure'. Correspondence with Dr A M Heagerty, June–September 1984. Unpublished

Ann Shaw. 'There's death on your plate. Keeping Britain unhealthy is big business'. Interview. Glasgow Herald, *2 July 1984*

Charles Bowden. 'Is milk image turning sour?' The Journal, *Newcastle, 3 July 1984*

Richard Dowden. 'Libel claim as diet book withdrawn'. The Times, *3 July 1984*

Professor Philip James. 'The food scandal'. Letter to The Times, *July 1984. Unpublished*

'Spotlight on food labels'. *New Health*, July 1984

'The great British diet: can you swallow the evidence?' *Company*, July 1984

House of Commons. Parliamentary debates. Hansard (official record). Heart disease. Jonathan Aitken MP, John Patten MP, *16 July 1984*

'Healthy eating guides'. Proposal to Health Education Council (Dr David Player), 17 July 1984. Unpublished

'Bread'. Correspondence with the British Nutrition Foundation (Dr Derek Shrimpton), July–August 1984. Unpublished

Avril Groom. 'Healthy eating, from the consumer's point of view'. The Daily Telegraph, *25 July 1984*

John Forsyth. Interview. City Limits, *27 July 1984*

'Advising on low fat diets – an alternative view'. *Health Visitor*, August 1984

'Merseyside's healthiest family competition'. Quiz. For Mersey Health Promotion Unit, August 1984. Unpublished

Julie Brackpool, Sibi Ramharry, John Ashton; Caroline Walker (advisor). 'Shopping and coronary prevention in Liverpool'. University Medical School: Department of Community Health, 1984

NACNE. Correspondence with British Nutrition Foundation (Dr Derek Shrimpton), August–October 1984. Unpublished

Elaine Cobbe. 'Meaty facts behind the great grub cover-up'. Interview. The Irish Independent, *28 August 1984*

(With Geoffrey Cannon) 'The food scandal continues . . .' Press release, 6 September 1984

Jane Lomas. 'Food's still a scandal'. Interview. Northern Echo, *7 September 1984*

'The fat connection'. *New Health*, September 1984

'Fitness: Get fit with the Green Goddess'. Advisor. BBC Enterprises: Video, September 1984

(With others). Coronary Prevention Group. 'The healthy heart guide'. Folder. London: CPG, 1984

'Diet and cardiovascular disease'. *Precis* 4, Autumn 1984

Kerry MacKenzie. 'Beanz meanz exactly what?' Interview. Womans World, October 1984

John Forsyth. 'Can you push a supermarket trolley and stay fit?' Interview. The Guardian, 26 October 1984

'Food'. BBC TV Scotland. 'The Afternoon Show', Interview, 1 November 1984

'Food for Thought'. *Home and Country* (Magazine of the National Federation of Women's Institutes), November 1984

(With others). Coronary Prevention Group/Health Education Council. You and your heart'. Booklet. London: CPG/HEC, 1984

(With others). Coronary Prevention Group/Health Education Council. *Blood pressure and your heart*. Booklet. London: CPG/HEC, 1984

'Food for babies and young children'. Correspondence with Dr Richard Cottrell. *Health Visitor*, November 1984

'Jam Tomorrow?' A pilot study of the food circumstances . . . of 1,000 people on low incomes in the north of England. Adviser. Manchester: Polytechnic Food Policy Unit, November 1984

'Heart beat. On sausages and socks!' *Modus*, December 1984

'Food for babies and young children'. Correspondence with Dorothy Francis. December 1984 – January 1985. Unpublished

(With Geoffrey Cannon) 'Just how well do we eat?' Wheel of Health – Part 1. The *Observer*, 27 January 1985

(With Geoffrey Cannon) 'How to start eating well'. Wheel of Health – Part 2. The *Observer*, 3 February 1985

(With others) Coronary Prevention Group. 'Healthier eating: a good foods guide'. Booklet. London: CPG, February 1985

'The gradual vegetarian'. Report for publisher, March 1985. Unpublished

'Diet, exercise and health'. Guidelines prepared for Inglewood Health Hydro, May 1985. Unpublished

(With Geoffrey Cannon) The Food Scandal. Enlarged, updated paperback edition. London: Century, 1985

'Food as therapy'. *Vogue Beauty and Health Special*, Summer 1985

Coronary Prevention Group. 'Nutrition in pregnancy and early childhood'. Conference chairman, 4 June 1985

(With Geoffrey Cannon) 'How to Eat Healthy and Hearty'. Feature for the *Daily Express*, July 1985. Unpublished

(With others) Coronary Prevention Group/Health Education Council. 'Healthier Eating and your Heart'. Booklet, London: CPG/HEC, August 1985

'Guide to Health Eating'. Correspondence with Health Education Council (Rosie Leyden), August–December 1985. Unpublished

(With others) *Food for Health*. Training pack. London: City and Hackney Health Authority, 1985

'Fat That's Good For You'. *New Health*, August 1985

'Meat'. Letter to Meat and Livestock Commission (Geoffrey Harrington), August 1985. Unpublished

'NACNE'. Feature written for *Health at School*, August 1985. Unpublished

BBC TV Food and Health Campaign. Continuing Education 'O'Donnell

Investigates the Food Connection'. Advisor, interviews. Four part series, 2, 3, 4, 5 September 1985

BBC TV Food and Health Campaign. Continuing Education 'Eat Your Way to Health'. Booklet. London: BBC TV, September 1985

(With Felicity Lawrence and others) 'Additives: The Case Against'. New Health, September 1985

Michael O'Donnell. 'One Man's Burden'. Br Med J 1985; 291: 612

Peter Ackroyd. 'Gnawing Obsessions'. The Times, 4 September 1985

Michael O'Donnell. 'Diet and Disease'. The Listener, 5 September 1985

Laurie Taylor. 'High Priests of Fibre'. New Society, 13 September 1985

'Nutritional Labelling of Food'. Report prepared for Coronary Prevention Group, September 1985. Unpublished

'NACNE'. Granada Television 'World in Action'. 'The Great Food Scandal'. Advisor, interview, 7 October 1985

'Additives'. Thames Television 'Good Enough to Eat?' Advisor, interview, 8, 9 October 1985

(With others) 'Good Enough to Eat?' Booklet. London: Thames Television, October 1985

'Additives: Legalised Consumer Fraud'. New Health, October 1985

'National Food Policy'. Correspondence with Parliamentary Food and Health Forum (Joycelin Hobman), October–November 1985. Unpublished

'The Great British Diet'. BBC TV Schools Broadcasting. Advisor, interview, 21 October 1985

Paul Levy. 'The Campaign Against British Food'. The Observer, 8 November 1985

Nigel Andrews. 'Out Damned Diet'. Financial Times, 9 November 1985

(With Geoffrey Cannon and others) 'Additives: Children at Risk'. New Health, November 1985

'Soup'. Complaint to The Advertising Standards Authority. November 1985 – January 1986. Unpublished

'Sausages'. Complaint to the Advertising Standards Authority, November 1985 – February 1986. Unpublished

'Modern Miracles'. Proposed column for New Health, November 1985. Unpublished

'Modern Miracles'. Correspondence with Oswald Hickson, Collier & Co (Solicitors), December 1985. Unpublished

'Food Labelling'. BBC TV 'Food and Drink Programme'. Advisor, November 1985

'Princess Diana's Breast Feeding'. Letter to 'Food and Drink Programme', November 1985. Unpublished

(With Maria Scott and others) 'Additives: The Good News'. New Health, December 1985

'Christmas Day in the Doghouse for Mr Jopling', Guardian, 13 December 1985

Bryan Christie. 'Shoppers' Revolt begins over the widespread use of food additives'. FACT launch. Interview. The Scotsman, 13 December 1985

John Young. 'Food Additives Under Fire'. FACT launch. The Times, 13 December 1985

Brenda Parry. 'Tougher controls urged on use of food additives'. FACT launch. The Daily Telegraph, 13 December 1985

'Additives'. The Jimmy Young Programme. Interview, 13 December 1985

Woodrow Wyatt. 'Give this secrecy the bird'. FACT launch. News of the World, 15 December 1985

Jill Moore. 'Feeding sick children'. Interview. Nursing Times, 18–25 December 1985

Anon. 'Additives action group praises trade moves'. FACT launch. Meat Trades Journal, 19 December 1985

Anon. 'Add a pinch of chemical to the Christmas fare'. FACT launch. New Scientist, 19–26 December 1985

Victoria McKee. 'Your guide to unfair Christmas fare'. Fact launch. Interview. Birmingham Evening Mail, 21 December 1985

Derek Cooper. 'Facing FACT'. FACT launch. The Listener, 2 January 1986

BBC TV Food and Health Campaign. 'You are what you eat: Mr and Mrs Average's diet and how to improve it'. Briefing document, January 1986. Unpublished

BBC TV Food and Health Campaign. 'You are what you eat'. Advisor, interview. Six part series, 5, 12, 19, 26 January, 2, 9 February 1986

(With Geoffrey Cannon, Maggie Sanderson and others) BBC TV Food and Health Campaign. 'You are what you eat. A Practical Guide to Healthy Eating'. Booklet. London: BBC TV, January 1986

(With Geoffrey Cannon and others) 'Additives: Plan of Action'. New Health, January 1986

(With Dr Ken Grant and Maggie Sanderson) Hackney Nutrition Survey. 'Physical Growth and Development of Hackney School Children'. Grant application to GLC, January 1986. Unpublished

(With Professor Michael Crawford) Hackney Nutrition Survey. 'The Composition of Meals Eaten by Secondary School Children and their Families'. Grant application to GLC, January 1986. Unpublished

Anon. 'The fact is . . .' New campaign launched on additives. Interview. London Food News, Spring 1986

(With Wendy Doyle, Felicity Lawrence) 'Nutrition for all ages. One to three-year-olds'. New Health, January 1986

(With Wendy Doyle, Felicity Lawrence) 'Guide to nutrition. Primary school'. New Health, February 1986

Weekly column on food and health. Proposal, February 1986. Unpublished

'Ribena'. Letter to Esther Rantzen of BBC TV 'That's Life', 23 February 1986. Unpublished

BBC TV 'Food and Drink Programme'. Coronary Prevention Group nutritional labelling competition results. Advisor, 25 February 1986

'Food Additives'. Lecture to the University of Bristol Department of Medicine, 28 February 1986

'Food facts'. Letter. New Scientist, 27 February 1986

'Nutritional labelling'. Correspondence with Ministry of Agriculture, Fisheries and Food (Valerie Smith), March 1986. Unpublished

(With Wendy Doyle, Alex Henderson) 'Guide to nutrition. Adolescence'. New Health, March 1986

David Fletcher. 'Row over teenage diet report'. The Daily Telegraph, 3 April 1986

'Diet of Schoolchildren'. The Jimmy Young Programme. Interview, 3 April 1986

Andrew Veitch. 'Survey on "chips and biscuits" diet to be released'. The Guardian, *4 April 1986*

Michael Leapman. 'Fish Fulfilment'. Radio Times, *April 5–11 1986*

BBC TV Food and Health Campaign. 'O'Donnell investigates the food business'. Advisor, interview. Four part series, 8, 15, 22, 29 April 1986

BBC TV Food and Health Campaign. 'Go for it!' Advisor. 13 part series, April–May 1986

BBC TV Food and Health Campaign. *Go for health.* Booklet. London: BBC TV, April 1986

BBC TV Food and Health Campaign. *Alcohol, friend or foe.* Booklet. London: BBC TV, April 1986

(With others) 'Food for health'. Report. London: City and Hackney Health Authority, April 1986

(With others) 'Food for health'. Training pack. London: City and Hackney Health Authority, April 1986

Diet of School Children. Granada Television World in Action. 'The threatened generation'. Advisor, 14 April 1986

(With Wendy Doyle, Alex Henderson) 'Guide to nutrition. Teenagers'. *New Health*, April 1986

(With Geoffrey Cannon) 'Nutrition labelling'. Submission to the Ministry of Agriculture, Fisheries and Food on behalf of the McCarrison Society, April 1986. Unpublished

Health campaign. 'Who decides what we eat?' *What Diet and Lifestyle*, April–May 1986

Health Education Council. *Guide to healthy eating.* Advisor. Booklet, April 1986

(With Geoffrey Cannon, Felicity Lawrence, Peter Mansfield, Melanie Miller) 'Additives: Your Complete Survival Guide'. London: Century, 1986

'The fats of life'. *Nursing Times,* 7 May 1986

'The proof of the pudding is in the chemistry'. *The Daily Telegraph*, 9 May 1986

'Caramel'. Feature for the *Guardian*, May 1986. Unpublished

David Southgate. 'Medicine and the media'. Br Med J 1986; 292: 1267

(With Wendy Doyle, Alex Henderson) 'Guide to nutrition. Young adults'. *New Health*, May 1986

'Food facts: to be taken with a pinch of salt'. *The Daily Telegraph*, 23 May 1986

'Eating for a Healthy Heart'. Lecture to Canterbury and Thanet Health Authority, 23 May 1986

(With Wendy Doyle, Alex Henderson) 'Guide to nutrition. Adults 23–50'. *New Health*, June 1986

Poverty and food. 'Tightening Belts'. Adviser. London: Food Commission, June 1986

'Making no bones about meat'. *The Daily Telegraph*, 6 June 1986

'Fertilisers'. Complaint to the Advertising Standards Authority, June–August 1986. Unpublished

'Food for the nation's future?' Precis 11, Summer 1986

Tony Webb, Angela Henderson. 'Food

irradiation: who wants it?' Report by the London Food Commission. Advisor, June 1986

'Irradiated food for thought'. *The Daily Telegraph*, 18 June 1986

'Scientists and the food industry'. Correspondence with Professor Don Naismith, June 1986. Unpublished

'Scientists and the food industry'. Correspondence with Professor John Yudkin, June 1986. Unpublished

'Scientists and the sugar industry'. Correspondence with the Sugar Bureau (Gerard Bithell), June 1986. Unpublished

'Scientists and the sugar industry'. Correspondence with Professor John Durnin, June 1986. Unpublished

'Food facts: to be taken with a pinch of salt' (second feature). *The Daily Telegraph*, 24 June 1986

'The health campaign for food labelling'. *What Diet and Lifestyle*, June–July 1986

'Eat, drink but be wary'. *Working Woman*, 1986

(With Wendy Doyle, Alex Henderson) 'Guide to nutrition. Middle age'. *New Health*, July 1986

'Food poisoning'. Feature for *The Daily Telegraph*, July 1986. Unpublished

'In support of school dinners'. *The Daily Telegraph*, 14 July 1986

Derek Cooper. 'Surviving with additives'. Review of 'Additives: Your Complete Survival Guide'. Quoted. Scottish Field, *July 1986*

'Buttering up the Royals'. *The Daily Telegraph*, 5 August 1986

(With Wendy Doyle, Alex Henderson) 'Guide to nutrition. Retirement'. *New Health*, August 1986

'Fair Game'. *New Health*, August 1986

'Food additives in perspective'. Correspondence with Bradford Food Policy Unit (Dr Verner Wheelock), August–October 1986. Unpublished

'The bread and butter battle'. *The Daily Telegraph*, 19 August 1986

(With Professor Philip James and others) 'Nutritional labelling of foods: a rational approach to banding'. Summary of report prepared by the Nutrition Advisory Committee of the Coronary Prevention Group. *Lancet*, 1986; II: 469

'Proving that we really do need food for thought'. *The Daily Telegraph*, 2 September 1986

'Food additives: for the benefit of the manufacturer or the consumer?' Lecture to the British Association for the Advancement of Science, 3 September 1986. Unpublished

Anon. 'Safety of food additives "uncertain"'. Report of the BAAS conference. Interview. The Times, *4 September 1986*

(With Wendy Doyle, Alex Henderson) 'Guide to nutrition. Vegetarians'. *New Health*, September 1986

'Additives'. Letter to the Food Advisory Committee (Professor Philip James), September 1986. Unpublished

'The future of British food manufacturing'. Correspondence with the Food and Drink Federation (Sir Derrick Holden-Brown), September–October 1986. Unpublished

'Additives'. BBC Radio World Service 'Science in Action', Interview, 12 September 1986

'Additives'. Letter to Food and Drink Federation (Michael Mackenzie), September 1986. Unpublished

'And you thought milk came from cows?' *The Daily Telegraph*, 23 September 1986

'It'll add years to your life'. *Telegraph Sunday Magazine*, 28 September 1986

'What we are not told about the food we eat'. *Secrets* **(Journal of the Campaign for Freedom of Information), October 1986**

'The risk in a rusk'. *The Daily Telegraph*, **8 October 1986**

'Year of the meal snatcher'. *New Health*, **October 1986**

(With Professor Philip James and others) 'Nutritional labelling of foods; a rational approach to banding'. Report of the Nutrition Advisory Committee. London: Coronary Prevention Group, October 1986

'The need for school meals'. Lecture to the Inner London Education Authority/ National Union of Public Employees Conference on School Meals, 22 October 1986

'Good riddance to half-baked ideas'. *The Daily Telegraph*, 28 October 1986

'Additives and nutritional quality'. Lecture to the International Conference on Food Additives, 29 October 1986. Unpublished

'Counterfeit food: additives as consumer fraud'. Lecture to the Food Additives Campaign Team (FACT) conference on Food Additives and Public Health, 30 October 1986. Unpublished

Paul Levy. 'Add red herrings'. FACT conference. Quoted. The Observer, *2 November 1986*

'How fresh is fresh?' *Taste*, November 1986

'Can food additives damage health?' *Pulse*, 8 November 1986

'Fast food fair'. Feature written for *The Daily Telegraph*, November 1986. Unpublished

'Food and Health'. HTV 'When the chips are down'. Interview, November 1986

'Food policy and the media'. Correspondence with Bradford Food Policy Unit (Dr Verner Wheelock), November 1986. Unpublished

'Old stodge, new stodge'. *Telegraph Sunday Magazine*, **7 December 1986**

'Dietary dissenters dish up a menu of misgivings'. The *Independent*, 9 December 1986

'Eat and be glad without fear of fat this Christmas'. The *Independent*, 23 December 1986

'The ABC of better health with extra vitamins'. The *Independent*, **13 January 1987**

Coronary Prevention Group. 'Diet'. Briefing paper no 4. Advisor. London: CPG, January 1987

City and Hackney Health Authority. 'Preventing coronary heart disease. A district approach'. Conference proceedings. Advisor, January 1987

'Heart Broken. Women and heart disease'. *What Diet and Lifestyle*, **February–March 1987**

'National nutrition policy. Healthy or unhealthy?' In 'Health policy aspects of dental caries prevention'. Edinburgh: Scottish Health Education Group, 1987

'Food and health'. Health Education Authority Action Pack. For the 16–19 HEA project. University of South-

ampton. Cambridge: National Extension College, 1987

'Baby Food'. The Food Programme. Interview, 12 October 1987

Heart. Magazine of the Coronary Prevention Group. No 7. Editor, December 1987

(With Geoffrey Cannon) 'The vitamin debate: a healthy attitude gives food for thought'. The *Independent*, 2 February 1988

Wooding D. 'Vitamins fail fitness test'. Interview. Today, 2 February 1988

(With Anne Dillon, Mike Rayner and others) 'Eating for a Healthy Heart'. With the Coronary Prevention Group. London: Ebury Press, 1988

Judy Sadgrove. 'Light on the dying'. Interview. The Guardian, 7 September 1988

'Christopher Baker of Cambridge: an organic Odyssey'. *The Living Earth* (Journal of the Soil Association), October–December 1988

Geoffrey Cannon, Judy Sadgrove, Professor Philip James. 'Food for the people'. Obituary. The Guardian, 24 September 1988

Felicity Lawrence. 'A crusader for better food'. Obituary. The Daily Telegraph, 27 September 1988

John Rivers, obituary. The Independent, 1 October 1988

Anon. Caroline Walker. Obituary. Heart (Journal of the Coronary Prevention Group), Autumn 1988

Anon. 'The battle for good food'. Obituary. Homoeopathy Today, Autumn 1988

Derek Cooper. 'Food'. Obituary. Listener, 3 November 1988

Anon. Caroline Walker. Obituary; report on The Caroline Walker Trust. The Food Magazine, Spring 1989

Anon. 'Caroline's work continues'. Report on The Caroline Walker Trust. The Food Magazine, Summer 1989

'Caroline Walker'. Report on the work of the Caroline Walker Trust. The McCarrison Society newsletter, April–June 1989

'Caroline Walker'. Report on the work of the Caroline Walker Trust. The Living Earth. (Journal of the Soil Association), April–June 1989

Anon. 'Food campaigner wins Rosemary Delbridge Memorial Trophy'. Press release. The Rosemary Delbridge Memorial Trust, 15 June 1989

Geoffrey Cannon. Celebrating Caroline. Report on the work of the Caroline Walker Trust. The Food Magazine, July–September 1989

THE CAROLINE WALKER
TRUST

When Caroline and I first talked about a Trust to be set up in her name, she was rather chuffed, and at the same time had some doubts. She had sometimes attended lectures meant to commemorate nutritionists. 'No dull talks, please,' she said. (We had often joked about studies on 'Molasses urea as a supplement to poor quality roughage' or 'The effect of daily baked-bean consumption on normocholesterolaemic men'.) Worse yet, a Trust might in time betray its original purposes; how could we be sure, she said, that her name would never be used as a vehicle for some Ministerial goon's Caroline Walker Lecture on, say, 'Sausages as a source of zinc' or 'The role of sugar as a means to prevent vitamin toxicity'?

Well, that's what Trustees are for, I said; and we discussed names, rather as a couple might cast a dinner party. I admired Caroline's fortitude. It's quite something to merit a Trust; it's something else to help set up your own Trust. Our friend Jonathan Aitken MP immediately agreed to be Chairman.

A Trust is rather grand. Talking about the Trust and its work, with Caroline and with friends, was for me like casting ropes over the chasm of her death; I didn't know if the ropes would hold, or whether a bridge could be made of them, or if anybody would want to walk to the other side. After all, 'she wasn't a bishop or a general, you know,' somebody said to me, a bit bewildered – as I was – by the scale of her obituaries in the *Guardian*, *The Daily Telegraph*, and the *Independent*.

Most people do seem to fade after they die. As I write now, nearly a year after Caroline died, her light is brighter; and I think this is because she set an example. What she stood for does not die. That is the thought expressed in many of the letters enclosing contributions to Caroline's Trust Fund.

'Her work is a lasting inspiration to me,' wrote Richard Austin from Rainbow Wholefoods in Norwich. 'Caroline's way of dying is a richness bequeathed to us all,' wrote Elizabeth and Richard Cook, authors of *Sugar Off!*, from Cambridge. Hetty Einzig, co-author with me of *Dieting Makes You Fat*, wrote, 'With much respect, and excitement at the future work of the Trust.' Clare Ford wrote from Unwin Hyman Books, 'I welcome the setting up of the Trust and wish you success in maintaining the spirited investigation of the food industry and the fight for better quality food.'

'A cheque is enclosed for Caroline's Trust as we are a family who have been touched by Caroline and wish to see her work continue,' wrote Dr Donald Gau of the Coronary Prevention Group and his wife Gillian. 'What a good idea!' wrote Sir Reay Geddes, in whose house Caroline lodged when she was studying for her second degree. 'Early deaths call for some act of remembrance more than older deaths,' wrote David Gee, shortly to become Director of Friends of the Earth. Maurice Hanssen, maestro of the health food trade, wrote, 'Her example can be appreciated now, and also by future generations.' 'We would like to help to support and sustain the continuation of her work,' wrote David Hargreaves, on behalf of BBC TV 'Continuing Education.' 'Many people here worked happily with Caroline and learned a great deal from her.'

The rope was holding.

'It's all finished,' Caroline said to me at occasional times of desolation. 'Everybody's forgotten already.' But they hadn't. 'I do hope that in time the voice of the Trust will prove to be as effective as that of the person whose name it bears,' Brenda Harris wrote from Sittingbourne. Also from Kent, Gwen Julius wrote, 'Although I never met her, I followed her work with enormous admiration; and her courage in fighting for the cause she believed in, and her bravery in her illness, will be an example to all the world.' Miss P Keats wrote from Rugby, 'Hoping that someone else will carry on her good work.' Dr Graham Langsdale wrote from his group practice in Bournemouth, '*The Food Scandal* is obligatory reading for my trainees, as I have become particularly interested in nutrition; and I hope the Trust will be able to continue the work started by you and your wife.'

So many letters came from people who never met Caroline. Another came from Deirdre Lyndon, a colleague from my BBC days in the 1970s, when I knew nothing of nutrition. She wrote, 'As far as I know, I never did meet Caroline Walker but I've read a fair bit of her work and often heard her talk on radio. I suppose I'm just one of many mothers whose shopping habits and cooking methods have been influenced by the work you and she have done together. Many have been the times when I've lightly sworn at you under my breath for forcing me to read the 6pt on packets and tins; many the times when I've wondered whether the eyestrain was worth the bother, or the anxiety justified.

Only time can test the theories and the fashions in nutrition, but our six year old John knows for himself that canned baked beans have sugars in them and that most sausages are packed with fat and preservatives. Caroline Walker is surely owed a lot of the credit for that; planting the seed of a notion in a child's mind is about all any of us can hope to achieve, and she went a lot further in her work than that. I was very upset to read of her death this morning. Please put this small sum into her Trust fund.'

The bridge was being built.

We British are shy of ceremony, which is a pity, because detachment robs ceremony of its human meaning. Caroline's Trust was first announced by Derek Cooper at the Service of Thanksgiving for Caroline, at Marylebone Parish Church, where we were married the year before; and it was the Trust, it seemed to me, that made a community from the congregation of our friends and family. For everybody, whatever other beliefs they may or may not have, can agree that those who live in the minds and hearts of others, although dead, do not die, but are immortal.

Response to the Trust let me see Caroline as others saw her. Her neighbour in Cambridge John McCall wrote, 'On one summer's afternoon in 1985 I was sitting in my back garden and Caroline passed on her way to a lunch party at her sister Olivia's house, carrying a large apple tart. She lifted a carton of cream and smiled a guilty smile. That is how I shall remember her.' And June Waters, once a student with Caroline, wrote after the Service of Thanksgiving, 'As a direct result I have now applied for an MA in Health Education and hope to add my small contribution to Caroline's cause.'

News of Caroline's Trust was broadcast in 'The Food Programme' and thence in the *Listener*, and in the publications of four professional and voluntary organisations Caroline was associated with: the Coronary Prevention Group, the London Food Commission, the Soil Association, and the McCarrison Society. Hundreds of people responded, and in the summer of 1989 the Trust's Appeal reached its first-year target of £20,000, uplifted by a generous grant from the Reader's Digest Trust.

The Trustees decided to celebrate Caroline's life and work every year, the first event to be held at the Royal Society of Arts. The celebration has three parts. First, annual awards are given to those who have done most to improve public health by means of good food, in four categories: consumer, media, science and industry. Then the Caroline Walker Award is given to the person whose achievement has Caroline's spirit. Cheeky, is her name for it.

Second, the annual Caroline Walker Lecture is given; the first year, by Jonathon Porritt, whose interests, like those of Caroline, range wider than daily baked-bean consumption or molasses urea. And then, the celebration having begun with a reception, it ends with a dinner.

Caroline had plenty of ideas about how her Trust Fund money could be well spent – research into the value of traditional agriculture, for example.

The funding of science is a grand idea, and Caroline's Trust is meant to flourish. Meanwhile, as a beginning, the Trustees have supported publication of this book, and also have granted a bursary to the student at London University whose work shows the best understanding of nutrition as a means to improve public health.

Donations to Caroline's Trust, and enquiries, should be sent to 6 Aldridge Road Villas, London W11 1BP; cheques to be payable to The Caroline Walker Trust. It is the intention of the Trustees to report on their work to everybody who donates £25 or more.

Three verses of the Bidding Prayer spoken at Caroline's Thanksgiving Service also speak for the spirit in whic'ı her Trust will work.

'We celebrate her gentle spirit as a daughter, sister, colleague, comrade, friend, godmother, aunt and wife; a light that will always illuminate the hearts of those she loved and who love her.

We celebrate her valiant spirit as a scientist, nutritionist, teacher, lecturer, campaigner, administrator, broadcaster and writer; a fire that will always refine the minds of those she moved and are moved by her.

We are brought together here and now; a new community. Let us rejoice in the gifts of her young life which we treasure and which, from the seeds she planted, we may grow into gardens, orchards, meadows and forests.'